ON BETRAYAL

†

AVISHAI MARGALIT

On Betrayal

HARVARD UNIVERSITY PRESS
Cambridge, Massachusetts
London, England
2017

Library of Congress Cataloging-in-Publication Data

Names: Margalit, Avishai, 1939– author.
Title: On betrayal / Avishai Margalit.
Description: Cambridge, Massachusetts : Harvard University Press, 2017. |
Includes bibliographical references and index.
Identifiers: LCCN 2016017878 | ISBN 9780674048263 (alk. paper)
Subjects: LCSH: Betrayal. | Interpersonal relations.
Classification: LCC BJ1500.B47 M37 2017 | DDC 179—dc23
LC record available at https://lccn.loc.gov/2016017878

In memory of Edna Ullmann-Margalit (1946–2010)
and Tziona (Margalit) Gerstein (1947–2013)

CONTENTS

PREFACE

I was trained in philosophy when the rift between continental philosophy and analytical philosophy still mattered greatly. The rift created more heat than light, but it didn't seem that way at the time. I strongly veered toward analytical philosophy. A teacher whom I greatly admired, a continental one, tried to dissuade me by quoting Hermann Lotze: "The constant sharpening of knives is boring if one never gets around to cutting." Analytical philosophy, he added, is an incessant sharpening of knives with nothing to cut. I piously retorted with a more soothing metaphor from Abraham Lincoln's famous adage "Give me six hours to chop down a tree and I will spend the first four sharpening the axe." Wrong you are, riposted my continental teacher; analytical philosophers live under the illusion that they work with a surgical knife, not with an axe. (Hebrew uses the same word for analysis and surgery: *nituach,* "dissection.") What lingered with me from this crossing of swords were two worries. One worry was about content, or rather the lack of it, in analytical philosophy ("no beef to cut"); the other worry was about method, about what sort of knife is needed in philosophy.

The topic of betrayal provides ample beef to dissect, but not of the kind analytical philosophers were bothered to stab their steely knives into. As for the second worry, with what knife, a reflexive answer is: with the analytical knife of making distinctions. But that is far from being the whole answer. The reflective answer is: with all the blades of a Swiss Army knife (to borrow Rudolf Carnap's simile). True, none of the blades of a Swiss Army knife is as sharp as a scalpel or as sturdy as an axe, but the combination of all the blades is probably the best way of dealing with a rich and chaotic notion such as betrayal.

In short, using many blades means using an eclectic range of methods. One blade for cutting political betrayal is the use of historical examples, another blade for dissecting personal betrayal is the use of literature, and still another blade for slicing into betrayal in general is the use of religious texts. Religion is particularly attuned to human vulnerabilities, which are related to betrayal. After all, even Peter, the rock on which the church was built, denied his master thrice. And then there is a blade of casuistry, of arguing and learning from cases, which is of great use in a work on betrayal. An exceedingly important blade is the one that is designed to unpack and unmask the uses of formative metaphors related to betrayal.

One useful blade goes under the heading of phenomenology, by which I mean an accurate description of the experience of betrayal, mainly by its victims. The idea is that such descriptions make us understand the specific character of what was betrayed. It is thick human relations that are betrayed in acts of betrayal. Where there is no love there is no betrayal, says a famous aphorism. My way of rendering it is: Where there is no thick relation there is no betrayal. This in any case is the theme of my book.

Writing a book about betrayal after writing a book about idolatry (with Moshe Halbertal) and another book about rotten compromises may create an impression that the book about betrayal is just the third volume in a trilogy. In a way the impression is right, but the book stands on its own, and its relation to the other two books is indirect.

So here is the plan of the book.

Chapter 1 asks: Why betrayal? What makes betrayal a subject worthy of philosophical discussion?

Chapter 2 deals with the vagaries of the concept of betrayal. It addresses various notions of ambiguity that are attached to betrayal. The puzzle is that, on the one hand, the concept of betrayal looks like a shifting sand dune and, on the other, acts of betrayal in whatever form and disguise seem to be readily understood across cultures, continents, and histories.

Chapters 3 and 4, the longest chapters, try to answer the question of what the effect of betrayal is—the answer: the undermining of thick human relations—and infer backward from that effect to what it is in betrayal that undermines thick relations. At the center of the two chapters is the idea of thick human relations, whose core is the idea of belonging. The guiding example in elucidating betrayal and its effects is adultery. Adultery for many people is not only the paradigm case of betrayal but also usually what they have in mind when talking about betrayal.

Chapter 5 deals with treason. If adultery is the paradigm case of personal betrayal, treason is the paradigm case of political betrayal. If the epitome of adultery is betraying the spouse with the spouse's best friend, the epitome of treason is offering aid and comfort to the enemy.

One line of concern with adultery and treason is carried over from Chapter 4 to Chapter 5, namely, have these two paradigm cases lost their grip in modern times?

Chapter 6 deals with collaboration as a particular form of betrayal: betrayal in the setting of military occupation. The mode of collaboration at the kernel of this chapter is patriotic betrayal, betrayal motivated by unmistakable (even if misguided) patriotic reasons. Here the example of Marshal Pétain looms large.

Chapter 7 is a short and direct continuation of the discussion about collaboration in Chapter 6. It deals with the case of Flavius Josephus and expands on one main theme: historical judgment ("the court of history") as betrayal.

Chapter 8 returns to the discussion about religious betrayal, not in the sense of betraying God (idolatry) but in the sense of betraying the religious community (apostasy).

Chapter 9 brings to the fore an altogether different form of betrayal, class betrayal, and withal the right setup to elucidate the notion of class solidarity. Class betrayal is betrayal of class solidarity, and the nagging question is whether class solidarity is a remnant of kitsch morality or a notion with ethical force.

Chapter 10 deals with the question of whether betrayal and hypocrisy are by-products of a society that lacks transparency, and if so, is transparency the remedy for betrayal, and is the medicine of transparency worse than the disease of betrayal?

The book revolves around a crucial distinction between morality and ethics. Morality is what regulates our relations to others on the basis of their humanity: it is our thin relations with strangers. By contrast, ethics regulates our thick relations such as relations to family and friends.

The claim is that betrayal is a notion of ethics, not of morality. This claim is not an exercise in mental administration, but a matter of supplying the proper grid for elucidating the notion of betrayal.

Betrayal, especially political betrayal, is far from being confined to personal relationships; indeed, betrayal may strongly involve institutions. Yet the book deals only tangentially with social institutions. The idea is that the concept of betrayal gains its currency and its potency from personal relations, whereas extending the notion of betrayal to large collectives that involve institutions is secondary.

I tried to keep the book to a conversational style, with frequent use of personal pronouns and a peppering of personal stories, partly because the different topics of the book were presented as lectures and discussed in settings in which the conversational style struck me as introducing the right tone. I retain a first-person tone of voice simply to convey my side of the conversation. The "lordly style" in philosophy (to use Bertrand Russell's expression) is usually the manifestation of a craving for generalities, whereas the plebeian conversational style expresses a yearning for concreteness. Betrayal calls for concreteness.

My list of references is very austere, yet what I owe to others is lavish. I simply accept Gilbert Ryle's advice that can be summed up as follows: In philosophy, try hard not to be a footnote nudnik. (Ryle's *Concept of Mind* has no references.) This is of course a controversial stand, especially for a book that deals extensively with the notion of gratitude.

ON BETRAYAL

†

1

Why Betrayal?

INDEED, WHY BETRAYAL?

Why choose such a moth-eaten topic? Why not stick with noble topics such as equality and liberty, instead of pursuing the seedy topic of betrayal?

I start with an indirect answer to the question "Why betrayal?" Then I suggest some direct answers to that very same question.

Robespierre suggested weaving the revolutionary triangle *liberté, égalité, fraternité* on the French flag.[1] His suggestion was not accepted. But the slogan became well inscribed on the revolutionary consciousness, and in a way set the agenda for all modern political thought. Almost all the effort in political thought has been devoted to two sides of the triangle, liberty and equality, and especially to the relationship between them. Indeed, one can view justice as finding the right balance between liberty and equality. The neglected side of the revolutionary triangle is fraternity. Fraternity, understood as a brotherly attitude toward people we don't know, strikes us as an elusive metaphor. Even worse, it strikes us as an invitation to dance to the tune of moral kitsch composed by propagandists; in short, it is a disinvitation to serious thinking. For some, fraternity reeks not only of senti-mentality but also of a precarious premodern leftover from a me-dieval guild's banquet. Fraternity seems to vitiate the liberal sensibility for privacy by granting license to interfere in people's private affairs under the sticky slogan of fraternal concern. Carlyle scorned forced "brotherhood" by quoting a pun on the revolu-tionary slogan that went "Fraternity or death: Be my brother, or I will kill you."[2] Some modern liberals view fraternity as pernicious communitarianism, a threat to our core sense of individuality. Liberal society should be inspired by liberty and equality and leave fraternity to families and cloistered undergraduates.

I believe that fraternity is important as a motivating force to bring about liberty and equality. Only a society with a strong sense of fraternity has the potential to bring about justice. There is nothing obvious in what I have just stated. I state it here dog-matically since my book is not directly about fraternity but about betrayal. The idea is not to tackle the idea of fraternity head-on but to deal with fraternity through its pathology, which is be-trayal. The basic claim in the book is that betrayal is betrayal of a thick human relationship. A thick human relationship comes very close to what fraternity means. So betrayal is the flip side of fraternity.

The business of medical doctors is health, but they deal with diseases: the way health goes wrong. Doctors hardly give an ac-count of what health consists of. They spend all their time and effort accounting for what undermines health. The same holds true for mental health. Sigmund Freud, for example, hardly said a word about what normal human beings are like, apart from what Erik Erikson quotes him as saying, which is that to be normal is to be able to love and to work.[3] Freud spent all his time dealing with pathologies that undermine normalcy. In the same spirit, I propose to deal with fraternity by dealing with what under-mines it. Betrayal undermines thick relations. The paradigmatic cases of thick relations are relations of family and friends. Fra-ternity is meant to stand for thick human relations, modeled on family and friendship. At center stage of my concerns are per-sonal betrayal, in the form of betraying family and friendship; political betrayal, in the form of treason; betrayal of religious community, in the form of apostasy; and betraying one's class. And so my answer to the question "Why betrayal?" is that it is a good indirect way to deal with fraternity.

A Basic Plot

A friend who spent years in Ceylon (present-day Sri Lanka) once told me that the price of a movie ticket, during his time there, was one rupiah. In buying a ticket one had to choose between queuing for love movies and queuing for war movies. The pro-ducers of the movies couldn't be bothered with editing their movies or giving them specific titles. Instead, viewers were pro-vided with a timeless overarching choice of topics: love or war. The idea is clear: for an admission price of one rupiah, basic human plots can be reduced to just two. The rest are mere varia-tions on these two Ur-themes. I would have squashed these basic plots even further, for a love plot is usually about love betrayed, and war plots are marred by treason, desertion, defection, col-laboration, and spying. In short, the only plot worth one rupiah is betrayal. One should of course take that description with a grand grain of salt, for there is more to human life than betrayal, but the point of the Ceylon story is that betrayal is such a basic and ubiquitous element of the human repertoire that there is no need to answer the question "Why betrayal?"

To be sure, you can dine out extensively by telling people that you are working on betrayal. People feel that the issue of betrayal touches their lives: some directly, others vicariously. Vicarious experience (*das Leben der Anderen,* "the lives of others") is no less a human experience than direct experience. Many people lead a vicarious life, either because they are terrified of daring and dangerous experiences or because they lack the opportunity. As a result, they become passive consumers of betrayal stories. By the same token, you may say that it is precisely the people who cannot live their own true life who become betrayers. Instead of leading one full life, they lead a double life.

One may retort that the broad underlying suspicion that comes with the question "Why betrayal?" is not whether betrayal is a subject worthy of general attention but whether it is a suitable subject for philosophy. To this last gambit there is a stock pious answer: nothing human is alien to philosophy. But the pious answer is not good enough. For it may very well be the case that artistic accounts are a better way of conveying what betrayal is. Reading or watching Harold Pinter's play *Betrayal,* or any scrap of paper written by John le Carré on that subject, may be a better way to gain insight into modern betrayal than reading a laborious philosophical tractate on the subject. Betrayal, like laughter, belongs to the basic fabric of human existence, and yet, like laughter, it may produce crushingly tedious philosophical stuff.

The last suspicion about whether the choice of betrayal is a proper philosophical topic has little to do with betrayal as such. It is a general suspicion about any choice of subject. That a subject is important doesn't mean that one has important things to say about it: one can write uninterestingly about an interesting subject, humorlessly about humor, and boringly about the exciting topic of betrayal. All of this is trite and true and should end with the cliché that the proof is in the pudding.

But the question "Why betrayal?" cannot be stonewalled by a cliché, for there is a genuine worry expressed by this question. The worry is that the concept of betrayal has lost its grip in liberal modern societies. True, the generic term "betrayal" still resonates with lots of people, but when it comes to its central species— political betrayal in the form of treason, marital betrayal in the form of adultery, and religious betrayal in the form of apostasy—the topic of betrayal rings archaic. Losing the grip on treason, adultery, and apostasy is not so much a matter of losing the sense of these terms as it is of losing their sensibility. What I shall try to do in this chapter is to inquire in what sense, if any, treason, adultery, and apostasy have lost their grip on the modern liberal imagination.

Treason

Our reactive attitude today to treason is greatly altered from the time of William Shakespeare. The horror expressed in "Treason! Treason!" *(Hamlet)* is not our horror. We seem to be removed from the paranoiac world of Henry's "Good tidings, my Lord Hastings; for the which / I do arrest thee, traitor, of high treason: / And you, lord archbishop, and you, Lord Mowbray, / Of capital treason I attach you both" *(Henry IV, Part 2)*. We do not shiver when dipping into Dante's frozen ninth circle (in the *Inferno*, the circle that is the lowest of the low, the seat of the betrayers). We may be puzzled as to why Brutus of all people ranks so high on Dante's list of traitors, which secures him a front-row seat in Dante's underworld, but these are the least of our worries. The worry is that the underpinning of "betrayal" and its semantic field seems so utterly entrenched in a feudal morality that it is not part of modern liberal sensibilities anymore.

You may protest and say that this worry about losing our grip cannot be true as stated. After all, treason is with us, enshrined, for example, in the U.S. Constitution, and the U.S. Constitution is an ongoing concern and not dead folios.

The handling of treason in the U.S. Constitution is, I believe, a poor counterexample to the claim that treason has lost its grip. The concept of treason in the United States Constitution is a response to the treason of feudal morality, with the aim of removing its sting.

I shall address the attitude of the U.S. Constitution to treason in more detail in Chapter 5.

Adultery

A parallel story to the loosening grip of treason on the Western world can be told about marital betrayal in the form of adultery. Adultery used to be a crime, which on occasion was punished by death or disfigurement. It stopped being a criminal offense in most liberal countries and was relegated to family law.

The decline in the hold of adultery, as a form of betrayal, in liberal countries has to do with an important shift in the attitude toward sexual morality. Liberal morality does not recognize sexual morality as an independent moral domain. It recognizes the importance of sex in human life as well as its vulnerability to exploitation and domination. It recognizes sexuality as a sensitive domain in applying general moral principles. But it does not recognize sexuality as an autonomous moral domain with principles of its own, any more than it recognizes eating as a separate moral domain. Indeed, in the liberal view there is no more room for sexual morality than there is room for a morality of eating. The counterpicture—shared by the major religions of the world—starts with the centrality of sexual morality. Sexual morality is at the core of religious morality. The rest of morality is taken as an extension of sexual morality. Adultery is a central category of the sex-centered picture of morality. The shift in attitude toward adultery, in secular liberal countries, expresses a deep shift from sex-centered morality to general morality. In liberal countries adultery lost its hold and was shunted to the private domain.

Apostasy

My third example of betrayal is religious betrayal in the form of apostasy.

The law in liberal states suggests the weakening of religious betrayal. Apostasy, "the right to replace one's current religion or belief," is a particularly curious case, for it is declared to be a basic human right, and is regarded as such by liberal states.[4] By contrast, apostasy may carry a death penalty in some illiberal states.[5]

We seem to be torn between two conflicting poles. On the one hand, betrayal seems an obvious concern for philosophy by being a basic human plot. On the other hand, major manifestations of betrayal—treason, adultery, and apostasy—from the perspective of a liberal way of life seem somewhat outdated concerns, and hence outdated philosophical concerns.

The Interest in Trust

While the concept of betrayal seems to have loosened its grip on liberal societies, an apparently inversely correlated notion, trust, finds its way to liberal societies' center stage. How can we explain the topicality of trust and the outdatedness of betrayal when betrayal seems to be the antonym of trust? Put differently, why is there an intense interest in trust, while there is wary disregard of betrayal?

The dialectics of trust and betrayal is more complicated than just presenting one as a close antonym of the other. It is important for my study to highlight the difference between the old-fashioned concern with betrayal and the current concern with trust in a market economy. It is a difference that, once understood, makes the need for answering the question "Why betrayal?" all the more pressing.

There are two notions of trust. There is thin trust and there is thick trust.

Here is a case of thin trust: Two strangers are sitting on the beach. Both are afraid to leave their belongings unattended. Suddenly one asks, "Would you keep an eye on my belongings while I take a dip?" "By all means," the other says. The first person returns wet and happy from her swim, finding her belongings in place. The other asks, "Will you keep an eye on my stuff? I feel like going in too." "Sure," she says. And off he goes. Both are showing thin trust: trust between strangers.

Here is a case of thick trust: It so happens that you and your companion have and hold each other in sickness and in health. Moreover, you vow to cherish each other from this day forward for better and for worse. In short, those familiar words do capture your thick trust in each other.

These two examples are in a way more than we bargained for. They are not just cases of trust, thick or thin, but cases of mutual trust. You and the stranger on the beach trust each other with your belongings; you and your companion trust each other to nurture and care for each other through thick and thin. But then the stranger may thinly trust you, without you trusting her, and you may thickly trust your companion, without your partner trusting you.

So what are the characteristics of typical cases of thin trust?

One cooperates with another in the belief that in doing so one promotes one's interests in comparison to being left on one's own. In cooperating you become vulnerable by becoming dependent on your presumed partner to do her bit in the cooperation. You expose yourself to exploitation. Being exposed to exploitation means that your partner is able to use your dependence and harm your interests relative to the situation in which you are left on your own. Exploitation strengthens by degrees: the degree to which your interests are ignored or actively harmed. The stranger on the beach may take your belongings and run away or, more benignly, may ignore your belongings and let others take them. Thin trust is a belief that usually you will not be exploited by the one with whom you cooperate, for the reason that the other is interested in the cooperation. Thin trust is a belief in trust in a non-exploitative relation. Of course, in trusting we assume more than the good intentions of the one whom we trust. We should be confident in that person's competence. The proverbial bear that hugs its master to warm him up, only to discover that it has killed him, can be trusted for its good intentions but not for its competence. In trusting others, we assume that they can deliver.[6]

Transaction Costs and Trust

There are good reasons for the surge of interest in thin trust with respect to democratic market societies, and even better ones with respect to societies that aspire to become market societies. Let me mention two: one economic, the other political.

There is a growing awareness among economists as to the importance of what are called "transaction costs" and "social capital" for the development of the economy. Transaction costs are the time and effort that are involved in carrying out a transaction. A transaction is basically a transfer of ownership. The point is that a great many such costs are due to lack of trust. A society based on trust has, in the economic lingo, a great deal of social capital. Social capital is a bad metaphor for an important concern—concern with the quality of human relations for the sake of economic cooperation and development.

One important advantage of having justified trust is the knowledge that the others do their share, even when they are not observed. Having such knowledge is a good test for justification of trust. It is useful to be reminded that in the old trusting world of the diamond bourse, expensive gems changed hands with no more than a handshake and the words *mazal u'bracha* ("luck and blessing" in Hebrew). There was no need to inspect whether the diamonds in the bag were the ones agreed upon. There was no need to measure and weigh them again, no need for lawyers to draft complicated contracts, and no need for expensive litigation in cases of dispute. A voluntary arbitration was all that was needed to enforce an agreement. In this trusting world, costs were confined to those involved in production and transportation.

This is not the market we now live in. Transferring property rights is very costly indeed. One has to be constantly on guard, equipped with an army of lawyers and inspectors. It may very well be the case that costs in the current world economy are growing not only in magnitude but also in proportion. High transaction costs hinder economic growth. In a global market, where commodities change hands across national boundaries and legal systems, there is fear that transaction costs will be prohibitively high. No wonder there is an interest in building trust as a way of reducing transaction costs. It is the relatively thin trust that allows northern Italy to prosper, and the lack of it that keeps the economy at bay in the south of that country, where trust is very limited, confined to family and clan.[7]

The basic insight of economic thought is that free transactions are capable of boosting resources to their highest value. Transaction costs due to mistrust are a friction in the movement of commodities and services that makes for an inefficient economy. Thin trust is needed in order to run the economy smoothly.

Trusting Political Representatives

The political reason for the interest in thin trust is not hard to fathom. There is, it seems, a growing suspicion among citizens in representative democracies that their representatives betray the interests of their voters. The mistrust of political representation has an acute manifestation nowadays in a growing demand for political transparency. The massive leak of government documents into the public domain by unauthorized individuals brings to the fore the serious issue of distinguishing between useful whistle-blowers and destructive traitors. If the concern with treason sounds archaic, the concern with whistle-blowing sounds squarely up to date. Moreover, whistle-blowing serves as a good answer to the question "Why (political) betrayal?"

Such nagging practical political suspicion is accompanied by theoretical unease with one main source of justification for our political obligation: the idea that a tacitly agreed-upon social contract is the main justification for political obligation. At the core of the unease lies a conflict between our notion of contract and our notion of trust. On the one hand, we need contracts because of our justified mistrust in one another. On the other hand, we need thin trust and a measure of good faith to make contracts work. No sovereign can make a contract enforceable if the parties to the agreement lack good faith. It is as hopeless as having a cease-fire agreement in the Middle East.

If we have to ascribe familiar faces to the tension between trust and contract, the names of Thomas Hobbes and John Locke come to mind, with Hobbes advocating the position that an enforceable contract is a substitute for trust, and Locke advocating the position that contracts hold because some measure of thin trust is already in place.

Contracts can never guard against all contingencies. A contract is essentially incomplete, and that is one of the reasons why we need trust and not just contracts. A liberal democracy based on a market economy is dependent on thin trust, if not for its very functioning, then at least for it to function well. It should come as no surprise that there is keen awareness of the role of trust in bringing about political and economic success. The accelerated pace of global economic integration in recent years has brought people from very diverse cultural and political backgrounds, real strangers, into contact. The economy counts on these strangers to cooperate, although they share no background on which to base trust. It is the possibility of thin trust among strangers that is at the focus of the current concern with trust. It is very different from the concern with betrayal of thick trust, which is my concern.

My Concern with Betrayal

I use here the concepts of thin and thick trust, but they are parasitic on more basic concepts: the concepts of thick human relations and thin human relations. My concern with betrayal is my way of dealing with thick relations, as distinct from thin relations. It is a concern with ethics. Morality is concerned with our thin relations, mainly our relations with strangers; ethics is concerned with our thick relations, relations modeled on our relations with family and friends. The notion of betrayal that I am interested in is, I believe, the primary notion of betrayal. In my division of labor, betrayal is predominantly an ethical notion, not a moral one.

We can brush aside the issue of decline in the topicality of major forms of betrayal in liberal societies by saying that philosophical concern doesn't usually come with an expiration date. We may say that topicality should concern newspaper editors more than philosophers. Moreover, we may add that liberal societies are a mere fraction of current humanity, and one shouldn't judge topicality by whether an issue tops the list of liberal concerns. In most societies betrayal in its major forms of adultery, treason, and apostasy is still an active concern.

All of the above is true, or almost true, but it misses the point. The point is that the tension between the ubiquity of betrayal and the loosening of the hold of betrayal is an indication—a symptom, if you like—of the tension between thick relations and thin relations, between ethics and morality. This tension is more pronounced in liberal societies. These societies are more troubled by the issue of how relations with strangers (morality) should constrain relations with kith and kin (ethics).

So the short answer to the question "Why betrayal?" is "Because betrayal sheds light on the nature of thick relations and what they should be." It also casts a long shadow over thick relations when they are not constrained by thin relations. Betrayal is a concrete way to get into the relation between thick and thin relations—in other words, the relation between ethics and morality.

This is the short answer. The long answer fills the length of the book. But we are not done yet with the question "Why betrayal?"

A Personal Twist

Betrayal has lingered with me from childhood. What always troubled me was the shifting nature in judgments of betrayal. Such judgments struck me as being like sand dunes, shifting with the wind. If such shifts take place and judgments of betrayal are not stable, then how can we account for betrayal, and how can we trust the evaluative use of the term? This is a general question, but the question "Why betrayal?" has a personal twist. The personal twist has to do with my childhood encounter with a shift in evaluating the loyalty and betrayal of two individuals. I was raised in a frontier society, which, rightly or wrongly, still perceived itself in heroic terms.

Meir Yakobi was a childhood hero of mine in Jerusalem. Milu, as we called him in our neighborhood, was older than I by a few years, a huge boy with soulful eyes and a dark complexion. He was the uncontestable leader of our neighborhood, fearless and fair, the defender of us young kids from older bullies.

At an early age Meir joined a kibbutz as an outsider child. Once on a school trip, I visited his kibbutz. As I stood with him at the entrance to the dining hall of the kibbutz I realized that he enjoyed in the kibbutz the same immense respect he enjoyed in our neighborhood.

From the kibbutz he joined the most elite unit of the military's paratrooper brigade. In this unit there was no regard for official ranking, and Yakobi, a sergeant, was made second-in-command to the legendary commander Meir Har-Zion. On a December night in 1954, Yakobi led a tiny squad inside Syrian territory to check an eavesdropping device. They were ambushed by a large force of Syrian soldiers and were subjected as prisoners to hellishly torturous interrogations. Uri Ilan, one of the squad's fighters and another kibbutz member, committed suicide in the Syrian jail. When his body was delivered back to Israel, it was found that he had written on nine scraps of papers by pricking holes into them and hiding them between his toes. On the papers he had written, "I didn't betray. I committed suicide." The last part, "I committed suicide," was dropped by Israeli army chief of staff Moshe Dayan when he read Ilan's last words at the funeral. He only read, "I didn't betray." Ilan became an instant hero. He had sacrificed himself so as not to reveal military secrets. But Ilan's "I didn't betray" implicated his comrades. When they returned from prison through a prisoner exchange, they were put on trial. Meir Yakobi was demoted.

Yakobi's mother fought hard to clear his name. She succeeded partially, and Yakobi then returned to the paratroopers. He died in action in 1956 in one the fiercest battles of the Sinai campaign, the battle of Mitla Pass. Later he was totally rehabilitated. Syrian intelligence documents found on the Golan Heights in 1967 attested that Yakobi took his captors to the eavesdropping device, knowing that the device was booby-trapped. He had the intention of blowing up his captors and himself with the eavesdropping device, but the explosive device didn't detonate.

A few years after Yakobi's death we reconstructed the battle of Mitla Pass in Israel's Negev Desert as part of our military training. At the end of that long day I spoke to one of my commanders who had mentioned Yakobi during the day. My commander (who later was the commander of the Entebbe operation and ultimately was the Israeli army's chief of staff) said that Ya-kobi was a victim of a Stalinesque kind of conception that any soldier taken as a prisoner of war is a traitor by definition. Stalin issued two famous orders: Order 270 on August 16, 1941, to the effect that there are no prisoners of war, only traitors, and Order 227 of July 28, 1942, the celebrated "Ni shagu nazad!" ("Not one step back! No retreat whatsoever!")

The Yishuv (the pre-state Jewish community in Palestine), my commander added, accepted Stalin's view. I believe that he also mentioned Abba Kovner, a Hebrew poet and a partisan leader in Lithuania who later served as *politruk* (political commissar) in Israel's War of Independence. Kovner made public a "combat sheet" in which he blamed the tiny kibbutz Nitzanim for surren-dering to overwhelming Egyptian forces: "To surrender while your body is still alive and your last bullet is breathing in its cartridge—is a disgrace. To agree to become the invader's pris-oner is a disgrace; it is worse than death." This attitude was a recipe for foolishly misplaced heroism, one that begins by turning any battle into a Stalingrad and ends by turning Yakobi, our best fighter, into a traitor. He placed my childhood hero on what I believed was a much-deserved pedestal. It taught me a disturbing lesson, however: what an easy shift it is from being a hero to being regarded as a traitor.

Another Meir, a different one, played a role in my anxiety about the shifting dunes of treason. It belongs to a childhood memory from the siege of Jerusalem in the War of Independence. The war on Jerusalem was bitter and the siege was biting: lack of food and water and plenty of bombs. As the scars of the war be-came more visible, the scare over the "traitors in our midst" grew to a fever pitch: "they" were directing the Arab cannons.

One didn't have to be a precocious child to understand the rumors and the fear of traitors from within. The salience of some of the targets made it seem as if the enemy was well informed by treacherous informers. Meir Tobianski, an officer in the new Israeli army in Jerusalem, was executed as a traitor for supplying the enemy, through British channels, with information about strategic locations in Jerusalem. He had access to this information because he was an employee of the electric company in Jerusalem. Tobianski was dragged to a deserted Arab village on the road to Jerusalem and after a short kangaroo trial was summarily executed. His widow fought to clear his name, and Tobianski was publicly exonerated.[8]

Nathan Alterman, a leading Hebrew poet, wrote a poem entitled "The Widow of the Traitor." The traitor is Tobianski and the widow is his wife, who single-handedly fought to clear his name and succeeded. If there is a medal for service to the nation, wrote the poet, she is the one who deserves it. She fought the horrendous reality of the "summary trial." Alterman also referred to confused "public opinion," which is "as quick to judge as a jeep that has lost its brakes."

Was the problem with the two Meirs simply a shift in evaluation because new facts were uncovered, or was it a shift in the notion of betrayal? The two, the sense of betrayal and the facts about betrayal, are tangled together, and practically it is hard to disentangle the conceptual from the empirical in the case of betrayal because of how often we shift from the act (of betrayal) to the actor (the traitor).

My father knew Tobianski. Later in his life he was tormented by the thought that he had been too quick to believe that Tobianski was justly punished. He kept returning to this sore topic, maintaining that ultimately Tobianski had been executed "for not being one of us," namely, for not sharing our lifestyle but rather choosing that of the British occupiers. Whether my father was right about Tobianski I don't know, but he pointed out an important guilt by association between betrayal and lifestyle. I shall return to my father's point in dealing with the grander case of Flavius Josephus in Chapter 7.

Tension over Betrayal

The question "Why betrayal?" may be countered by "Why not?"

I raised two sets of worries that, on the face of it, look like arguments for why not: the topicality of betrayal judgments, or rather the lack of it, and the stability of betrayal judgments, or rather the lack of it. The first set of worries, about topicality, has to do with a sense of the current irrelevance of the concept of betrayal, as judged by the apparent loosening of its grip. The second set of worries, about stability, has to do with the rapid change in evaluation and reevaluation of betrayal: from a hero to a traitor and back to a hero. If evaluative judgments of betrayal shift like sand dunes, then the stability of the concept of betrayal is in question.

I detect a tension here: on the one hand, a feeling of rapid changes in the evaluative judgments of betrayal, and on the other hand, a feeling that we do understand the use of the concept of betrayal across time and space. The feeling is that when we read, for example, ancient biblical stories, which tell us a great deal about betrayal, we do understand what we read. The same can be said about understanding betrayal in ancient Greek tragedies. Indeed, I shall count on this feeling of understanding by using the Bible and Greek tragedies as a wellspring of formative examples and keen observations. Nowadays we can also travel to remote places on earth, visiting cultures different from our own, and yet when we encounter their notions of betrayal we don't seem to find them incomprehensible.

So how do we reconcile the tension that the concept of betrayal produces in us: the feeling of "now we see it, now we don't," with no firm grasp of the concept, and the opposite feeling of understanding across seemingly insurmountable cultural and historical barriers?

The next chapter addresses some germane aspects of this tension between the stability and instability of the concept of betrayal. The idea is not to remove the tension as much as it is to expose its mainsprings that contribute to the tension. I do so by dealing with various notions of the ambiguity of betrayal.

2

The Ambiguities of Betrayal

THE TITLE OF THIS CHAPTER IS BORROWED FROM JUDITH Shklar. She wrote a justly celebrated essay on betrayal that was included in her collection of essays *Ordinary Vice.*[1]

In what sense can betrayal be taken as an ordinary vice?

Shklar's notion of ordinary is strained. In the case of betrayal, ordinary means having frequent occurrences, but in that sense death is also ordinary. And ordinary as attributed to betrayal cannot mean boringly common.

"Who hasn't been betrayed?" asks Shklar rhetorically, but familiarity with betrayal doesn't make it trite, any more than the question "Who hasn't been sick?" indicates that sickness is trite. Moreover, if it is true that everyone has gotten a hold of betrayal from both ends of the stick, by betraying and being betrayed, it neither reduces the shame of betraying nor alleviates the pain of being betrayed. "Ambiguity" is Shklar's way of saying that betrayal is intricate and "ordinary" is her way of playing down the drama of betrayal. Betrayal, she believes, is common enough to take in stride.

With the phrase "ambiguities of betrayal" I would like to introduce a conceptual worry about betrayal without playing down its drama.

The worry is that the concept of betrayal is irredeemably afflicted with the curse of being an *essentially contested concept*. That is, betrayal is a concept whose proper application is an issue no one can hope to resolve, because its application is ideologically contested. By "the concept of betrayal" I am casting a wide net over the whole semantic field of betrayal, covering terms such as "perfidy," "treachery," "treason," "double-crossing," "sellout," and the like.

Let's take "traitor" as an example. "Traitor," like "terrorist," has a highly contested use along ideological lines.

We know the routine: "You are a terrorist, I am a freedom fighter; you are a traitor, I am a patriot." It seems that there is nothing useful left to say about such divisive concepts. The idea of essentially contested concepts originated with the Scottish political philosopher W. B. Gallie.[2] He had in mind concepts that had gained positive evaluative status across the board—in short, "good words." Thus, in the setting of the Cold War the contest was over the good word "democracy." Each side of the divide between East and West tried hard to arrogate "democracy" to its depository of good words, while denying it to the other side.

There is a mirror-image phenomenon with regard to "bad words." Just as you arrogate good words to yourself, your ideological self, so you hurry to unload bad words on your rival. Bad words such as "traitor" and "terrorist" are two glaring examples of essentially contested bad concepts. When a concept is essentially contestable, there are no facts of the matter and no logical constraints for resolving their legitimate application. Their use is all in the blind eye of the ideological beholder. Whenever there is a clash of ideologies, one ideology's "traitor" is the other ideology's "hero." A concept such as traitor can be contested as a matter of fact without being contestable as a matter of principle: being *contestable* means that it can be contested with justification, whereas being *contested* merely points to the fact that people debate its use. Yet if a concept has been contested for a long time when all the facts about its use are known, it is usually a good sign that the concept is not only contested but also contestable.

Morris Cohen was an American-born citizen of the United States and a confirmed communist. As a courier in a ring of atomic spies, he passed the Manhattan Project's top secrets to the Soviets.[3] There is no question that he was branded a traitor by the Americans, but the Soviets awarded him the Order of the Red Banner, and even after the downfall of communism he was declared a hero of the Russian Federation. His face can be found on Russian stamps. Is there anything useful to say about Cohen's case above and beyond the fact that he was regarded as a traitor by the Americans and as a hero by the Russians?

What exactly is contested in a case such as Cohen's? A concept is not a proposition. A concept does not bear truth or falsity. So how can something that doesn't bear truth or falsity be contestable? One possible answer is that it is not the concept that is contestable but the whole *conception.* A conception is a set of propositions in which the concept plays an essential role. The clash is between two sets of propositions that constitute two conceptions that share a concept but are mutually incompatible.

Another answer is that what is contestable is what count as paradigm cases for the application of the concept. The disagreement over an essentially contestable concept is over its application not so much to borderline cases as to central cases, which are supposed to be clear cases.

A Paradigm Case and Ideal Type

A paradigm case is a clear case, by which one can be taught the use of the concept. But a paradigm case is more than that. It is an object of comparison. Especially in cases of hesitation about how to apply a concept to borderline cases, comparison of the concept to paradigm cases—comparison means weighing similarities and differences—serves as justification for applying (or withholding) the concept.

For a paradigm to serve as a model, an object of comparison, and not just as a clear case for application, it may need some accentuated salient features. This need for salient features may bring about a clash between a paradigm case and what is regarded as a typical case. The typical is bland; the paradigm is vivid.

But is it true that "traitor" and "betrayal" have neither paradigm cases nor clear cases for their application?

I have lumped together actor and action, traitor and treason, betrayer and betrayal. But the inference from the action to the actor is very much at the heart of our problem with the contestable nature of these terms.

It is the gap between the action (the betrayal) and the actor (the betrayer)—that is to say, between treason and traitor—that plays a role here. One can admit that an act is an act of betrayal without admitting that the actor is a betrayer. Richard Sorge could admit to stealing Nazi documents from the German embassy in Japan and handing them over to the Soviets and yet rightly deny being a thief. Filling the gap between action and actor is not always straightforward. There might be cases in which the action is clearly a case of political betrayal, and yet whether the one who committed the act of betrayal is also a traitor remains essentially contestable.

We may even make a much stronger claim based on the gap between assessing the action and assessing the actor. Some great political acts in the second half of the twentieth century were made by leaders who betrayed their constituency by doing the opposite of what they had promised their voters. Charles de Gaulle greeted his ardent supporters in Algeria with his celebrated "Je vous ai compris," only to betray them by proclaiming the independence of Algeria. The same holds for F. W. de Klerk and apartheid in South Africa, Richard Nixon and China, and Menachem Begin and Sinai. Betrayal in the sense of a serious breach of trust did take place in each of these cases. What made it serious was not just the weight of what was at stake but the sense that the constituency stood in a thick relation with their leader. Still, whatever these leaders may have been, they were not traitors. They acted with authority and in the best interests of their constituency, and for no other reason—unless doing the great thing is "another reason."

Indeed, in the case of treason, what is contested is more likely to be the attribution of the appellation "traitor" to the actor than the attribution of the appellation "betrayal" to the act.

Uncontestable Traitor

With the gap between action and actor and between contested and contestable in mind, let us go back to the claim that the concept of traitor is an essentially contested concept. That is to say, in all its uses the concept of traitor is always subject to dispute along ideological lines.

I have been told that schoolchildren in America used to get milk and cookies along with the story of Benedict Arnold, the most perfidious traitor in American history. Arnold, it will be recalled, was the general in the Continental Army during the American Revolution who defected to the British enemy, but not before he treacherously offered to hand West Point over to them.[4] The British never contested the American description of Arnold as an archtraitor. They handsomely rewarded Arnold with rank and rent, but they never rewarded him with respect. In their eyes he was too much of an opportunist to be respected. He was useful but not honorable. For the epithet "traitor" to be contested, the side that benefits from the betrayal must recognize the purity of the actor's motive in order to counter the ascription of betrayal by the suffering side. Selfish motives such as money and sex are exploited but not respected, not even by the benefiting side.

American children perfectly understand the Benedict Arnold story, but one irony probably escapes them. It is an irony best conveyed by a tale about the late Gideon Schwarz, an Israeli mathematician and a great wit. The story has it that an ultraconservative senator once visited the university where he taught in the United States. "All they teach you here is sex, drugs, and treason," said the senator. "Quite right," retorted Gideon, "but here we call it gynecology, pharmacology, and the history of the American Revolution." The barb for my purpose is the last bit, which refers to the American Revolution as treason. This, I suspect, eludes the children of America. They cannot believe that the United States was conceived in an act of treason against the crown.

Be that as it may, there is no question that the issue of whether the American Revolution was an act of liberation or an act of treason is different from the issue of whether George Washington and Benedict Arnold were traitors or patriots.

Here, then, is the main claim. In the case of alleged public traitors, essentially contested terms come to be essentially contestable
if the alleged traitor is caught between two sets of recognizably
incompatible deserving loyalties. In opting for one loyalty at the
expense of the other, one may become a traitor to one and a hero
to the other. The stress is on *deserving* loyalties. What about a
contest between deserving and undeserving loyalties—say, between undeserving loyalty to Nazi Germany and deserving
loyalty to the Norwegian underground, as in the case of Willy
Brandt? The use of "traitor" in this case may have been contested, but it shouldn't be regarded as contestable, let alone essentially contestable. Willy Brandt is an uncontestable hero.

There are two elements in my claim: purity of motive and deserving loyalty.

The question is, of course, in light of what, and in light of
whom, should judgment about a deserving loyalty be made? The
answer is that whatever the source of light may be, morality
should be a main source of light. A thick relation that is governed
by ethics but doesn't meet certain moral constraints is not a thick
relation that deserves loyalty. Nazi Germany doesn't deserve loyalty. I hope this claim will become clearer as we go along.

The concept of traitor is contested on many occasions, but it is
contestable only on some occasions.[5]

Moral Ambiguities and Ambiguity of Motives

I have mentioned that Judith Shklar titled her essay "The Ambiguities of Betrayal." I believe Rebecca West had a similar idea in
mind in retitling her book *The New Meaning of Treason* in later
editions.[6] The idea is that our sense of betrayal is not what it used

to be. Betrayal used to be a simple notion that elicited a strong and simple reaction. Talking about the ambiguities of betrayal need not mean that we have more than one robust sense of betrayal. It might mean that we don't have even one.

"Moral ambiguity" is an expression usually reserved for a situation of dubious morality, straddling a gray zone between moral behavior and immoral behavior. "Moral ambiguity" in this common understanding is a case of vagueness rather than a case of ambiguity. The word "day," in the sense of the period between sunrise and sunset and in the sense of twenty-four hours, the period of a complete rotation of the earth on its axis, presents a case of ambiguity. By contrast, the issue of whether "dusk" is in the realm of day or the realm of night is a case of vagueness. "Morally ambiguous character" is akin to the vagueness of "dusk" and not to the ambiguity of "day," for we hesitate to say on which side of the fence between good and evil the morally ambiguous character, who constantly straddles it, belongs.

So the expression "morally ambiguous" should be glossed as vagueness rather than ambiguity. Conceptual ambiguity conveys doubtful meaning; moral ambiguity conveys doubtful morality. It is the moral ambiguity of the means used by both sides that troubled John le Carré so much.[7] A lofty end such as defending freedom is just too abstract and remote, whereas a nasty means such as forsaking your loyalists when they become a liability rather than an asset is immediate and concrete. Abstract ideals can hardly justify the nasty means required for their defense. Does the end justify the means? But of course, said Sidney Morgenbesser whimsically; what else can justify the means if not the end? The end does not sanctify the means, however; a noble goal does not confer nobility on the means.

Ambiguity as Ambivalence

Freud made famous the claim that from early development on, we are caught in contradictory desires that are expressed in conflicting emotions. On the one hand, we harbor sexual desires toward the parent of the opposite sex. On the other hand, we are in competition with the parent of the same sex for the love of the parent we desire. It is competition with the parent of the same sex, whom we both admire and hate, that creates ambivalence. This universal complex of ambivalent desires is resolved with varying degrees of success. A great deal of pathology in many individuals is due to an inability to resolve this basic ambivalence. Ambivalence in this picture is a conflict of desires and emotions, mostly unconscious. Unconscious emotions have the power to exert subversive influence, which may determine one's behavior.

What does the Freudian idea of ambivalence have to do with betrayal? A great deal, I believe.

Betrayal presupposes unequivocal human relations and wholehearted loyalty. It is these kinds of relations that are undermined by betrayal. But we might be ambivalent in our relationships even toward those to whom we declare utter loyalty, to our nuclear family, say. Declarations aside, ambivalence may turn betrayal into a psychologically ambiguous attitude. The recognition of basic ambivalence erodes our sense of betrayal. Nothing in our attitude toward others lacks ambivalence. So the notion of betrayal cannot have the simplicity it requires.

But do we need simple attitudes to be a betrayer?

I once heard Byron Bland give an account of a powerful leader of the militant Protestant militia in Northern Ireland, who had a great deal to do with violent activities during the Troubles. This

leader later turned into a major force in bringing peace and rec-
onciliation to this conflict. "What made you undergo such a radical shift?" he was asked. "I didn't undergo any radical shift," he
answered. "All that happened to me is that in my former violent
stage, I was 51 to 49 percent in favor of violent struggle, which
meant that I opted for violence and acted in a way that was
100 percent violent. Now, in my peace stage, I have switched to 51
to 49 percent in favor of nonviolent activities for bringing about
peace, and I stand 100 percent behind it, acting peacefully." This
is possible, albeit unlikely: a dramatic change in behavior due to
a change only in the margin. In big decisions we expect something akin to a wholehearted conversion of outlook to bring
about such a dramatic change in behavior.[8]

Mixed Motives

Betrayal for money seems to be an unambiguous case of betrayal.
Doing it for sex is another. But even these straightforward cases
may be simplistic rather than simple. Human motives are mixed
motives. One may become a traitor not just for want of money
but also because one wants sex and communism, and there is
no more point in asking which was the motive than in asking
whether a doctor works to save lives or to make money. You
would do better not to try to disentangle motives in such complex matters, especially if you read the astonishingly subtle psychological account by John Banville in *The Untouchable* on the
motives of Anthony Blunt, one of the celebrated Cambridge Five,
for becoming a betrayer.

In saying that human motives are mixed motives, we normally
do not mean that human action is overdetermined by the motives that bring it to pass; that is to say, each of the many motives

in the mix could on its own bring the agent to act the way he acted. What we usually mean by mixed motives is that a combination of motives, none of which was sufficient on its own, made him a betrayer.

Sex, money, and a mild form of communism triggered Admiralty clerk William John Christopher Vassall to betray Britain to the Soviets.[9] All of these motives worked together, and none of them on its own would have made him a traitor. But we are still free to weigh the relative strength of his motives and to say that sex was his main motive. The claim is that when the motive for betrayal is predominantly self-regarding, as it is with money and sex, betrayal is not ambiguous. But self-regard may be too broad a category. We may very well say that the motive that drives many people to betray is the thrill of one-upmanship, the excitement of living dangerously, the kick of living a double life, which is more than one life. Self-regard has more to it than does money or sex.

Ambivalence accompanies mixed motives. The French Moralists, those shrewd connoisseurs of the human race, expressed in their epigrammatic style pretty skeptical views about the purity of human moral motivation.

Oscar Wilde was full of scornful mistrust of any avowed moral motives by human actors. Wilde would speak of those who love only once in their life as "shallow people": "What they call their loyalty, and their fidelity, I call either the lethargy of custom or their lack of imagination." Betrayal, by such an account, is the expression of a free, active imagination, whereas loyalty is nothing but tedious timidity.

By this cynical account, there is no moral ambiguity. Noble moral emotions should appear in the periodic table of human emotions as by-products of base moral emotions. Thus there is not much difference between the emotional makeup of a patriotic investigator and the ideological traitor whom he confronts. Who is broken on the wheel and who turns the wheel is sheer accident from a psychological point of view. It is not a clash between the integrity of a patriotic spy catcher and the perfidious nature of a traitor. The clash has very little to do with their character and everything to do with the relations they are in.

High-Minded Betrayer

The mixed motives claim is the claim that in the case of betrayal, we cannot extricate base motives from idealistic ones, and hence the concept of traitor is an essentially contestable concept: there are no clear cases of betrayers.

This doesn't seem right. Moreover, it is not right. But then the interesting question is not how base betrayers' motives are but how to account for high-minded betrayers, or, rather, how high-minded betrayers account for themselves.

There are various images that accompany high-minded ideological betrayers. For example, they may cast themselves as being caught in a Shakespearean moral dilemma of the sort "not that I loved Caesar less but that I loved Rome more."

Indeed, a common self-understanding of political betrayers is that of individuals fixed on the horns of moral dilemma. The dilemma involves a conflict of loyalties: opting for one choice means betraying the other. The choice is a forced one with no escape route. Political betrayers fairly often present themselves as having opted for the higher and nobler choice. It is a choice that demands courage and fortitude, unlike the conventional and cozy choice adopted by everyone around them.

Klaus Fuchs, the noted German atomic physicist who described himself as a "controlled schizophrenic," believed at the beginning of his spying operation during the war that there wasn't a conflict of loyalties for him to face. Britain, his adopted country, and the Soviet Union, his "ideological country," were both fighting Germany, his native country, a country that had betrayed him. The Soviets, he thought, should get all the information needed for the common struggle against Nazi Germany. He thought that the blame should fall on the policy of not providing the Soviets with the information needed, rather than on him. Fuchs apparently went on spying for the Soviets even after the war was over.[10]

Betrayers with communist convictions believed that they faced a dilemma between being loyal to humanity and being loyal to their parochial community. They quite often believed that they were serving the working class, which was the universal class that stood for humanity at large. In betraying the capitalist state they were not even betraying petty local loyalties, but only the state as a ruling-class agent of exploitation, if not downright oppression. In their view, betraying the capitalist state shouldn't be regarded as a genuine moral conflict of loyalties. The choice was between being loyal to a sham state apparatus and being loyal to humanity, the humanity of the future. This was not a moral dilemma, though it could be a serious prudential one due to the risk involved in betraying a powerful state. For the true believer in communism, there was no room for moral ambiguity: the dilemma was resolved and the choice was clear. If a comrade was still on the horns of an unresolved dilemma, it meant that he was still in the grip of an old bourgeois morality.

Indeed, many political betrayers make a sharp distinction between being loyal to the government, which they shouldn't be, and being loyal to the people, which they should be. Loyalty to the government is devoid of true moral force, whereas loyalty to the people has a great deal of moral force to it. Ideological betrayers may readily admit that they betrayed the government, but they would vehemently deny that they betrayed the people. On the contrary, they would argue that by betraying the government, they most effectively served the true interests of the people.

It is an obvious yet highly significant fact about our life that we are given over to many loyalties. These loyalties may clash and often do. On occasion the clash is so severe that each side demands total loyalty and views dual loyalty as betrayal. "He that is not with me is against me," says Jesus (Matthew 12:30). But on another occasion Jesus amazes his disciples by telling them: "Give back to Caesar what is Caesar's and to God what is God's" (Mark 12:17).

We don't have a moral or ethical framework to rank all our loyalties so as to decide, in time of conflict, which loyalty we should uphold and which we should give up. Moral ambiguity seems to be the proper description for facing an unresolved case of incompatible loyalties. With moral ambiguity upon us and no way out of our dilemma, we face a tragic choice: we are damned if we betray the one and damned if we betray the other.

Some resolve their moral dilemma of, say, loyalty to society or loyalty to personal friends with ease, at least theoretically. E. M. Forster opts for personal loyalty over public loyalty, and all he asks is to have the courage to abide by this conviction, whereas the elder James Mill claims that he would unflinchingly sacrifice his friends for the public good.

The most serious claim about the ambiguity of betrayal is the claim that betrayal almost always involves dual loyalty; at least dual, and possibly more. So it has to do not with lack of loyalty, which is the core of betrayal, but rather with the claims of more than one loyalty.

The accusation of betrayal is the accusation that one let the wrong loyalty trump the other, rather than the accusation of being simply disloyal. This point is well taken, but how does it relate to Forster's choice of always preferring the concrete to the abstract? Indeed, Forster in his 1938 essay "What I Believe" too cheerfully proclaimed the celebrated dictum "I hate the idea of causes, and if I had to choose between betraying my country and betraying my friend, I hope I should have the guts to betray my country."[11]

For most people "my country" means, among other things, "my family." This is true as a matter of concrete fact and not as a matter of abstract cause. On the whole, one's family lives in one's country. Betraying one's country usually does involve betraying one's family. Even Forster would have been hard put to betray his aunt Marianne for the sake of a friend. True, he did not choose his aunt and she did not choose him, but from the time of his father's death a year after he was born she helped his mother look after him with great care. If betraying England means intention-ally putting its people at risk, then in betraying England for the sake of a friend, Forster puts at risk Aunt Marianne, among others: it is a betrayal of her and not just a betrayal of the idea of England (or Britain for that matter). It is here that Forster fails to heed his own heroine's wise sermon to "only connect!" He did not connect his aunt with England.

It took such a keen connoisseur of betrayal as Joseph Conrad to tell a story of "my country"—as opposed to "my friend"—that was free of family connections. Razumov, the hero of *Under Western Eyes*, is "as lonely in the world as a man swimming in the deep sea."[12] He does not know his family. All he knows is that he is Rus-sian. He believes that a certain Prince K is his illegitimate father. This is as far as his family ties go. He faces the Forster predicament in its pure form: the friend or the state. He betrays his friend. I mention Conrad's story to indicate how unusual Forster's predicament is. At a certain point the self-conscious Razumov declares: "Betray. A great word. What is betrayal? They talk of a man betraying his country, his friends, his sweetheart. There must be a moral bond first."[13] I believe that Razumov makes an important point. Thick relations provide the ethical bond that the act of betrayal presupposes. It is in the credentials of this presupposition that I am most interested in my discussion of betrayal.

The ambiguity of betrayal currently of topical interest is not any of the ambiguities I have mentioned so far but rather the ambiguity delineated by the thin line between nasty traitor and noble whistle-blower.

Between Traitor and Whistle-Blower

A person who voluntarily reveals to the public a well-kept secret of actual or potential wrongdoing by an organization is a whistle-blower. There are many ways to reveal wrongdoing to the public: one way is to inform the authorities anonymously, another way is to leak information to the media, and still another is to tell the story to the public without hiding one's identity. By "whistle-blowing" I mean predominantly an inside job. This can be done with the encouragement of outsiders—journalists, undercover police agents, and whatnot—but still the main burden is on the inside informant. The suspected organization will most likely defend itself by depicting the informant as a snitch who cannot fit in any organization and exacts revenge out of irrepressible resentment. We know the script. The organization under fire hopes that the whistle-blower will be discredited for performing an act of disloyalty.

The whistle-blower is usually a conscientious figure: maligned by some, idolized by others. The law halfheartedly protects whistle-blowing, but only halfheartedly, for fear that whistle-blowing will disturb the government itself as the organization involved in the wrongdoing.

The notion of the whistle-blower is important to our dealings with betrayal. Many betrayers claim for themselves the moral status of a whistle-blower.

The metaphor of the whistle-blower is based on a referee blowing the whistle to indicate foul play. The referee is presumed to be impartial to the teams on the playing field, treating all the players equally, without bias. The referee is the enforcer of the rules of the game.

Should there be a parallel presumption in favor of the moral integrity of the whistle-blower? Is the presumption rebutted if the whistle-blower's moral integrity is found to come up short? In the case of a metaphorical whistle-blower, the presumption means that one is presumed to be clean as a whistle. This means that one uncovers one's findings out of genuine concern for public well-being and takes special care to be as accurate as possible in reporting wrongdoings. The whistle-blower should blow the whistle with a clear conscience.

Another possible source for the metaphor of the whistle-blower is the British bobby, the constable who used to be equipped with only a whistle and no gun. But even if we switch from the referee to the bobby, the presumption of good intentions remains the same.

Note that we are dealing here with assessing the actor, rather than assessing the act, for we are interested in the comparison between traitors and whistle-blowers. The overt connotations of "traitor" are bad, whereas the connotations of "whistle-blower" are on the whole good.

Whistle-blowing does not just refer to a revelation of what is morally wrong but also addresses illegal practices that do not necessarily amount to moral wrongdoing, such as reporting on evasion of a tax that is used to finance an unjust war. My concern here is not with legal whistle-blowing but with moral whistle-blowing.

Let's draw a distinction between whistle-blowing on government agencies and whistle-blowing on nongovernmental organizations. It is an easy distinction to draw, but not an easy distinction to apply. Subcontractors for the government, such as the RAND Corporation in the celebrated case of Daniel Ellsberg, belong to the category of government.

But then there is whistle-blowing aimed at wrongdoing by nongovernmental organizations, such as corporations that pose grave public health and safety hazards.

The business community tends to treat whistle-blowers as informers who not only spoil the reputation of the firm but also destroy the firm's sense of hierarchy. The business community on too many occasions wants to present whistle-blowers as full-fledged traitors who engage in practices akin to treason. In their eyes, the enemies whom the whistle-blowers help are "the enemies of business," whatever that means. Ratting by employees helps the enemies of business, and the informer is nothing but a traitor who shouldn't expect immunity from retaliation by the firm he let down.

Firms are not friends and family: they do not stand in thick relations with their workers. But does a whistle-blower betray her coworkers?

Workers, even those who feel estranged from the organization they work for, may form thick relations with their fellow workers. The formative story of whistle-blowing in my youth was *On the Waterfront*. It was terribly important for me and my friends that the fellow workers of Terry Malloy (Marlon Brando) stood by him, a whistle-blower about to testify against the mobster union boss Johnny Friendly (Lee J. Cobb). We didn't see breaking *omertà*, the Mafia code of silence, as a problem. But breaking solidarity with coworkers by breaking the union was a problem. It was, however, mitigated when we realized that this particular union was a Mafia-run operation. This in any case was the situation that was presented in the movie, modeled on a true case at the Hoboken docks. As long as there was a reign of fear on the docks, *omertà* was kept. Once the fear was dispelled by the sheer courage of a whistle-blower, the union turned from a Mafia organization into a locus of worker solidarity. At the end of Budd Schulberg and Elia Kazan's *Waterfront* fellow workers showed solidarity with the whistle-blower: the dockworkers refused to work till the whistle-blower was reinstated to his former position. But this is only at the end. We were all struck by the scene in which Terry's young friend and fan Tommy, who helps him raise pigeons, hurls a dead pigeon in front of Terry, saying, "A pigeon for a pigeon." Tommy expresses a culture of deep mistrust of the authorities, of whatever kind: any information provided to the authorities is snitching. In this view, the union boss can be recognized for the villain he is, but he is still our villain, whereas the anonymous authorities—police and judges and whatnot—are not "us" but the enemy with whom we do not cooperate, no matter what. The waterfront workers coming from New Jersey's ethnic neighborhoods may have shared this attitude. They needed the authority of the waterfront priest to overcome this deeply held attitude of suspicion. A deaf and dumb attitude when it comes to cooperating with the authorities of the law is an outcome not only of fear of a local bully but also of a deep-seated mistrust of state authorities as such. The coworkers of a whistle-blower may manifest this kind of mistrust, and may feel bitter hostility toward whistle-blowing.

Waterfront had a hidden agenda that was well recognized at the time of its release in the mid-fifties. Both Kazan and Schulberg voluntarily testified before the House Committee on Un-American Activities and named names of former friends. Kazan named members of the celebrated Group Theater, which Kazan had once described as "his first family," that is to say, as people with whom he had the thickest of relations. The hidden message of *Waterfront* was that by naming names to the Committee of Un-American Activities, Schulberg and Kazan, much like Terry Malloy, were acting as whistle-blowers, not as traitors.

A story has it that Arthur Miller, once a close friend of Kazan's, sent Kazan his play *A View from a Bridge,* in which a Sicilian waterfront worker in a moment of rage informs on his illegal immigrant nephew. Kazan, the story has it, mistakenly thought that this was an invitation by Miller to direct the play. Miller straightened him out: "I didn't send it to you because I wanted you to direct it. I wanted you to know what I think of stool pigeons."[14]

From reading the literature on real-life whistle-blowing, one gets a distinct impression that fellow workers of whistle-blowers are on the whole far from being sympathetic to them. This should come as no surprise: whistle-blowers may threaten the livelihood of their fellow workers by revealing to the public wrongdoing by the firm they work for. It may force the firm to close and the coworkers to be unemployed. But there is another element in whistle-blowing that may alienate fellow workers from a whistle-blower. It is the air of moral superiority that the whistle-blower assumes. The whistle-blower is bravely exposing the truth, in contrast to other workers' sheepishly complicit behavior in helping the firm's cover-up. Moral superiority is not something easily forgiven.

Ralph Nader famously stands for the right of workers to expose with impunity any wrongdoing by the organization they work for, be it in its policies, its production, or the daily running of the workplace. Nader, perhaps more than anyone else, promotes the idea that accountability means both responsibility and total transparency. The concept of whistle-blowing is recent, and Ralph Nader in the early 1970s was at its origin. However, the practice is far older. Yet once the concept as a sign of overt recognition of the practice was in place, it may very well have affected the practice itself, not only in terms of the number of cases of whistle-blowing but also in the reevaluation of the practice itself.

Nader had a great deal to do with making whistle-blowing a civic virtue of high order and thus loosening the hold of the corporate world on the loyalty of its employees. This belongs to the political backdrop of whistle-blowing, but the main thrust of the concept is its moral underpinning, namely, putting public interest before corporate interest, even by those who make their living in the corporate world. As I already mentioned, the corporate world presents whistle-blowing in a very different light, as an act of gross ingratitude: biting the hand that feeds you.

This is feudal morality: gratitude comes before everything else. There is no question that firms try to arrogate the loyalty of thick relations with family and friends to their side, but this has hardly any credibility in the current corporate world, where one can be fired on a whim.

I am trying to separate the issue of moral justification for whistle-blowing from the issue of whether whistle-blowing is an act of betrayal.

Henrik Ibsen's 1882 play *An Enemy of the People* is far from being a play about corporate whistle-blowing, yet some features of the plot are remarkably pertinent to some of our ethical and moral concerns with whistle-blowing. In a small seaside town an enormous bathing compound was built, endowed with a great deal of public and private funding with the aim of attracting health tourism. Stockman, a respected and beloved doctor, discovers that the drainage system is badly contaminated by waste from a local tannery. At first he is feted as the man who saved the town, but once the economic implications for the future of the huge investment in the bath become clear, the idealistic incorruptible doctor is ostracized, most painfully by his own brother, the chair of the powerful bathing compound committee. The worthy whistle-blowing doctor is treated as a worthless nuisance and his idealism is regarded as an advanced form of insanity.

Whistle-blowers do not necessarily get respect and recognition for their service to the public good. They may be tarnished even to the point of being regarded as the enemy of the people they serve. This point can be stressed by traitors who are treated as enemies of the people yet view themselves as unrecognized whistle-blowers: Yes, we betrayed information without authorization, but we did so for the greater good of the people.

Recall that the context of our discussion is the ambiguities of betrayal and the issue in this last section is the relation between betrayal and whistle-blowing. It seems that we need a referee's meta-whistle to toot when the fine line between moral whistle-blowing and ideological betrayal is crossed.

Is Snowden Snow White?

Edward Snowden recently raised the stakes of whistle-blowing in a way no one had before. He disclosed hundreds of thousands of classified documents, most prominent among them ones on the massive surveillance program carried out by the National Security Agency (NSA) in the United States. Reports based on the leaked documents were published in the *Guardian* and the *Washington Post* in May 2013. It created a tremendous uproar when the extent and the depth of the surveillance became clear. The organizations involved in the scheme were government agencies as well as private corporations. Snowden constantly moved between public and private agencies, and his whistle-blowing has to do with both types of organization. Snowden became an emblem of the controversial whistle-blower: hero to some, traitor to others. Indeed, he himself vacillated in different periods of his life between two extreme positions: the belief that anyone who leaks classified documents "should be shot in the balls" and the later attitude that one should "inform the public as to that which is done in their name and that which is done against them."

U.S. Army Private First Class Bradley Manning (later to become Chelsea Manning) outclassed Snowden in the number of classified military and diplomatic documents he leaked. The charges against Manning were severe, but the severest charge of all, aiding the enemy, which amounts to treason, was dropped. Manning was exempted from the charge of treason because his leaks were directed to the public at large. Leaking to the public at large may help the enemy, but the intention in leaking was not to help the enemy. "Manning was viewed as both a 21st-century Tiananmen Square Tank Man and an embittered traitor," notes Wikipedia.[15] He was credited with sparking the Arab Spring by leaking cables referring to the corruption of the First Family in Tunisia, which coincided with the famous dramatic suicide of a fruit vendor protestor. The content of the cables spread among Tunisians at the time like the fire that sparked the revolutionary flame in the Arab world.

Both Snowden and Manning by their leaks raise a very serious problem: Can governments govern innocently?[16]

Dirty Hands

Manning's detractors, and they are many, claim that the damage he caused to the conduct of vital secret diplomacy is irreparable.

The two cases of Manning and Snowden and the controversy that ensued provide a diffuse sense of ambiguity about betrayal. That is, betrayal can quite easily split the public into those who view it as whistle-blowing in the service of a noble cause—to educate the public of what has been done in its name—and those who believe that without secrecy there is no security and security requires the use of dirty hands, or the use of nasty means to fight evil forces. Surveillance, even on a massive scale, is just the price that we, as a community, have to pay for our security and stability.

The attitude toward political and military whistle-blowers—as despicable traitors or supreme patriots—rests on a more basic divide, namely, the attitude toward the use of dirty hands in politics.

Hands may get dirty at two different tiers: an elevated tier that involves decisions of life and death and a mundane tier of dreary decisions about how to stay in power. Breaching morality on the elevated tier has to do with crimes, while breaching morality on the mundane tier has to do with misdemeanors. I use "crimes" and "misdemeanors" in a moral sense and not necessarily in a legal sense.

Nixon's decision to carpet bomb Hanoi on Christmas Day 1972 rests on the elevated tier of crime. Nixon's Watergate cover-up is on the mundane tier of misdemeanor. The first, as Bernard Williams used to say, involves criminals; the second involves crooks.

Exposure of crooks acting crookedly out of sheer selfishness is usually welcomed by the public. By contrast, the reception of leaks about the use of dirty hands by government and army officials, supposedly working for the public interest, is mixed: mixed, roughly, between those who believe that dirty hands are just dirty and that there is no way to wash them with the detergent of necessity and those who believe that there is no way to govern innocently and that dirty hands are a necessity of life and should be kept in the dark.

States need to keep some information classified. Classified information should be accessible only to those who are authorized. If this is true, then the government, and not hackers, should have the authority to decide what information must be classified and who is entitled to have access to it. This is an argument in favor of the presumption that the government and none but the government is entitled to control classified information. But like any other presumption, this presumption in favor of government authority can be rebutted: for example, with evidence that the government is trying to cover up its gross misuses of power. The issue then becomes what counts as a gross misuse of power and, more important, who will decide. People who believe in the necessity of dirty hands for a good cause won't accept any rebuttal of the presumption that the government should be the sole arbiter of state secrets, even if it must use dirty-handed tactics.

On the whole, when a cover-up by the government is perceived as a mere means to save the government from embarrassment, the public is edgier than in cases of a blatant use of dirty hands for what is claimed to be done in the public interest. Indeed, classified information is on too many occasions nothing but a protective belt for politicians caught with their pants down, as, for example, in political sex scandals. More important, the cover-up of political embarrassment is due to momentous incompetence: censorship gives the impression that classified information is quite often about avoiding embarrassment, and rarely about national interest.

People who are hostile to political whistle-blowing feel that shaming their government in the eyes of the world is akin to betrayal. For them political embarrassment is by no means trivial. It erodes political authority and creates a climate of irreverence. It dispels a much-needed mystique of power without which no government can govern successfully. Respect is power. In this view, whistle-blowing exposes the government as either incompetent and out of touch with reality or, worse, as being too much in touch with reality by being downright corrupt. For an authoritarian, eroding authority is a subversive act that leads to anarchy, and anarchy is the ultimate political sin, whereas stability is the highest virtue. Authoritarianism doesn't look kindly on whistle-blowing, not even of the gossipy, embarrassing kind.

Authoritarianism is in the grip of a paternalistic picture of politics: the public is a bunch of unruly children who need a disciplinarian father to set them straight. Whistle-blowing is a subversive act that holds the pater authority in contempt. There can be no authority without mystery, believes the authoritarian. De Gaulle mustn't be accessible to the people, nor must his reasons for action be accessible; they must be shrouded in mystery as reasons of state, all for the glory of France. Once one demystifies de Gaulle's stance and presents him as a melodramatic figure, one undermines his authority as the father of the nation, and that is very bad. Whistle-blowing is an act of political anarchism. It is an act of demystification, and as such, it is an act of subversion and a step on the slippery slope of betrayal.

What emerges from this account of whistle-blowing and whistle-blowers is the ambivalence of public opinion toward it. Part of the ambivalence is motivated by the direct interests of those who are afraid of being exposed, for they have so much to hide. This kind of fig-leaf hostility to whistle-blowing is pretty straightforward and not terribly interesting. The interesting case is raised by those who claim that one cannot govern innocently, by which they mean transparently, for there is a need for dirty hands and mystification in order to govern successfully. The clash here is between morality and ethics. Morality rules against dirty hands and mystification on grounds of falsification, but ethics in the service of a community of thick relations may require both.

The clash between ethics and morality is a recurrent theme in this book, always in support of the claim that betrayal belongs predominantly to ethics, and only derivatively to morality.

The distinction between ethics and morality is based on the distinction between thick and thin human relations. Betrayal is the betrayal of thick relations. This is the main claim. The next two chapters are meant to clarify the main claim.

3

Betraying Thick Relations

BETRAYAL IS UNGLUING THE GLUE OF THICK HUMAN RE-lations. This is an admittedly puzzling opening statement. Saying that betrayal does to human relations what acetone does to glue does not make things any clearer. I shall start by elaborating the glue metaphor and only then move to unpack it in more literal terms.

Relation as Glue

Concern with betrayal brings me to thick human relations. In thinking about relations in general we are in the grip of a picture that has a particular hold on our thinking about thick human relations.

The idea is that our intuitive notion of relations in general comes with a picture: a relation is two (or more) things glued together. The glue, metaphorically speaking, *is* the relation. It is what makes things stick together. The metaphor for relation may go by many names—cement, tie, knot, stitch, fetter, cord—but the idea is the same: a relation is something above and beyond the things that stand in the relation. The Fascist emblem of a bundle of reeds tied together, borrowed from ancient Rome, is a pernicious expression of this picture: people tied together under the authority of the axe. On their own, individuals are feeble reeds, but tied together they are formidable.

Logically, the glue metaphor is cause for an old concern. If we have a relation, say, between Abraham and Isaac, and the glue that connects them ("the father of") is a third thing, then the question is: what is the relation between Abraham and the glue and Isaac and the glue? In accounting for this über-relation we need superglue, and the road to infinite regress is paved. The picture of the glue becomes sticky.

Logicians have tried hard to dispel the attractiveness of the glue picture, namely, the need for a third element in the relation, by reducing relations to sets. Norbert Wiener, Felix Hausdorff, and Casimir Kuratowski each suggested a way of reducing relations to sets. W. V. O. Quine viewed the reduction of relations to sets as a philosophical triumph: the paradigm for philosophical analysis.[1] Whatever clarity and economy are gained from the use of Ockham's razor to reduce relations to sets, the glue picture still plays a significant role in our day-to-day understanding of human relations and especially family relations. Indeed, "blood relations" as the expression of family relations provides such glue, for blood is meant to be the sturdiest human glue there is. The Bible has another bodily substance to glue the family together for generations and generations: "seed" (Hebrew *zerah* and Greek *sperma*).

Jews, for example, understand themselves as related to the "seed of Abraham," which makes the Jewish glue of "the seed of Abraham" doubly awkward. For rabbinic Judaism, it is the mother, not the father, who determines who is a Jew: a Jew is anyone who is born to a Jewish mother. Being born of the seed of a Jewish father doesn't make the running, probably for the reason that only the identity of the mother is certain. Another reason for the awkwardness is that "the seed of Abraham," which was meant to refer exclusively to Jews ("in Isaac shall thy seed be called" [Genesis 21:12]), cannot deny that Ishmael is very much of the seed of Abraham, and in the Quranic tradition Ishmael is the ancestor of the most noble of the Arab tribes. This seedy problem alludes to a weighty theme: metonyms of nature, such as blood and seed, perceived as gluing thick relations are not enough to make the glue stick. Thick human relations are not constituted by mere raw biological facts. The atavistic social concern with so-called illegitimate children tells us that blood and seed are not enough. Thick human relations are ultimately determined by social facts and fictions: sperm are brigands harnessed by brigades of norms. Seed plays havoc with the notion of betrayal. Is a bastard child expected to be the most loyal or rather the most treacherous of one's children? Are bastards to be deemed as trustworthy as King Arthur, himself an illegitimate son, or as untrustworthy as Mordred, Arthur's vicious illegitimate son? But even without the issue of legitimacy, the "natural glue" is not always a sufficient condition for establishing thick relations. Those who donate their sperm to a sperm bank or surrogate mother can and should be kept in the dark and not establish thick relations with their seed.

Fostering is an interesting case of thick family relations: it involves no blood and no seed. But a form of fostering in Arab societies, whereby "milk kinship" is established between babies breast-fed by the same wet nurse, creates secondary kinship, with a strong obligation of loyalty and protection. Milk, a vital substance, is the glue. It is not as thick as blood, but thick enough.

There is no institution of fostering in the Bible. The God of the Hebrew Bible has no son, let alone sons, but he adopts the people of Israel as his sons and, as Ezekiel 16 tells it, he even adopts Israel as a daughter. God adopts an exposed girl on the day she is born: "And when I passed by thee, and saw thee wallowing in thy blood, I said unto thee: In thy blood, live; yea, I said unto thee: In thy blood, live." There is blood all over the adoption of the girl, yielding the impression that blood glues the relation between the God of the Hebrew Bible and the adopted Israel. The Israelites, the adopted sons and daughters of God, instead of being eternally grateful, as helpless adopted children should be, betray God by whoring after strange gods. These adopted children turn into bastards: ungrateful adopted children.

If blood and seed are perceived as examples of concrete substances that establish family relationships, what can we say about friendship, the other paradigm of thick relations? With friendship we would expect pure spiritual glue. But even in the case of friendship some old concrete pictures creep in. First among them is the effort to mold friendship on family glue. "Blood brother," in the sense of comrade turned brother by an oath of loyalty and the rite of mingling blood, attests to such effort. Mingling blood is supposed to provide the thickest glue of friendship in arms and is a familiar rite in warrior cultures.

The business of blood brothers is indeed blood: "For today who sheds his blood with me shall be my brother."[2] Henry V is talking not about the ritual intermingling of blood but about the serious business of shedding the blood of others in battle.

Blood may serve as an emblematic glue of camaraderie, but it can hold for soul mates. In the book of Deuteronomy (12:23) blood is the soul *(nefesh),* but since then the soul has been greatly spiritualized, conceived in disembodied terms.

Yet even a "spiritual" relation is not immune from the concrete hold of the glue picture. Think of Christian communion. The word "communion," used for fellowship in faith *(koinonia)*, is glued with flesh and blood: "The Lord Jesus, on the night he was betrayed, took bread, and when he had given thanks, he broke it and said, 'This is my body, which is for you; do this in remembrance of me.' In the same way, after supper he took the cup, saying, 'This cup is the new covenant in my blood; do this, whenever you drink it, in remembrance of me'" (1 Corinthians 11:22–25). In the rite of "breaking the bread" members of the community are glued to each other by sharing the consecrated bread and the blessed wine. The glue is the body of Christ. The Christian glue is transmitted by eating and drinking the consecrated bread and wine.

It is interesting to note that the account of Jesus breaking the bread is preceded by "on the night he was betrayed." Betrayal is contrasted with the glue that unites the disciples and friends, namely, the bread and wine of the Last Supper. It is not God the Father who is betrayed on that night but Jesus the friend, or so I shall argue in Chapter 9. Betrayal, in any case, is the act of removing the glue from thick relations.

A Reminder: Blood Talk

Thick blood relations and living space are inflammable stuff that not a long time ago set Europe aflame. Discourse on thick blood relations and territoriality is thoroughly tainted by the Nazi ideology of blood and soil: blood means ancestry, exemplified by pure race, and soil means homeland *(Heimat)*, exemplified by rural countryside. Together they formed the fundamental notions of the Nazi expansionist plan of race and space *(Rasse und Raum)*.

Karl Kraus allegedly said that the mixture of blood and soil is a recipe for tetanus. However, Nazi ideologues made blood and soil the fountainhead of healthy relations and their negation the drainpipe of cosmopolitanism and big-city degeneracy.

I think that blood and soil should serve us as a constant reminder of how badly wrong these ideas can go. But as dangerous as "thinking with blood" can be, it should not restrict our probing into the picture underlying thick relations. If anything, the opposite should be true, and more probing should be the order of the day.

Thick Relations

Using "thick" as an attribute of human relations is a figurative extension of "thick" as physically dense, like trees in a thick forest. This figurative extension is evident in expressions such as "thick friends," which means very close friends: friends who stay friends through thick and thin.

When it comes to human relations, family and friends are core cases of thick human relations, and it is for us to examine which figurative extension is a natural extension and which is overstretched. If a corporate manager tells his employees, "We are one big family," it sounds hollow, if not preposterous. It sounds hollow partly because of its manipulative use in trying to recruit for a cold, calculating corporation the loyalty and warmth of affection that are associated with family relations. I shall return to the theme of family and friends in contrast with firms later.

Checking the credentials of the figurative extension of an expression above and beyond its core cases belongs to philosophy in its critical role of policing the boundaries of sense. But it is also the role of philosophy to patrol the boundaries of sensibility.

Sensibility is the range of emotive associations and attitudinal connotations that systematically accompany the sense of an expression.

Some of those metaphorical extensions of family and friends are familiar instances of moral kitsch, which sentimentalizes family and friendship beyond recognition. By sentimentalizing I mean turning the object of sentiment into an object of great purity.

Moral kitsch is not just an expression of bad taste; it can turn nasty. C. G. Jung was quick to point out that sentimentality is a superstructure erected on brutality.[3] The reason, I believe, is that a perceived threat to relations that are like relations to family and friends—relations taken as an emblem of purity—justifies any brutality in response.

The role of family and friends in shaping our notion of thick relations goes way beyond the fact that family and friends are clear examples of thick relations. They are the objects of comparison for all thick relations, and they shape the way we think about thick relations. It should be no surprise that family relations and relations between friends loom large in what follows.

Thick relations are the relations we care about most. Caring about our thick relations makes them important to us. If betrayal has the potential to undermine something important in our life, it should concern us a great deal. By "we" I mean normal people who are in need of thick relations. By "we" I exclude desert hermits, Diogenes-like cynics, and some labeled as Stoics.

Indeed, some Stoics seem to entertain an argument against developing thick relations of any kind. Being tied by thick relations, they believe, makes one a puppet to fortune, since one becomes dependent on the vagaries of fortune, which are not under one's control. Autarky and autarky alone immunizes one from the vagaries of time. What is truly good in life must withstand all contingencies. Thick relations are no good in that regard, for losing loved ones is wretchedly bad. Whereas having courage is good in all circumstances, and therefore good without qualification. Good things are not relational. Relation calls for dependency. Good things are character traits. They are captured linguistically by one-place predicates such as "wise" and "courageous." Ethics as a guide to good living should deal with virtues rather than with human relationships. This does not, according to the Stoics, mean that thick relations are not on occasion preferable to having no relations at all. Thick relations are of limited value, however: they are not good in the Stoic sense of good as that which is valuable under all possible changes.

Most people most of the time in most places care most about their thick human relations. The relation between caring and importance is complicated, but caring is at least a strong indication of what caring people hold important. So we have now identified two features of thick relations: caring and importance.

In saying that paradigmatic cases of thick relations are relations with family and friends, I take "paradigmatic" to mean not only clear cases of correctly applying the expression "thick relations" but also, and perhaps more important, paradigmatic cases in the sense of models. By "model" I mean an exemplary case that guides the use of an expression when applied to new and less clear instances.

Thus, for example, tribes, ethnic groups, and nations make claims on their members by giving the impression that they establish thick relations like the ones that hold family members together. Tribes, ethnic groups, and nations view themselves as extended families, claiming for themselves the intensity that the model of the nuclear family provides. One may think that making family an object of comparison for the nation is a precarious move, but it is hard to deny the influence of its use in shaping the idea of the ethnic nation.

Thick relations manifest three orientations that are of great moment to our concern with betrayal: *belonging, memory,* and *meaning.* These headings are placeholders. Let's view each in turn.

Belonging

Thick relations are based on belonging rather than on achievement. Your relation to your children does not hinge on their achievements, nor does their relation to you depend on your achieving anything, or so you hope. You are bonded together in thick relations because you belong to each other. I wish for my children to achieve a great deal in their lives, but they are my children in virtue of who they *are,* my children, and not in virtue of what they *do* and how well they do. My thin relation with, say, a chance street vendor is normally based on her ability to sell me what I want and my readiness to pay for it. You may think that something more ambitious and perhaps loftier than a pedestrian exchange of buying and selling should be called achievement, but buying and selling is an achievement all right, and it is enough to establish my thin relation with the vendor. This thin relation would be handily dissolved if she could not provide the good or I could not provide the money. The chance street vendor and I do not belong to each other in any way except in the way we do business.

The distinction between the two types of orientations in human relations, between *belonging* and *achievement,* is similar to the distinction between two types of social status, one based on *ascription* and the other based on *achievement*: gaining status for who you are (by birth) and gaining status for what you do (say, being a painter). The distinction in status goes with the idea that in modern society there is a discernible shift from status based on ascription to status based on achievement. There is room for a parallel idea: in modern times more weight is given to relations based on achievement than to relations based on belonging.

Thick relations are based on belonging. Belonging means that the relation holds irrespective of the evaluation of the actions of those who are thickly related. As such, how can an act of betrayal undermine a thick relation if the relation is based on unconditional belonging?

"Undermining" may mean one of two things: weakening or destroying. Understanding how betrayal can weaken thick relations is not much of a problem. But how can it destroy a relation based on unconditional belonging? The idea of Catholic marriage takes the idea of unconditional belonging seriously, but this is hardly true of all or even most thick relations.

Ernest Renan compared the nation to a "daily referendum": people can dissolve their national ties and stop living together. This is a bad metaphor. Most people do not view their national ties as something that can be dissolved on the whim of a moment. But even between the whim of a moment and strong ties of nationalism there is a similarity. For in the case of nationalism, we should distinguish between *ethnic* nationalism and *civic* nationalism with respect to the role of belonging. Ethnic nationalism views national ties as based on a strong sense of belonging, a relation that can hardly be dissolved, whereas civic nationalism thinks of national ties not in terms of ethnic belonging but as a contractual relation, the strength of which is the strength of a contract, which is always conditional.

The contrast between the two orientations, between belonging and achievement, is quite obviously related to two other orientations manifested in *instrumental* and *non-instrumental* relations. In an instrumental relation—say, between a film actor and a film producer—the relation is an instrument for achieving something, such as a role in a movie. In a non-instrumental relation the relation is an end in itself. Achievement goes together with instrumental human relations, whereas belonging goes together with non-instrumental relations.

Immanuel Kant famously warned against having purely instrumental relations with other human beings: the imperative is not to treat others *only* as means. This is a moral constraint on all instrumental human relations. Human relations based on belonging may be of immense instrumental value for the parties involved, but the very existence of such relations does not hinge on their instrumental value. Again, belonging *should not* be dissolved for lack of achievement. Yet it is wrong to think that a relation of belonging *is not* affected by achievement, or rather by the lack of it. Failure to achieve may cause deep disappointment and thereby strain even the thickest of relations. The elder son who refuses to carry on the solid, traditional family firm and tries instead to pursue a shaky career in the arts is a proverbial type. No matter how disappointing his choice is to the family, he is not a betrayer. There are extreme cases, however, in which lack of achievement, if that is the word, should adversely affect thick relations. One such example is parents who neglect their children to the point where the children must be taken from their custody.

Thickness and Nearness

The prototype for the paradigm cases of thick relations, namely, family and friends, consists of people who know each other on a face-to-face basis. However, thick relations extend far beyond personal face-to-face relations. Thick relations permeate secondary social groups, which, unlike primary groups, are far removed from face-to-face encounters.

The English idiom "near and dear" is not confined to family, but on many occasions that is what it is. "Near" may of course mean something figurative: near to one's heart. However, I am interested in the literal sense of near and, in particular, in the relation between nearness in space and thickness in relations. Before the technological revolution in transportation, there was a very strong correlation between nearness in space and thickness in relations. The dear lived near. Yet there were some glaring conflicts. The Hebrew Bible tells the story of how Abraham, living in the land of Canaan (Palestine), sent his most trusted servant to fetch for his son Isaac a bride from Haran, which was a long way off in Upper Mesopotamia (in present-day Turkey), because he rejected the prospect of marrying his son to one of the local Canaanite women. The point of the story is that in a conflict between blood relation and spatial proximity as criteria for forming a family, blood relation takes precedence. This motive repeats itself with the twin sons of Isaac: Esau married into a neighboring Canaanite family, to the intense chagrin of his parents, but Jacob married a blood relation living far away.

In general, though, proximity breeds children. One may even add the far-fetched evolutionary speculation that for a long time proximity served as a proxy for genetically related relatives.

Jan Gross wrote a shattering book on tragic thick relations between Jews and their gentile neighbors in Jedwabne, a tiny Polish town of 2,500 people. The very title of his controversial book, *Neighbors (Sasiedzi),* makes the distressing point of thick relations most horribly betrayed. The Jews of the town were herded by their Polish neighbors into a huge barn, where they were burned alive. Very few Jews of the town survived, and one of them, Shmuel Wasserstein, is the main witness in Gross's book on the events that took place on that horrid day in July 1941. In Gross's account, half of the adult male population, "ordinary people," participated in the massacre. The instigators of the crime were German Nazis, but the genocide-abiding executioners were the Polish neighbors.

Are Neighbors Expected to Hold Thick Relations?

The biblical book of Job tells us that when Job's friends *(reai Iov)* heard about his troubles they set out from their homes and went to comfort him (Job 2:11). *Reah* here is correctly translated as "friend." But in the Book of Leviticus, where it states "You shall love your neighbor as yourself" (19:18), the translation of *reah* is "neighbor." The three friends of Job, like the three wise men (magi) of the East, came from three different places, possibly three distant places. Proximity, spatial proximity, is not a condition for friendship in Job's case.

Jesus' celebrated parable of the Good Samaritan comes in answer to the question "Who is my neighbor?" The Samaritan was not a neighbor of the Jew, who was on his way from Jerusalem to Jericho. He didn't habitually live near the one whom he helped. But Jesus did not obliterate the moral hold of spatial proximity in this case. The Samaritan and the robbed and wounded Jew who encountered each other were strangers, but once they met, direct proximity established a direct moral claim. The Samaritan was not a neighbor, but he was near, very near, by virtue of a mere chance encounter.

In the ancient world of the Bible, family, clan, and tribe lived in proximity, and Job's story of long-distance friendship is very much the exception. In this sense "neighbor" correlates well with "comrade." Deserting a place might mean betraying one's near and dear. Leaving one's place wasn't a neutral act of drifting away, unless you moved together as a wandering tribe. One needed reasons such as famine, war, and other threats to life to move away from the proximity of the family. The expectation was that one would stay in proximity to one's people. Distance calls for justification.

There is *blessed* proximity and *menacing* proximity. Blessed proximity invites the picture of literal face-to-face relations. Menacing proximity invites the picture of a stab in the back.

Home and Homeland

Proximity starts at home. The question is whether home and homeland are proxies for our thick relations with the dwellers at home and the inhabitants of the homeland or whether home and homeland are associated with the dwelling itself. If they serve as proxies, then betraying one's home and homeland by, say, desertion is just a roundabout way of betraying one's family and people. "Homeland" in English is more of a bureaucratic invention, as its post-9/11 use in an expression such as "homeland security" attests. It lacks in English the evocative power of equivalent terms such as *Heimat* in German, *rodina mat* (motherland) in Russian, *patria* (fatherland) in Italian and in some dialects of Spanish, and the like. But the relation between home and homeland is important. For the idea is that the nation-state is in the grip of two pictures: the nation as *extended family* and its territory as *home*. One question, then, has to do with the relation between family and home and the relation between nation and homeland. Another question is whether one can betray one's home or homeland as places, with no human beings involved in it.

Robert Frost expressed the idea of home as a locus of thick relations beautifully in "The Death of the Hired Man":

> "Home is the place where, when you have to go there,
> They have to take you in."
>   "I should have called it
> Something you somehow haven't to deserve."

He succeeded in succinctly expressing the sense of unconditional belonging as something that has nothing to do with being deserved. But it is clear that it is the people at home who take you in. It isn't the inert empty dwelling he has in mind as home; it is the dwellers who turn the dwelling into home.

But what about the exiles by the rivers of Babylon who took an oath, "If I forget you, Jerusalem, may my right hand wither away" (Psalms 137:5)? On the face of it, it seems that the psalmist's oath expresses a thick relation with Jerusalem, the place of domicile, rather than with the people who are related to Jerusalem. I don't deny that people may have a strong attachment to a place, but the question is whether the attachment amounts to a thick relation between a human and a location.

The psalmist's attitude to Jerusalem is a proxy for complicated relations with human beings, rather than an attitude toward a mere piece of land. Attachment to land—or, better, landscape—may play an important role in such complicated thick relations. Jerusalem for him is not a piece of real estate but a locus of shared memories that constitute the community of exiles he is with. There is more to a thick relation than mere attachment: the "more" requires human beings, at least for the memories involved in the thick relation.

Proximity, as I have already mentioned, can nourish thick relations and can menace human relations, both thick and thin.

Indeed, it is this ambiguity of proximity that was the experience of the Jews in their many years of exile. Their own proximity bred children, whereas the proximity of others bred contempt.

Jews lived in proximity to their fellow countrymen for long stretches of time, but they felt not like fellows but like strangers. There was a deep failure to establish thick relations with people near to them: not always and not everywhere, but in many places and for long stretches of time.

Freud made famous the idea of the uncanny, that which is familiar and yet utterly strange. If the unambiguously familiar is *heimlich* (homelike), then its antonym, the uncanny, is *unheimlich* (unhomelike). *Heimlich,* as Freud, citing the dictionary, was quick to point out, is the idea of belonging to a home, of not being strange, of being familiar, tame, friendly, intimate, comfortable, agreeable, restful, and secure. By contrast, the uncanny *(unheimlich)* is the eerie, weird, ghostly, and fearful. A great deal of human ambivalence dwells between these two poles: a sense of home, on the one hand, and a sense of the uncanny, on the other.

Freud is a latecomer to the conceptual scene of the uncanny: his essay is from 1919.[4] Ernst Jentsch had published his essay "On the Psychology of the Uncanny" in 1906. Both essays had at the core of their concern the use of the uncanny as a literary device and especially in the hands of E. T. A. Hoffmann. Yet years before Freud and Jentsch wrote their respective essays, Leo Pinsker, a Russified Jew who became a Zionist, had had this very idea. Pinsker had hopes that the Jews would find a home in a liberal Russia, but his hopes were dashed by the pogroms of 1881. Being a medical doctor, he treated the Jewish problem as a medical case. He wrote a pamphlet dubbed *Auto-Emancipation* in 1882. This was a formative statement for Jewish self-understanding. The upshot of it was that the Jew is everywhere a guest and nowhere at home. Jewish existence is the existence of the uncanny. He writes:

> The world saw in this people the uncanny form of one of the dead walking among the living. The ghostlike apparition of a living corpse, of a people without unity or organization, without land or other bonds of unity, no longer alive, and yet walking among the living—this spectral form without precedence in history, unlike anything that preceded or followed it, could but strangely affect the imagination of the nations. And if the fear of ghosts is something inborn, and has a certain justification in the psychic life of mankind, why be surprised at the effect produced by this dead but still living nation.[5]

Pinsker viewed the fear of ghosts as the mother of the fear of Jews, who lead a ghostlike existence, both familiar and uncanny: "Since the Jew is nowhere at home, nowhere regarded as a native, he remains an alien everywhere. That he himself and his forefathers were born in the country does not alter the fact in the least."[6]

Pinsker was wrong in believing that being permanent strangers, as mythologized by Ahasver, the "eternal" wandering Jew, is unique to the Jews. Yuri Slezkine is definitely right in writing: "There was nothing particularly unusual about the social and economic position of the Jews in medieval and early modern Europe. Many agrarian and pastoral societies contained groups of permanent strangers who performed tasks that the natives were unable or unwilling to perform." From the Sheikh Mohammadi of eastern Afghanistan to the Yao of Lake Malawi to the Armenians, Nestorians (Assyrians), overseas Indians, Lebanese, and Chinese, all lead an uncanny mode of existence in the midst of a native agrarian society that is wedded to the land. They, the permanent strangers with whom "one does not eat or intermarry"—merchants, craftsmen, entertainers, entrepreneurs—were "wedded to time, not land: people seen as both homeless and historic, rootless and ancient."[7]

Indeed, such nomadic service tribes observe dietary restrictions, are endogamous, and retain a "secret" language of their own, and though these customs are typical of Jews, they are by no means confined to the Jews. Moreover, the stereotype of service nomads is almost invariably the same: greedy, devious, crafty, pushy, clannish, crude, acquisitive, and indecent. Jews were probably more mythologized than others because of their role in the formation of Christianity and Islam, to the extent that with the shift from agrarian to industrial urban society Jews became the emblem of modern existence. The Jew became a metaphor for modernity. More and more agrarian societies, "first in Europe and then elsewhere, had to become more like the Jew: urban, mobile, literate, mentally nimble, occupationally flexible, and surrounded by aliens."[8]

Sharing territory, even for long periods, is no guarantee of forming thick relations. Some people feel at home in the territory and some don't. Some people feel homesickness when they are away from home and other people feel sick and homeless even at home.

The distinction I am drawing is between *attachment,* which is a strong feeling of affection for something, and a *thick relation* with someone. I have already made the point that one can feel attachment to something but that attachment, however strong, doesn't amount to a thick relation, which takes place only between humans. Only humans with a historical consciousness can be in thick relations. Historical attachment to a place is parasitic on the historical element in constituting thick relations between humans.

An attachment to a place can be a proxy for a thick relation. Home is a combination of thick relations with the dwellers and an attachment to the dwelling. The dwellers don't even have to be current dwellers; they can be dwellers from the past.

Stab in the Back

The stab in the back became a graphic expression of betrayal. Julius Caesar had no problem identifying his betrayer: he was stabbed in the chest. But the noble Siegfried was stabbed in the back by the wicked Hagen in Richard Wagner's opera. Apparently this operatic scene from *Twilight of the Gods (Götterdämmerung)* was evocative enough in the mind of many Germans after the defeat in World War I for the image of the stab in the back to become a foundational myth, according to which the German army was not defeated but betrayed. It was a

Hagen-like assortment of Jews, Bolsheviks, antiwar dissidents, and Weimar's "November Criminals" (who signed the armistice agreement of November 1918) who stabbed the army in the back. The fearless German army was not defeated; it was massively betrayed by treacherous civilians who never really belonged to the nation.

Like many kids of my generation, I was addicted to western films. There was no moral ambiguity in those movies: you could tell the good guys from the bad guys by the cowboy hats. And yet there were strict rules of fair play, such as the face-off between gunslingers at high noon, when the good guy and the bad guy gave each other a chance to shoot from the hip. But then the stunning "spaghetti westerns" of Sergio Leone arrived and a terrible beauty was born. The protagonists were dirty and sweaty, they looked like ambiguous types, but the most shocking thing was that they played dirty. They were shooting each other in the back without giving each other a chance for a fair fight. It was a paradigm shift.

The idiomatic metaphor "straight shooter," referring to an honest man, belongs to this genre. The foil is the dishonest, corrupt, and unscrupulous shooter, the one who is capable of backstabbing.

German cartoons of backstabbing are realizations of this metaphor. They show the straight-shooting helmeted German soldier taking aim at the enemy across the trenches but being stabbed in the back by the enemy within in the form of a swarthy hook-nosed Jew. The stab-in-the-back myth was based on the contrast between naive and knave, between German soldier and archetypical Jew, at times a Bolshevik, at times a plutocrat, but always a foreign element ready to betray from within.

Fifth Column, Trojan Horse, Sabotage

In time of war the fear of betrayal from within—the encompassing group's fear of being betrayed by the encompassed subgroup—can turn into existential panic. Existential panic is related to moral panic, but it is different. Moral panic is when there is fear that a whole value system is collapsing because a social taboo was crossed. Existential panic is when the fear is for the physical existence of the society rather than for its soul.

The idioms "fifth column" and "Trojan horse" are based on extant pictures of sedition, sabotage, and subversion in the service of the enemy without. Even the term "sabotage" is based on the forgotten picture of sixteenth-century Luddites breaking mechanized looms by throwing their wooden shoes (sabots) into the works. Indeed, sabotage can be an important element of betrayal. We may distinguish between material sabotage, acts aimed at disrupting or destroying equipment and material needed for the war effort, and morale sabotage, acts aimed at lowering the morale of the combatants or the civilian population.

The term "fifth column" originated during the three-year siege of Madrid by four columns of Francisco Franco's Falange during the Spanish Civil War. The fifth column referred to the supporters of the Falangists inside the besieged city, who were set to undermine the war effort of the Republicans from within. The Trojan horse is based on a story from the ancient Trojan War in which an enormous wooden horse was deceitfully left behind by the besieging Greeks as an offering to the goddess Athena to ensure their safe voyage back to Greece. Inside the horse were chosen fighters ready to open the gates of Troy to the Greeks once the horse was towed inside the city walls. The ostensible motive of leaving behind the Trojan horse was that it was a gift to Athena, an offering to atone for the desecration of her temple by the invading Greeks. But the lesson of the story is that there cannot be gift relations between mortal enemies like Greeks and Trojans. In Laocoön's words, "Do you think any Greek gift's free of treachery? . . . I fear Greeks, even those bearing gifts."[9] In other words, don't delude yourselves that you are now in thick relations with the Greeks.

Love Your Friend and Hate Your Foe

The ancient Greek term *philia* is habitually translated as "friendship." But it has been pointed out that its scope is far wider than friendship between intimate individuals who are not related by family ties. *Philia* in a way covers a great deal of what I have termed thick relations. Its paradigmatic examples are a fusion of family and friends. The closest friends are contrasted not with family but with one's friends in the narrower sense of the term. Friends used to be made predominantly in one's family: cousins were expected to be friends. The guiding principle of the Greek notion of a thick relation is to side with your relative and friend and to hate *(echthra)* and harm your foe. The idea of *philia* was not unlike a configuration of concentric circles, expanding from friends and close family at the center to the city-state and on to some of the rest. The expansion of *philia* from the inner core to the outer rim changes its nature. The commitment to *philia* in the close circle of family and friends is unconditional. It becomes more strategic as the circle becomes wider. It ends with shifting coalitions: the friends of today are the foes of tomorrow, as was the case between Athens and its allies. The shift that should interest us is that between the inner core of unconditional *philia* and "civic *philia*" (John Cooper's expression), namely, *philia* in the city-state.[10] This shift presents our general problem of whether enlarging the scope of thick relations, say, to the whole nation, doesn't already stretch the metaphor of thickness to the ripping point.

Sophocles's *Antigone* is probably the most-discussed Greek tragedy. It is evident that at the center of the tragedy there is a tremendous clash. But the nature of the clash is open to inter-pretation. The suggestion here is to view the clash as a clash be-tween family *philia* and city-state *philia*. The point is that there is no simple extension from family *philia* to city-state *philia*. By burying her treacherous brother, Antigone acts on family *philia;* Creon, the ruler, acts on city-state *philia*. Creon's commitment to *philia* means hating the enemies of the city. Antigone's brother is the enemy. Hence, from the point of view of the city, he doesn't deserve an honorable burial. For the Greeks, hating a common enemy is part and parcel of the idea of a thick relation. It is against this idea of hating the enemy, as a vital element of a thick relation, that we should appreciate Jesus' revolutionary notion of love.

Jesus famously said: "You have heard that it was said, 'You shall love your neighbor and hate your enemy.' But I say to you, love your enemies." It is not clear where his audience had heard that one must hate one's enemy. But the maxim to both love your family, friends, and community in the sense of affectionately caring *(philia)* for them and hate your enemy does capture the ferocious attitude of the Qumran community at the Dead Sea. Jesus' adage is a radical break from the demand to hate one's enemy.

The idea that being in a thick relation encompasses not only the idea that we affectionately care for one another but also the complementary idea that your enemies are my enemies and mine are yours cuts deep into the human psyche, to the point where loyalty and betrayal are often judged as much by one's hatred of enemies as by one's love of friends. This attitude of hating the enemy lingers on in modern times and current relations. Let me describe a familiar and rather tacky scene. For many good years my wife and I were close friends with a certain couple. After years together they broke up and went through a bitter and ugly divorce, hating each other from among the ruins of their relationship. Both asked for our undivided loyalty. Each demanded that we sever all relations with the monster ex-spouse. In short, they wanted us to take sides, very tough sides. We were not allowed to be neutral in the rift. They took our "understanding" of the other side as nothing short of betrayal. This scene has many variations and intensities, but the idea behind it is clear: my friends are your friends and, no less important, my enemies are your enemies. Enemy is the petri dish of betrayal.

The Unholy Trinity of Betrayal

"Jacob loves Rachel" is a dyadic relation. It is a relation between two objects: Jacob and Rachel. Whereas "Laban betrays Jacob with Leah" is a ternary relation. It holds between three objects: Laban, Jacob, and Leah. Betrayal is a ternary relation. Betrayal in its paradigmatic cases involves a third party on top of the betrayer and the betrayed.

With regard to betrayal, we may distinguish two canonical forms:

(1) A betrays B with C.
(2) A betrays B to C.

The second form (2), "betraying to," roughly means handing over to the enemy, whereas the first form (1) correlates well with "she betrays him with his best friend."

Betrayal with the best friend means that there was a double betrayal: both by the primary betrayer and by the best friend. Betrayal to the enemy does not imply a double betrayal, for the enemy doesn't usually stand in a thick relation with the betrayed.

There is a typical emotion toward the third party that goes hand in hand with betrayal. It is jealousy. Jealousy is most conspicuous in a love triangle. It is jealousy, not envy. Here is the difference: if I envy you, I desire to have what you have, but I don't mind you having it too, whereas if I am jealous of you, I want what you have, but I don't want you to have it. In a love triangle that involves betrayal, jealousy is to be expected, since it is precisely the exclusivity of a particular thick relation that was betrayed. If you betray me in a love triangle, I don't want you to have the love of the third party; I want the love of the third party all to myself.

Morality and Love

In our search for the glue of thick relations we skipped the possibility that morality itself can serve as glue. But can it?

In a famous debate about the enforcement of morality, known as the Hart and Devlin debate, Patrick Devlin makes the claim that "society is not something that is kept together physically; it is held by invisible bonds of common thought. If the bonds were too far relaxed the members would drift apart. A common morality is part of the bondage. The bondage is part of the price of society; and mankind, which needs society, must pay its price."[11] He goes on to state: "Society is entitled by means of its laws to protect itself from dangers, whether from within or without. Here again I think that the political parallel is legitimate. The law of treason is directed against aiding the king's enemies and against sedition from within."[12]

Society in distinction from a collection of individuals, Devlin believes, is a group cemented by common morality. The morality of society is expressed by a shared strong disapproval of unbecoming conduct, such as homosexuality. Moral disapproval is manifested by a combination of emotions such as intolerance and disgust. This combination of negative emotions is a guarantee that the disapproval is intense. In suppressing sinful behavior, according to Devlin, society should act as if it were facing subversive behavior. Erosion of morality is erosion of what cements society and turns it into a meaningless collection of individuals. The cement of society amounts to a strong emotional reaction.

By morality Devlin understands something akin to what G. W. F. Hegel dubbed *Sittlichkeit*: the norms and mores that govern habitual conduct in a given society (in particular a nation) and are regarded as proper. *Sittlichkeit* is neither morality nor ethics in my terms (even though the habitual English translation of *Sittlichkeit* is "ethical life"). It is the conventional ethics of a given society: the mores of a society that contribute to its cohesiveness.[13]

For H. L. A. Hart, the analogy between suppression of sexual immorality and suppression of treason is absurd. Hart assumes that homosexual acts are committed in private and should be confined to the realm of the private, whereas a subversive act of trying to overthrow a legitimate government is a public act. Though I share with Hart the sense that Devlin's analogy between transgression of conventional sexual morality and subversion of the government is grotesque, Hart's line of exposing the absurd along the line of private versus public won't do, either. Conspiracy to overthrow the government can take place in private and homosexuality may go public: one such example is gay parades. But Hart has another line of attack: Devlin commits a fallacy of division. Even if it is true that the cement of society is its shared morality, and even if it is true that dismantling shared morality dismantles society as a whole, it does not follow that any deviation from any conventional norm of a society's shared morality dismantles society. What is true of the whole is not necessarily true of each and every part.

Shared Memory

Thick relations are oriented toward a shared memory of the past. Shared memory does not mean that the individuals who are in thick relations with one another remember the same thing. There is a mnemonic division of labor in thick relations. Those who stand in such relations are plugged into one another and can fill in the memory gaps. What gives thickness to human relations is to a large extent their historical depth.

Memory is veridical: if you remember p, then p is true. If the two of you remember having your first kiss in the train station, then it is true that the two of you had your first kiss in the train station. But what is shared in shared memory is hardly veridical, especially when the shared memory involves many individuals.

Jews have religious obligations to remember certain things. Most of the requirements to remember have to do with the exodus from Egypt. But does the memory of Egypt mean that the events told in the Bible about the exodus are historically veridical? Or is the exodus story a foundational myth no truer than the legend of the foundation of Rome? Is the tale of baby Moses

being set adrift on the Nile no truer than the tale of baby Ro-
mulus and Remus being set adrift on the Tiber?

Shared collective memory is in many cases a shared memory of
an alleged memory; the exodus seems to be such a case. But even
when it is veridical, shared collective memory is shrouded in a fusion of facts and fiction. The further back in the past the remembered event is located, the more assured we can be that in the battle
between fact and fiction, fiction wins. This is the advantage of old
religions, which anchor their foundational stories in a dim ancient
past, whereas new religions such as Mormonism have a much
tougher sell. In any case, mythos, mixed with genuine memory,
constitutes the orientation toward the past in thick relations. The
more people there are involved in the relation, the smaller the ratio
of fact to fiction. Shared collective memory of the past is more a
memory of past memory than a memory of a veridical event.

Nationalism, as an ideology of thick national relations, was in
the last generation subjected to tough scrutiny: is the nation a
primordial social entity predating the nation-state, or is the nation a Johnny-come-lately, a product of the nation-state? Put differently, is the nation antecedent to the nation-state, or is the
nation-state antecedent to the nation?[14]

I believe that this is a wrongheaded choice. What is antecedent
to the nation and the ethnic nation-state is the community of
memory. The institutions of state and religion, with their writs
and rites, contribute a great deal to sustain a community of
memory, but it is wrong to view a community of memory as a
sheer product of manipulation by such institutions. In any case,
thick relations, whether national or personal, are based on a
shared past, that is to say, on shared memory.

No, claims Richard Rorty, it ain't necessarily so. Solidarity, he
believes, can be solely oriented by a vision of a shared future. The

past is excess baggage, to be dropped by liberal democratic states. There is no need for a shared past. Accordingly, in a country of immigration, citizens can and do cement their solidarity around a vision of a better future for themselves or, more important, for their children. The past is a divider; the future can be a unifier. It seems that for Rorty the project of the United States is future-oriented: solidarity should be building a decent society free of cruelty and humiliation.[15]

The idea that the United States or its individual states have no useful past is a myth. "Remember the Alamo" was invented not by immigrants in Staten Island but by settlers with a past. Whether the useful American past is shared enough to form thick relations among U.S. citizens is another question. However, to think of the United States as an Aphrodite country arising from the sea foam fully grown, having left the past behind in Old Europe, is as flimsy as Aphrodite's foam. Rorty's claim that there is no need for the past in shaping sustained solidarity is an empirical claim. Judging by the past, I don't see much support for his claim.

Conferring Meaning

Thick human relations can be viewed as an instrument for satisfying interests and desires, but they can also be viewed as a vehicle for conferring meaning on human actions and on human life in general. Conferring meaning differs from bestowing advantage. An exchange in thick relations is less like a market exchange and more like a gift exchange. Both are exchanges, but in a gift exchange, ideally, we are interested in the meaning expressed in the exchange, and only derivatively in the use value of what we give and what we get, whereas in a market exchange we are interested only in the use value of what we give and what we get.

A common claim is that social identity, such as being Irish or Catholic or working-class, supplies matrices for the meaning of important actions. I maintain that it is not so much *identity* that confers meaning as it is *identification,* such as identification with Irish people, et cetera. Identification involves an active adoption of the relations with the individuals who are in the relation. Identification turns inert, inactive thick relations into active relationships.

What does conferring meaning mean? It does not mean giving a sense of purpose (goals). Thick relations do not necessarily have a purpose. There are efforts to assign purpose to thick relations, such as bearing and raising children in family relations or culti-vating culture and keeping the traditions of the past in the case of national relations. Thick relations may bring about children and culture. Indeed, from a third-person point of view, a thick relation may have an extrinsic evolutionary or social function, but from a first- or second-person point of view, such a function is rarely the goal. If there is a goal, it is the *intrinsic* goal of keeping the relation in good form.

One way of thinking about how meaning is conferred on thick relations is by way of stories. Thick relations are important rela-tions and as such are essential elements in the life story of their participants. The meaning of one's life is expressed in one's life history, which weaves together descriptions of life events of the road taken and shadows of the roads not taken. The meaning of our life is expressed in the best story we can tell about our life. In such a story thick relations contribute to the overall sense of the story and are in turn understood through the overall sense of the story. In good thick relations the stories of thick relations are calibrated by those who stand in the relation. Each provides some reality check for the other, or so it should be in a good thick relation. As in shared memory, in composing the story of our life there is room for division of labor. But calibrating stories with others through division of labor doesn't mean dictating the story to others or being dictated to by others. We negotiate our stories. Still, ultimately, each one of us has his or her own life story, and each one of us is the author of his or her life story. There are good authors and bad authors. A good author doesn't necessarily mean a good life and a bad author doesn't necessarily mean a bad life. The two do, however, correlate with a meaningful life and a less meaningful life. The gap between the two is due to the fact that there is more to life than the literary model of life suggests. There are many good things in life that don't register in the plot of our life, but they are daily good experiences all the same, even if not memorable ones, such as drinking good coffee in the morning. But we hardly measure out our life with coffee spoons.

Thick Relations: Natural, Imagined, Constructed

It is interesting that lovers are depicted as facing each other, whereas solidarity is depicted as standing shoulder to shoulder.

Shoulder to shoulder assumes that they stare in the face of a common enemy. Lovers standing face-to-face are engrossed in each other, oblivious of an outward gaze. A face-to-face relation has to do with physical presence.

The core cases of thick relations suggest face-to-face relations, or at least a meeting at a certain point in time. The question is what happens to thick relations once they are extended beyond face-to-face relations.

Ibn Khaldûn, the fourteenth-century theoretician of thick relations in the form of tribal solidarity (*asabiyya*), was keenly aware that thick tribal relations cannot be confined to face-to-face relations.[16] But he did correlate the thickness of relations with their distance from face-to-face relations.

One concern in moving from core cases of thick relations involving face-to-face relations to thick relations at some remove from face-to-face relations is that the remote relations cannot be *core* cases of thick relations. They are derivative. But this is not the end of our worries. Thick face-to-face relations are relations between individuals who are related as specific people. In moving to a derivative group of thick relations, say, between an Irishman and his fellow Irishmen, the relation is not a relation between specific individuals. It is very different from his relation with, say, his close family in Galway.

The Hobbits, the diminutive humanoids in J. R. R. Tolkien's fiction, are an imagined community, namely, a product of sheer imagination; the Irish community is not imagined in the sense in which the Hobbits are. It is misleading to view every group that is formed by a projection from observed members to unobserved members as an imagined community in the Hobbit sense.

True, the Irish people do not form a natural kind. They do not, for example, share a distinct natural property such as type A blood. Sex is a natural kind, based on chromosomes and hormonal profile. But gender is not. It is based on cultural and behavioral features that are associated with masculinity and femininity. However, neither the Irish nor a gendered group is thereby an imagined community in the sense of a fictional community.

We can view a collective concept such as the Irish people, which is based on thick relations, as an "inference ticket" (or "season ticket") to the relation that would obtain between any couple of Irish individuals if they came into a face-to-face relation.[17] This way of looking at collectives cuts through the division between collectivism and individualism. The collective is a ticket for taking a bus to the dwellings of couples.

Nevertheless, Benedict Anderson is within his rights to call a national community such as the Irish community an imagined community. The reason, as we just noticed, is not that any group that is formed by projection from the observed to the unobserved is thereby an imagined community. The imagination in Anderson's case is needed for viewing the Irish people as standing in thick relations. Forming a group of blood type A individuals calls not for imagination but for discovery. But turning individuals of blood type A into a community of mutual-aid blood donors calls for social imagination.

Calling a nation an imaginary community captures something important: in forming thick relations with people whom we don't really know firsthand, we determine not just how we relate to them but also how our relation with them is important to our life. The subjective element, which determines the intensity of the relation, is fed by features that are an amalgam of fact and fantasy. In thick face-to-face relations we have specific people in mind and we don't have to idealize them, for we care about them in the specific way they are. It is different when collectives make demands on our thick relations. They recruit ideologies such as nationalism, socialism, and religion to spur the imagination to forge or maintain thick relations. There is less ideology in face-to-face relations.

Inelasticity of Thick Relations

How malleable are we in being forged into thick relations? This is indeed a double-edged question: How easy is it for us to form thick relations, and how difficult is it for us to sustain them?

The issue of "imagined," "constructed," or "invented" thick relations is, I believe, of great moment. These terms in quotation marks are meant to counter a picture of thick relations as "organic" and "natural" and hence unalterable, in the sense in which the relation between the root and the trunk of a tree is unaltered. But then, even a new branchlet can be grafted onto an old trunk. Or, as in Jesse's tree, a new rod can come forth from an old stem and branch into a new tree (Isaiah 11:1). The idea of depicting a family genealogy as a family tree attests to the hold of the organic picture in thinking about family. But then again, there are hardly any part-whole relations in nature that are irredeemably organic, not even those concerning real trees. This doesn't mean that we cannot make use of the idea of "natural." We say English is a *natural* language, unlike Euphoria, which is a *constructed* computer language, programmed for specific purposes. The English language has no creator; it emerged spontaneously and not as an outcome of planning and design. Its rules, like laws of nature, are discovered rather than programmed. The natural language English is also contrasted with *artificial* languages such as Esperanto, which, like English, is used for all human purposes, but which, unlike English, is governed by rules that were not spontaneously created but rather constructed and postulated by its creator, Ludwik Zamenhof. Yet natural languages are constructed by human beings in a sense in which animal communication is not: they are conventions, and as such, they are subject to change, including changes at will.

The stress here on the distinction between natural and constructed is meant to be a move in unmasking ideologies that depict human patterns as immutable and immune to change. The idea is that ideologies, in the service of ruling powers, tend to

depict as *natural* patterns of behavior that are conducive to retaining the status quo, which favors those in power. By treating
such patterns as constructs, rather than as natural, they would
be exposed as patterns that could be subject to change.

This unmasking move is fine as far as it goes, but it is useful to
remember that one can drown in an artificial lake. The lesson is
that the artificial and the constructed can successfully imitate
many features of what goes under the label "natural." Many thick
relations are natural in the sense in which natural languages are
natural, namely, evolutionarily spontaneous; but they are also
constructed, much the way natural languages are constructed,
namely, conventionally.

It may very well be the case that the picture of blood relations
as a model for thick relations is responsible for viewing nations
or ethnic groups as natural kinds. Yet this is a misleading picture, indeed a dangerous picture, as the horrendous histories of
purity-of-blood doctrines attest. But the fact that thick relations
are not organic in the biological sense shouldn't lead us to believe
that thick relations are a mere figment of the imagination, to be
undone by fiat. It is sometimes easier to manipulate natural kinds
such as diamonds and daffodils than to manipulate the Dutch
language or Dutch nationalism.

Imagined collective thick relations were and are greatly helped
by modern means, such as newspapers and printed books, stan-
dardization of language, mass education and mass communication, political parties, and urbanization. But easy access to tools
that help form extended thick relations do not necessarily make
it easy to manipulate thick relations. A comparison between
family members and employees of firms makes the point about
the difficulty of manipulating phony thick relations to look like
genuine ones. Imagination in thick relations does not mean total

fabrication and easy manipulation. Firms with achievement-oriented relations trying to masquerade as belonging-oriented relations usually fail. There is more rigidity and stability in thick relations than scholars of nationalism—as one example of extended thick relations—are willing to admit.

Thick relations can be *vertical* relations and they can be *horizontal* relations, namely, relations among equals. The relations between the father and the other family members in a patriarchal family are strongly vertical, whereas the relations between siblings are usually horizontal. The two models that guide us with respect to thick relations are family and friends. Family, especially the traditional family, is a grid of vertical and horizontal relations: vertical relations with the father and horizontal relations between the children. Family as a formative political metaphor can be used both for *paternalistic* vertical relations—the ruler as the father of the nation—and for republican horizontal relations of *fraternity*. When friendship is couched in family terms, it is "brother" and "sister" that are picked to depict the relation, namely, the horizontal vocabulary of family relations.

So much for showing that thick relations are the relations that are betrayed. What does it mean to betray thick relations? This is the question at the center of the next chapter.

4

What Is Betrayal?

THE METAPHOR FOR BETRAYAL IS UNGLUING THE GLUE from a thick relation. It is time to look at the metaphor in more literal terms.

There are two elements in betrayal. The first element is the harm and the offense to the victim. But harming the interest or seriously hurting the feelings of the victim is not enough to constitute betrayal; there is a need for another element. For betrayal, the harm and the offense must take place between people who are presumed to stand in thick relation. Only when the harm and the offense serve as good reasons for questioning the meaning of the thick relation can we talk of betrayal.

It is the injury to the relationship that makes it betrayal. This injury is expressed by the metaphor of ungluing the glue of the thick relation.

Ungluing the glue means that betrayal is an act or acts that undermine the specific meaning of a thick relation. Undermining the meaning of a thick relation is undermining the relation, or, rather, its thickness. Betrayal of a thick relation is the *primary* sense of betrayal. Betrayal may be ascribed to other forms of human relations that are not thick, such as those between doctor and patient, lawyer and client, or psychoanalyst and patient. Normally these relations are professional relations, oriented by achievement, rather than thick relations, oriented by belonging. These professional relations mimic one important aspect of thick relations, which makes them resemble some thick relations, namely, the principle of entrusting the professionals with one's vulnerabilities or secrets.

It seems that by concentrating on betrayal as an act that undermines the meaning of a thick relation I am ignoring the obvious, namely, that betrayal is simply a serious breach of trust. The idea here is that betrayal should be accounted for in terms of trust and breach of trust, rather than with the notion of thick relation, which seems to be foggier than trust.

There is nothing wrong with treating betrayal as a breach of trust. Yet only a *serious* breach of *serious* trust counts as betrayal. The minute we try to account for the notions of serious breach and serious trust we are in the thicket of human relations, namely, dealing with thick relations. A serious breach of serious trust is nothing other than a betrayal of a thick relation. It is the thickness of the relation that makes the breach of trust serious.

I have already made the distinction between thin trust, expressed to a stranger at the beach by "keep an eye on my stuff," and thick trust, expressed in the famous Anglican marriage vow to "love her, comfort her, honor and keep her, in sickness and in health, and, forsaking all others, be faithful to her as long as you both shall live." The Anglican vow is a very tall order, but if you do all you said you would do, then you are trustworthy, and she can put her trust—thick trust—in you. Thick trust is simply the manifestation of a thick relation. There is no independent account of the two notions. In being subjected to a breach of thin trust, on the other hand, you may feel disappointed, even deeply so, but to say in such a case that you are within your rights to feel betrayed is too much of a stretch.

Can You Betray Only in Your Heart?

Betrayal is an act that undermines a thick relation. What counts as an act? Can a pure mental act, for example, constitute betrayal?

You share your life with someone and your fantasies, by day and by night, with someone else. Are your acts of the imagination, whether memories or fictions, acts of betrayal? Do they cast a shadow on the presumably thick relation you have with the one you presumably share your life with? Do they undermine the meaning of the relation with the one you share your life with? Does the incongruity between your inner life and your outer behavior count as betrayal?

Incongruity between overt disloyal behavior and loyalty "in the heart" is recognized by some religions as a legitimate mode of existence in time of persecution. Loyalty in the heart matters more than the professed behavior. There is hardly a consensus on this point even in religions that condone dissimulation in time of danger. The need to serve as witness—martyr, *shahid* in Arabic—to the glory of God and not to hide one's faith is tested in such a trying time, but professing one's faith in the open goes beyond the call of duty and is reserved for saints and heroes. Others believe that professing the faith in the open is the duty of everyone and not a supererogatory left for saints and heroes. The Donatists in North Africa at the time of Augustine were ferociously against allowing in the church priests who in trying times had let the faith down and dissimulated their disloyalty by burning the sacred books. The idea is clear: one cannot be loyal only in one's heart. Incongruity between the inner and the outer is a sign of betrayal.

Peter's three denials of Jesus are obviously overt acts. He denied "being with Jesus." This may be taken as a denial of being a disciple, or a denial of being a friend, or a denial of the mission of the master: all are possible understandings of his denial of being with Jesus. Does the denial under any of these interpretations constitute betrayal for not standing up and being counted when it mattered? There is no question that Peter, when he heard the rooster crow at midnight, recognized his denial as a betrayal. His denial of Jesus is not as bad as handing over Jesus to the enemy, which is exactly what Judas did. Nevertheless, Peter did shed tears of remorse over his betrayal. Peter had never suspected that he would be capable of betraying: "Even if all fall away on account of you, I never shall" (Matthew 26:33).

The idea in Peter's story is that even the sturdiest believer, who seems to be unshakeable as a rock, is deeply susceptible to betrayal. The need for repentance for the sin of betrayal is universal. Loyalty cannot be left only to the heart.

But the orthogonal question is, can betrayal take place only in the heart? By "only in the heart" I mean by mental acts with no outward manifestation, such as that of the tenth commandment: "You shall not covet your neighbor's wife."

Does the covetousness mentioned in the tenth commandment constitute betrayal? Jesus' answer is yes, it does: "You have heard that it was said, 'Do not commit adultery.' But I tell you that anyone who looks at a woman lustfully has already committed adultery" (Matthew 5:27–28).

Adultery in this case means that the one who stares is a married man. He betrays his wife with a lustful look at another married woman. If he stares lustfully at an unmarried woman, it is harlotry, not adultery, and if he is unmarried, it is not adultery, for he betrays nobody. Adultery, like the tango, takes two consenting adults.

If we insist on this pedantry, let us present the Matthew case a bit differently: A married man and a married woman stare at each other lustfully. Do they each betray (in their heart) their respective spouse? Couched in my terms, do their states of mind—sexual desire for each other—absent any overt action, let alone consummation of their lust, undermine their thick relations of husband to his wife and wife to her husband?

Dona Flor in Jorge Amado's novel "lives" simultaneously with two husbands: her reckless and sexy late husband and her respectable and dull current one. She constantly fantasizes about the one, who is not even alive anymore, while living with the other. Dona Flor conjures up her fantasies quite willingly. She is the agent of her daydreaming.[1]

The formula "betrayal is an act" does not preclude mental acts of the kind I attribute to Dona Flor. Her willful daydreaming seems to undermine the meaning of her presumptive thick relation to her dull current husband. Her case is different from the case of Oedipus in Sophocles's *Oedipus Rex* (lines 1068–1078). He is disturbed at having dreamed of sleeping with his mother. Jocasta quite rightly, if not quite properly, tells him not to worry—lots of people have such dreams.[2] Dreams are mental acts in the neutral sense of mental events, without conveying a sense of agency and control. They are not acts that undermine thick relations; they may be symptoms of thick relations the way blushing is a sign of infatuation. They have natural causes but are not reasons guided by conventional rules. As such, dreams have natural meanings in the sense in which dark clouds mean rain, but not in the sense in which *il pleut* means—conventionally but not naturally—"it's raining."

Voluntary mental acts with no overt manifestation can provide a reason to question the meaning of a given thick relation, but they cannot by definition serve anyone other than the actor.

What Does Undermining a Thick Relation Mean?

Is "undermining" in the expression "undermining the meaning" an empirical concept? As an empirical concept, undermining means that betrayal tends to terminate or seriously erode, as a matter of fact, thick human relations. Or does "undermining" have a normative meaning such that betrayal provides a good reason or even a decisive reason to reconsider the meaning of one's thick relation? Undermining the meaning can be either undermining the meaning of the *relation* or undermining the meaning of its *thickness*.

What does the meaning of a thick relation mean? Thick relations are relations under a description: my sister, my friend, my fellow Jew. The meaning of each of these thick relations has a different role in my life and in the lives of those with whom I stand in such relations. Undermining the meaning of a thick relation is undermining the specific description the relation goes under. To undermine the meaning of a thick relation is to undermine a specific form of a thick relation, be it family relation or friendship relation or any other form of thick relation. Each relation has its own set of expectations and norms, which may vary from society to society, from culture to culture, and from time to time.

By the meaning of a thick relation I mean the meaning of the specific form that the thick relation takes. By specific I don't mean just the conventional type under which the relation goes, but a token of it. What I have in mind is not just a type of thick relation, say, friendship, but rather a token of a thick relation, say, the friendship between *you* and *him*.

Being betrayed by a friend is a very good reason for you to reconsider your particular relationship with *this* particular friend. It may also be a reason for you to reconsider the meaning of your relationship with other friends of yours. It may even be a reason for you to question friendship in general, but it would not be a *good* reason. The distinction I am counting on is between having a reason and having a good or even very good reason. You know the story about Napoleon and the delegation from Moscow. Napoleon said, "Give me three reasons to trust your promise not to shell my forces." The head of the delegation replied, "One: You can count on our integrity. Two: We are committed to saving human lives. Three: We have no ammunition." The first two are reasons, but only the third one is a good reason.

It is a curious fact, if it is indeed a fact, that people in United States are getting married for the second time at the same rate that people are getting married for the first time. One way of understanding this curious fact is that people refuse to infer from the experience of their failed marriage that it is the institution of marriage that is to be blamed. They blame themselves or their spouses or both. They don't seem to say, "It is a wretched institution; not for me. I have already had a taste of it, a bitter one at that. Never again." It is this sense of specificity that I have in mind, namely, individuals assessing their particular relationships in cases of betrayal, rather than assessing the value of the institution under which their particular relation falls.

Undermining Thick Relations

What does "undermining" in the expression "undermining thick relations" mean? Note that the question is about undermining the relation and not about undermining the meaning of the relation. There is a relation between the two, but they are separate issues.

It may mean that betrayal as a matter of fact may cause people who are betrayed to terminate the relation by not regarding it as thick anymore. One cannot stop being a brother to a biological brother. The two might be totally estranged from each other, but they don't stop being brothers. Undermining suggests erosion of the foundation on which the relation is established. There is ambiguity here between a relation that becomes shaky and a relation that is destroyed. But still, these two readings of "undermining" (shaking or shattering) are empirical claims about what betrayal may do to the relation. It claims that as a matter of fact, in many cases, betrayal may compromise a relationship either by weakening it, by changing its character, or by terminating it. The empirical claim should be hedged by saying that the act of betrayal must be known, or suspected, by the betrayed party, so as to bring about this possible array of reactions. The claim should be hedged even further: an imagined act of betrayal, unfounded but intensely believed and feared, may bring about the same array of reactions. The empirical understanding of betrayal, as an act that undermines human relations, is pretty straightforward.

Viewing betrayal as a shattering experience, which erodes one's sense of a particular thick relation, does not mean that betrayal, as a call for a total reevaluation of one's relationship, is not mediated by a social understanding of the relationship. Here is an example. In Theodor Fontane's great masterpiece *Effi Briest,*

Baron von Innstetten learns after many years that Effi, whom he married when she was seventeen, once had a brief extramarital affair with the dashing Major Crampas.[3] Since no one else, apart from the couple involved, knows about the affair, the Baron has the option of acknowledging the fact and letting it pass, thereby saving his marriage, his wife, and his children from suffering disgrace. Yet the Baron is a victim of his class notion of honor. He challenges Crampas to a duel. He kills him. He divorces his wife. She is socially ostracized. He remains miserable regardless of his later political successes. The Baron acts not out of sexual jealousy but out of a sense of duty. It is the conventions of his class that make the Baron view the meaning of his relation with his wife in a new light, a rather dim and grim one.

This is very different from the story of *The Doctor's Divorce* by another great writer, S. Y. Agnon, about a physician married to a nurse who one day tells him that she was once, before they ever met, involved with another man.[4] The doctor is seized with irrepressible jealousy: he divorces the nurse not because of an internalized social pressure but because of retroactive sexual jealousy.

Reactive attitudes to particular cases of betrayal give us a sense of the erosion of thick relations that comes with betrayal. The point is that we expect strongly held strong emotions as typical reactions to betrayal. We may, for example, expect bitter resentment from the betrayed, but also stern indignation from a third party, and on occasion pangs of guilt and stabs of remorse from the betrayer. Then there are other sorts of reactions to betrayal that might take place: epistemic shock, rage, despair, and more.

The strength of the reactive attitudes to betrayal is a good index to the seriousness of the betrayal, as well as to the way the betrayal undermines thick relations. The reason is simple: it is hard to sustain thick relations under the stormy pressure of such negative attitudes. People's reactions to betrayal are hardly emotionally simple. But no matter how sophisticated and nuanced the reactions are, it is simply true that, emotionally, betrayal hurts bitterly.

Undermining the Meaning

There is, on top of undermining thick relations as a matter of fact, a normative sense of undermining thick relations. The normative sense is the sense I am mostly interested in. Betrayal provides the betrayed party with a good reason to reevaluate the meaning of the thick relation with the betrayer. After my description of stormy reactive attitudes toward betrayal, an appeal to reevaluation sounds tepid and timid. It is not.

Human relations oriented by achievement can be constantly reevaluated, according to the level of achievement reached by one's performance. Each statement from your broker provides you with a good reason to reevaluate her performance. To be sure, laziness and mindless inertia may prevent you from either reevaluating the performance or acting on your reevaluation. The point is that you could, and maybe even prudentially should, if you so wished.

By contrast, thick relations oriented by belonging are not, by their very nature of belonging, up for constant reevaluation. Your friendship shouldn't be dependent on each twist and turn in your friend's behavior. Once she is your friend she has enough emotional "capital" in your joint emotional bank account to sustain your relationship. Friendship and a policy of constant reassessment do not get on well. You know the people for whom every day is another day. You constantly start your relations with them from scratch. These people are not built for sustained friendship. This holds true for other thick relations. One needs very good reasons to reassess one's thick relation, and betrayal is the strongest of such reasons.

What do we reevaluate when we reconsider a thick relation due to betrayal? The point was already made: thick relations are usually very important in our life. The hedge "usually" is not a nervous tic but a serious possibility. Only a few people don't establish or don't value thick relations at all. Most people, most of the time, greatly value some of their human relations, first and foremost their thick ones. A shattering experience of betrayal may bring one to question the value of thick relations in general or the value of a particular type of thick relation, such as friendship.

But what does undergo reevaluation when a relation is challenged by betrayal? It is expressed by tormenting questions such as "Was I wrong about our relationship in the past? I thought we were friends, but were we?" I have already stressed the point that thick relations are built on a shared past. The shared past is constitutive of the relation. It is the shared past that is colored by the betrayal.

By reevaluation here I mean judging the worth and the significance of the relation. But the context of the reevaluation is the context of belonging. Following the betrayal, what is questioned about the past is the sense of belonging: "I thought we belonged to each other, but now I know that we didn't." This voice of one crying in bewilderment has many variations, such as "I thought I belonged to you and you belonged to me, but I was wrong about what I meant to you and what our relation meant to you"—"you" being the betrayer. Reevaluation has another context, the context of achievement, where it means reassessing performance and setting a value on performance. In the case of a thick relation and the context of belonging, however, the only performance assessed is the quality of the relation (now in the shadow of the betrayal). The language of reevaluation is the language of the past tense. The present tense is "Now I know." The present tense can express a more confused state of mind: "I thought we were friends, but now, after you did this and that, I don't know what to think." This may be taken as an expression of despair, but it can also express deep doubt about the relation and, in particular, about it being a thick relation. There is an important future tense to it all: "What shall I do? I cannot go on as if this didn't happen." This can be an invitation to renegotiate the relation starting with a joint reevaluation of the relation, or it may mean an end to the relation. But whatever the tense might be, it is parasitic on evaluating the past.

Can Thick Relations of Belonging Be Terminated?

After leafing through one's Stasi file one can say, "My ex-son-in-law betrayed me to gain promotion in the Party." But one cannot make literal sense by saying, "My ex-son betrayed me to gain promotion in the Party." The difference is not in the content of the files but in the difference between son and son-in-law. One can turn from a son-in-law into an ex-son-in-law, but one cannot turn from a son into an ex-son: once a son, always a son. Suppose that to your horror you discover that it was your son and not, as you had suspected, your son-in-law who informed on you to the Stasi, with the goal of facilitating his climb up the Party ladder. Now what? "The bastard," you mutter. Well, he may be a bastard in the sense of a despicable person, but he is your son, born in wedlock, if this makes any difference, and you cannot—conceptually, that is—terminate the relation of father and son between you and him. This is all true but in a way irrelevant: you could, after all, terminate the thickness of the relation and regard the father-son relation as nothing but a mere biological fact.

The words "relation" and "relationship" are usually used interchangeably. True, there are contexts in which replacing one expression with the other looks forced: it would look forced to replace "race relations" with "race relationships." However, it is hard to tell what nuance is lost in replacing the one with the other. It seems that "relationship" suggests interaction in a way "relation" does not. We may even say that the term "relationship" is more suitable for thick relations, whereas "relation" carries a more neutral sense and as such is less suitable. This is evident in the use of "relationship" to connote a close romantic friendship between two individuals. In this vein we may say that the betrayed man cannot terminate his *relation* with his flesh-and-blood son, which is a biological fact, but he can terminate his *relationship* with his son, which is a social fact. Yet I shall use "relation" and "relationship" interchangeably unless the difference matters.

Traditional societies put a great premium on belonging, and hence on thick relations. Nonetheless, traditional societies devised quite effective policies for terminating thick relations. The policy of shunning an individual or a group by carefully keeping away from them is a generic policy. It has many different manifestations, ranging from stealth shunning—not letting the victim of this policy know about it, but making sure that everyone else does—to elaborate rituals of total exclusion. The Balinese policy of *kasepekang* and the various forms of Jewish *cherem* are examples of the variety of practices devised to terminate thick relations. The warmth of belonging turns into ferocious acts of aggression, aimed at destroying any relation with the one who is ostracized.

Disownment, disinheritance, expulsion from home, and refusal to recognize or maintain any familial connection with one's child are equivalent in parent-and-child relations to divorce in husband-and-wife relations. Thick relations by this account are social relations, not biological relations. There are of course less exotic ways of terminating thick relations, including parent-child relations: discreet alienation without formal renunciation is a more common sort of termination. Reevaluation in the shadow of betrayal can end in the termination of thick relations.

An Undermining Effect in an Act of Betrayal

I have characterized betrayal as an act or acts that undermine the meaning of a thick relationship. But what makes an undermining act an act of that nature? There are many damaging acts that hurt human relations. Some of them are pretty serious, but we don't regard all acts that damage thick human relations as acts of betrayal. Let's return to the Anglican wedding declaration of consent to "love her, comfort her, honor and keep her, in sickness and in health, and, forsaking all others, be faithful to her as long as you both shall live."

The formula of honoring and keeping in sickness and in health is an important formula for conveying the idea of belonging, which should be independent of achievement (in this case health). Abandoning or being indifferent to her in time of serious illness impairs the pillar of thick relations, namely, *belonging*. Belonging is constitutive of thick relations. Damaging the sense of belonging by not "honoring and keeping" her in time of sickness, because she becomes a burden, is what makes such an act of omission the kind of act that undermines the meaning of marital relations. It is a betrayal. But suppose something else happens. Suppose she discovers your personal diary and she reads that you don't forsake her, you keep your vow to the letter, because you are an honorable man. But she goes on to discover that you don't love her anymore. She realizes that you still value her and your concern for her hasn't been shaken, but then you quote Bertrand Russell: "I went out bicycling one afternoon, and suddenly, as I was riding along a country road, I realized that I no longer loved Alys. I had had no idea until this moment that my love for her was even lessening."[5] Your diary goes on to say, "The same happened to me." Your passion faded away. In light of what she reads, she may reconsider the relationship between the two of you, but it would be strange of her to infer that once your passion was gone, you had betrayed her. You are still motivated in the right way to keep the thick relation between you and her. The lack of passion is a sound source of dire disappointment, but it is not a sound source of being betrayed and feeling betrayed. When you vowed to love her, it wasn't love as passion—an emotion that comes, as it were, from the outside and not as a volitional act—but rather it was love in the sense of keeping an unshakeable sense of "we" between you and her. This sense of love you determined to keep till death would keep the two of you apart.

We and Us

I draw a distinction between a sense of *we* and a sense of *us*. In general, the difference between "we" and "us" is purely grammatical: "we" is a subject pronoun and "us" is an object pronoun. But the way I am using the distinction is between "we" as the agent, who acts, and "us" as the patient, who suffers the acts of others. You may identify with the passive "us," the sufferers, and at the same time feel estranged from the active "we."

The great poet Julian Tuwim identified with "we," the Poles, when the blood of the Jews flowed in their veins, but he identified with "us," the Jews, when Jewish blood was spilled out of the veins. He used the expression *my, Zydzi polscy* ("we, Polish Jews") in both cases, but my unpacking of his position is along the distinction between "we Poles" and "us Jews."[6] (I shall expand on Tuwim's expression in Chapter 9.)

How does this distinction between "we" and "us" fare with the example of passion gone out of a marriage?

There are acts that are recognized as undermining the identification with "we." There are acts—usually different ones—that are recognized as undermining the identification with "us." They too may serve as candidates for acts of betrayal. The fading of passion may weaken the conviction in "we," but it leaves "us" intact: the combined effect doesn't justify viewing it as betrayal.

Now we reach the sticky item of the marriage vow. You did all that the vow required, but for one exception: you were carrying on an affair. In the language of the vow, you forsook your spouse and were unfaithful to her. For most people this is what betrayal in marital life is.

We are trying to figure out what betrayal consists of by dealing with the question of what in betrayal erodes the meaning of a thick relation. There are many forms of thick relations, and the meaning of each form is different: a sibling relationship is different from a comrades-in-arms relationship. Yet adultery is a good paradigmatic example for dealing with the question of what erosion in the meaning of a thick relationship is. And this is how I use this example. The Anglican declaration of consent is an old-fashioned way of presenting married life and its betrayal, but for our purposes, namely, to clarify what erosion of meaning amounts to, it is a helpful paradigm. For one thing, in the Anglican ceremony as well as in the Catholic ceremony, the marriage vow is utterly symmetrical between the genders: only grammatical gender differentiates between the spouses. True, it does not make room for same-sex marriage, but it still gives meaning to marriage. This meaning differs from the meaning of marriage in many other religions, in which there is a blatant asymmetry between man and woman. In the symmetrical understanding of the marriage vow, adultery is any voluntary sexual intercourse between a married individual and an individual who is not his or her spouse.

The vows of symmetrical Christian weddings can be understood as a mutual promise of sexual exclusivity and emotional monogamy. Betraying one of these promises counts as an erosion of the meaning of the marriage.

In dealing with the meaning of marital relations, as in dealing with the meaning of other thick relations, we should draw a crucial distinction. The distinction is between *exterior* reasons and *interior* reasons for understanding human relations. In dealing with betrayal we deal with interior reasons, namely, with reasons related to the particular relation of husband and wife, say, between Charles and Diana. Our concern is with the marriage token, not with the marriage type, and hence with interior reasons. Exterior erosion of the meaning of marriage has to do with the marriage type: for example, questioning the very idea that marriage is between opposite genders. General objections—say, to asymmetry in marriage, or to monogamy, or to exclusive opposite-sex marriage—are based on exterior reasons.

Exterior reasons may change the meaning of a relation's type. Mormons of the old school, quite rightly, pointed out that the biblical meaning of marriage as modeled on the lives of the biblical patriarchs was polygamous marriage. We may agree with the Mormons' historical claim and yet regard the change to monogamy as a good thing. We may also admit that the meaning of marriage is undergoing change by being extended to same-sex marriage, but we view it as a change for the better. Sometimes there are excellent reasons to change externally the meaning of certain thick relations. Sometimes there are poor reasons for such a change. But be that as it may, our concern so far is with the erosion of the interior meaning of a thick relation due to betrayal, rather than with the exterior meaning.

The Meaning of the Meaning of a Relationship

A human relationship is not an obvious bearer of meaning, much as life is not an obvious bearer of meaning. Obvious bearers of meaning are words and sentences. Yet we talk about the "meaning of life" as well as the "meaning of our relationship."

Let's focus on the good-making features of thick relations and, in particular, of thick personal relations, which are our model for thick relations. By wholesome good-making features of thick relations I have in mind traits such as caring, ability to converse intimately, commitment, sympathetic understanding, goodwill, shared humor and shared cherished memories, mutual respect, considerateness, and, somewhere down the line, sincerity (telling the vulnerable truth about me) and honesty (telling the painful truth about you). We could go on, but for our purposes this is already enough. These wholesome features loom large in all thick personal relations, but they are differently manifested in different kinds of relations. Even in close family relations these wholesome features are manifested differently in the relation between mother and daughter than in the relation between two cousins. There are various ways to list the wholesome features. They can be listed as abstract values or they can be prescribed as norms.

But then there are less lofty wholesome features of thick relations that are manifested in shared activities that individuals bonded in thick relations may cherish together, such as solving jigsaw puzzles, watching Monty Python, comparing performances of *The Well-Tempered Clavier,* collecting wild mushrooms, and being fanatical fans of the Spurs and avid supporters of Old (pre-Blair) Labour (or, for that matter, fervent competitors for the distinction of who better remembers Jane Austen's novels).

Let's call the first list of wholesome abstract features of thick relations the *lofty* list, and the second list of wholesome concrete features of thick relations the *lowly* list. As you can see, the lofty list consists of features that are wholesome for all those who are involved in the thick relation, though they may differ over the importance they attach to each feature. One may give honesty precedence over humor and the other may reverse the order, but both take these features as relevant wholesome features of thick relations.

The *relative importance* of the features in the lofty list can be negotiated by the people who stand in the relation, and they may end by agreeing to disagree. Less open to negotiation are the very features that are to be included in the list. These features may be negotiated by the whole culture, for they have to do with thick relation types and not with their specific tokens. A "type" question is, for example, whether sharing religious faith should be included in the lofty list or not, whereas a typical "token" question is "Shall we celebrate Hanukkah with a bush?"

I shall draw a distinction between negotiation *of* the meaning of thick relations and negotiation *for* the meaning of thick relations. "Meaning" here means the value and the significance that a given socially prescribed good-making feature imparts to the lives of those who are negotiating the terms of their relationship. As mentioned previously, the lofty features are imposed from the outside, and it is the culture in which they are embedded that provides their common understanding. Nevertheless, there is room to negotiate the relative importance of features in the lofty list by the ones who are involved in a relation. A couple may decide to lead an open marriage and ascribe zero value to sexual fidelity. They may negotiate ground rules that would prevent sexual jealousy, but those ground rules are already part of the negotiation *for* meaning, namely, the specific forms established by the two who have already adopted the good-making features.

Negotiation *of* is, so to speak, an external negotiation about the framework of the relation. Negotiation *for* is an internal negation within the framework of the relation about the weight of the different features in the frame. Negotiation *of* and *for* meaning does not necessarily mean strategic bargaining and power games, but rather a lifelong process of clarification as to what should constitute in general the relation, and what features are good for *their* specific relation. Damaging thick relations is done by damaging a good-making feature, be it a default feature adopted from the social environment or a negotiated feature the two settled on.

Betrayal is damaging by unilateral act an important good-making feature that was taken by both sides to be a *constitutive* feature of their thick relation. The overarching feature that looms large in all thick relations and is the most threatened by betrayal is the sense of belonging. It is manifested in different ways in different relations, but it can be identified across a variety of thick relations by what counts as being replaced. In betrayal you are replaced: replaced by a lover, replaced by an enemy state, replaced by another god. Replacement is the nemesis of belonging.

Betrayal cannot be displayed on the continuum of the ongoing negotiation *of* meaning or *for* meaning of a relation. Betrayal is a deal breaker rather than a new deal maker. It is an act that is off the chart of negotiating the meaning of the relation. This is why it calls for a radical reassessment of the assumed meaning of the relation, and especially the features that make the relation thick. This, as I have already stressed, includes the shared history of the relation. The history cannot be changed, but the memory of the history and the meaning of the past can be revised; moreover, it can be revised dramatically.

Drifting into Betrayal

We may feel that betrayal in personal relations is an overdramatic notion. We claim that betrayal is a good reason to reconsider the meaning of our thick relation to someone, but we may drift into thick relations and, more important, drift out of thick relations for no reason at all. We may, for example, move to a different town because we find a suitable job there at a time when our thick relation with an old friend is wearing out. No big decision—indeed, no decision at all—is involved: being busy in the new place and neglecting to keep in touch, or some such humdrum explanation, may account for our drifting out of the relation.[7] If such a commonplace cause can account for ending our thick relations with friends, why make a fuss over betrayal and turn it into a momentous event?

What stands between betrayal and drifting away? The short answer is the meaning of the relation. Betrayal undermines the meaning of the relation. It colors the past in a way drifting away does not. Drifting away affects the future of the relation, but it does not affect the meaning of the relation in the past. Betrayal robs one of an important part of one's past. The relation of the past looks to the betrayed at present like an empty shell. Drifting does nothing of the sort. It leaves the memory of the past intact.

But can one drift into betrayal? Can betrayal be not an outcome of a conscious decision but a result of small incremental decisions, none of which on its own constitutes betrayal, yet whose end result amounts to betrayal? Drifting toward betrayal is usually a consequence of self-deception. There is a recurrent theme in spy novels of the character who cannot bring himself to spy for his country's enemy but desperately needs the money. He meets by "accident" an intermediary, who presents himself as a Norwegian military attaché or some such harmless figure. Our character tells himself that there is no real harm in handing over some sensitive information about his country to an inoffensive country such as Norway. Then there is a meeting with an Australian friend of the attaché, and after a chain of secret meetings arranged with the help of his new Norwegian friend, our character ends up working directly for what he had regarded as the enemy, the Americans. There are infinite variations on this trashy theme, but the general hang of it is not trivial: no matter how murky the details are, the big decision to betray one's country is sliced into small decisions, so the betrayer never faces a big terrifying decision but instead drifts aimlessly, half suspecting (but only half), toward betrayal.

Whose Perspective on Betrayal Should We Adopt?

Betrayal is betrayal of a relationship; that is, betrayal is first and foremost betrayal of friendship, marriage, and the like. But betrayal of a thick relation not only hurts the relationship but badly hurts the betrayed side of the relation. The question is, is the betrayed side entitled to a privileged position in assessing the relation by virtue of being the suffering side? Or does the fact that the betrayed side is the suffering side cloud her judgment, so there is a need for an impartial, sympathetic observer to assess the relation? By sympathetic I mean sympathetic to both sides.

Let's allocate names to the perspectives. The perspective of the betrayed is the *first*-person perspective. The perspective of the betrayer is the *second*-person perspective. The perspective of a sympathetic bystander is the *third*-person perspective. But first we need to make a distinction between *private* relationships and *personal* relationships. Private relationships are, as a first approximation, the concern of those involved in the relationships, and none of the business of others. We may hedge our claim by making a private relationship not the exclusive concern of those directly involved ("it is no one else's business") but rather the privileged concern of those directly involved in the relationship. The concern of the involved should greatly outweigh the concern of others: it is more or less their own business, as long as they don't harm others. It is for the individuals having the relationship to work out their differences by negotiating the terms of their relationship. Personal relationships are interpersonal too, but not necessarily private. Personal relationships may involve concern of a much wider scope: they are personal in the eyes of the public. What is considered personal and what is considered private vary widely among the cultures of the world. Thus, for example, marital infidelity in many cultures is not confined to the first- and second-person perspectives: a third-person perspective in the form of the public eye has a stake and a say in the matter. Till not so long ago, infidelity was criminalized in almost all countries. The historical shift in what is termed "modernity" in matters of personal betrayal is a shift from the personal to the private: the third-person perspective in such matters of marital fidelity seems to be losing its standing. It still keeps tongues wagging in gossip, which shows that others are interested, but being interested does not mean being concerned.

One can be betrayed without even knowing it. It seems that this fact alone is a good reason to transfer judgment about betrayal from the first-person to the third-person perspective. On the other hand, it seems that the erosion of the meaning of a thick relation due to personal betrayal should not be the concern of the public but should be left to the individuals involved and to no one else.

The betrayed may adopt the general policy expressed by the cliché "What I don't know won't hurt me." I don't ask and you don't tell. Only when I know there is a problem is there a problem. If I know that I have received a placebo from my doctor, the placebo effect disappears. I prefer a placebo human relationship with its placebo effect to no relationship, which in the medical case amounts to no treatment.

But then, the betrayed victim may adopt a very different attitude: What I know about the betrayal doesn't really concern me. I am far more concerned about what others know about it. The third-person perspective is my worry, not my first-person knowledge. Betrayal known to others brings public shame on me; it is insult added to injury. Moreover, I am willing to keep up appearances and not react, on condition that the betrayal is kept a secret between me and the betrayer. Betrayal is for me first and foremost public shame, and my relationship with the betrayer is secondary. Betrayal for me amounts to being indiscreet; the rest for me has very little to do with my relationship with the betrayer.

Which perspective we adopt toward betrayal hinges on what we think about thick human relations. If we advance from the view that a dyadic thick relation assumes antecedently two individuals with their own individual objective interests, then the right perspective on betrayal should be an objective third-person perspective. For the interests to be objective means that they are advantageous to the individuals involved irrespective of their beliefs and desires. If betrayal consists in undermining objective interests and it behaves analogously to illness, then it is in the interest of a patient to get effective medicine to cure her disease, rather than a placebo. A placebo may provide a good feeling and even a marginal objective effect, but the true interest of the patient with a curable disease is determined by the third-person perspective, best presented by a sympathetic, competent doctor.

It is possible that one may be willing to settle for a placebo relation, finding it preferable to no relation at all. But that is another issue. In the case of betrayal the danger is that the meaning of the relation as a thick relation is gone, and what remains is a placebo relation.

Unless we get clearer about the nature of thick relations, there is no hope of answering which perspective to adopt. Before we carry on with the question of which perspective to adopt, then, let us make a detour through the thicket of thick relations.

For Whose Sake?

My view on thick relations is different from the view that takes as antecedent to human relation individuals, with their interests and desires, and only then views the relation as an added component. Let's call the view I would like to challenge by the tendentious name of the *conventional* view. A thick relation, in the conventional view, admits that on occasion the two sides to the relation are willing to act for each other's sake, even if it is at their own expense. Indeed, acting for one's friend's sake is taken as a constitutive element of friendship. Aristotle talked about wishing a friend well for his own sake. I am concerned not with wishing but with doing something for one's friend's sake. Doing something for the sake of one's friend may be understood in various yet connected senses. In one sense, it means that the overriding motivation for one's action is one's concern for one's friend's well-being. This is patently wrong.

I am your friend. I am supposed to do things for your sake, as I expect you to do things for my sake.

But it is our friendship that makes you special in my eyes, and so, I believe, is what makes me special in your eyes. I would hardly consider doing things for your sake, at considerable cost to myself, if we weren't friends. There is nothing intrinsically precious and admirable in you. If you were on your own—without us being friends—I would probably treat you with the same courtesy I treat strangers, but with nothing beyond the call of minimum duty.

True, I might have done things for Nelson Mandela for his own sake, even though we were complete strangers, out of admiration for the man, but you are no Nelson Mandela. Besides, you don't want me to treat you as a Nelson Mandela; you want me to treat you as my friend. We are both heavily invested in our friendship, and there is a great deal that we are willing to do for the sake of maintaining our friendship. Friendship needs maintenance: mending temporarily strained relations, and quite often minding one another's business. Friendship is first and foremost a joint venture. A joint venture means we are acting for *our* sake.

What does acting for our sake mean? An example may help. We play as a team. I pass you the ball to score. I do it neither for your sake nor for my sake: it is for the sake of our team. I may pass you the ball out of the goodness of my heart, even though I am in a better position to score. This I do for your sake. I might try to score rather than pass the ball, even if you are in a better position to score, acting selfishly for my own sake, which is for the sake of my personal glory or whatever. In the last two cases I don't act for our sake as a team. But then there are things that we deliberately do for the sake of keeping our friendship going.

I stay with friendship since friendship is an Ur-model of thick relations. Acts—or, rather, interactions—that constitute thick relations in general, and friendship in particular, manifest both a past orientation and a future orientation. Michael Stocker aptly and helpfully distinguishes between "out of" explanations and "for the sake of" explanations.[8] It would be in line with the common usage of these expressions to view "out of" explanations as explanations that appeal to *motives,* whereas "for the sake of" explanations appeal to *reasons* in the narrow sense. Reason in the narrow sense is a forward look. Motive is a backward look.

Thick relations have a history and a memory. Indeed, actions motivated by thick relations such as "out of friendship," "out of familial love," or "out of solidarity" mention the relation in the explanation of the action. Motives habitually have a heading term such as "love," "jealousy," "envy," "spitefulness," and so on. Not every backward-looking reason has a handy heading label, but motives, as the term is commonly used, do, and so we shall view motives as a subgroup of backward-looking reasons. Motive headings in turn are closely related to terms for emotions, such as "love" or "grief," and they play a much deeper role in our account of thick relations than in thin relations. Along this line I would say that emotivism (the claim that all moral statements are expressions of emotions or attitudes) has more initial plausibility when viewed as an account of ethics (thick relations) than as an account of morality (thin relations).

Acting toward a friend out of friendship contributes to the friend and to the friendship. In that innocuous sense, it can be viewed as acting for the sake of the friend as well as for the sake of the friendship. But what about acting out of love?

Jane Austen tells us in her celebrated *Pride and Prejudice* that Mr. Darcy is willing, out of love for Elizabeth Bennett and at significant financial cost to himself, to settle the marriage of Elizabeth's reckless young sister, without having thick relations with Elizabeth, let alone with her sister. He makes the settlement secretly, out of love. It is an act done purely for Elizabeth's sake. Darcy acts discreetly, without assuming that Elizabeth is to know of his outstanding generosity, and with only scant hope of forming a thick relation with her.

La Rochefoucauld, who once said that anyone who thinks he loves his mistress for her own sake is mightily mistaken, would have doubted the sincerity of Darcy's motive. But if Darcy's motive is good enough for the shrewdly humane Jane Austen, it should be good enough for us. He does what he does for Elizabeth's sake.

And so there is a sense of acting for someone else's sake, be it out of admiration for Nelson Mandela or out of love for Elizabeth Bennett. But these are not cases of healthy thick relations. In healthy thick relations such as friendship, a friend acts for friendship's sake. This is not just the causal sense of acting out of friendship; it is also its purpose. In friendship you don't act for your sake or for your friend's sake; you act for the sake of the friendship.

As friends, we do things *out of* our relationship (our friendship) and *for* our relationship. We may personally benefit differently from such acts of friendship, but as long as we are friends
we refrain from counting our personal gains and losses and instead count our joint blessings. What we do for each other jointly
and each other separately constitutes our friendship, but doing it
for each other jointly or separately does not determine for whose
sake we do what we do. The best way to look at a thick relationship
is not to fall into the trap of accounting for it in terms of serving
the interests of one another, but in terms of the goodness of the
relationship. There is asymmetry here. When we view the goodness of friendship, we don't do it in terms of serving the interests
of one another, but when one grossly vitiates the interests of the
other, the goodness of the relation comes into question.

A great deal of what goes into a thick relationship such as
friendship has to do with concern for one another. Concern has
to do with the importance we hold for each other in our life, with
the attention we pay to the others in the relationship, with our
regard for their well-being, and even with the anxiousness and
nervousness we feel when their well-being does not go as well as
it should.

Can an Act Done with No Intention of Harming the Victim Be Called an Act of Betrayal?

The answer is yes. It happens all the time. Acts of betrayal in personal relations are rarely acts that are deliberately done with the
intention of harming the betrayed. Marital infidelity, for example, more often than not favors the third party, "the lover,"
rather than being meant to harm the betrayed. The result harms
the betrayed, but that is rarely the primary intention of the

betrayer. The issue in betrayal is not the intention to harm but the indifference to the victim, the lack of concern. The true insult in betrayal is the discovery by the betrayed that he wasn't at all on the mind of the betrayer. Indeed, what was done was not directed against him but instead was done with utter disregard for him. The maddening indifference is what hurts. Betrayal gives the betrayed a glimpse of not being important in the eyes of the betrayer. It is not the betrayed's *interests* that are ignored. *He* is ignored. The shocking discovery in betrayal is the recognition of the betrayer's lack of concern; the issue is not one's interests but one's significance. The betrayed realizes that he is not the significant other and not special.

Specialness

There is something deeply missing from my account of for whose sake we act in friendship. Saying that in our friendship you act for our friendship's sake, rather than for my sake, is only half the truth. True enough, I am not special in the way Nelson Mandela was, nor even in the sense in which José Mourinho, the celebrated soccer coach, famously declared, "I am a special one." But in our friendship there is a sense in which you are special in my eyes, and I hope I am special in your eyes. It is our friendship that confers specialness on each one of us in the eyes of the other. It is not for any admirable antecedent trait that we find each other special. Think of an analogy between being a special person and being a holy place. A holy place can be a place that is sanctified because it is believed to be "objectively" holy, as, for example, when there is a history of divine presence in the place. The Church of the Holy Sepulcher is holy in this first sense: the site is venerated as the place where Jesus was crucified. But a place can become a holy place because it is consecrated as such. It is the consecration that makes the place holy and not any antecedent trait ascribed to it. An ordinary church is a holy place in this second sense: there was nothing holy about the place before it was consecrated, but now it is a holy place, and its holiness manifests itself in the way believers behave in the place.

Our friendship confers specialness the way consecration confers holiness. You, my friend, are special in my eyes because of our friendship and not because you are Nelson Mandela. Once you are special in my eyes, due to our friendship, it is natural to say, the way Aristotle says, that there are things that I shall do for your sake. Indeed, one important thing that a thick relation does is to make us special in the eyes of those with whom we stand in the relation. We know all too well that there is nothing unusual about us. We know that no objectively valuable, unique qualities readily distinguish us from others. We are not outstanding. But ideally, thick relations, and especially the ones with our family and friends, make us special in the sense of being important and loved by them, in the specific and peculiar way we are.

We want to be special, to command affection and esteem, if not admiration, even though there is nothing unusually distinctive about us. It is our special relations that make us special in some meaningful sense. In the limited environment of our thick relation we are special. Betrayal tells us in a brutal way that we are not. This is what undermining the sense of belonging implies. Once our belonging is in doubt it is not just our thick relation that gets hurt; our sense of being special is crushed.

On Mother's Day 2014 my daughter Ruth wrote in the *New Yorker* about a motherless day (her mother, my wife, Edna, died in 2010):

Once, when I asked her whom she loved more, my sister or me, she answered, simply, "You." Incredulous, my sister posed the same question. "Who do you love more, *Ima?* Ruth or me?" "You," my mother said. We tried again. Each time, my mother invariably told whoever asked that she loved her more. "This doesn't make any sense," we finally said. She smiled and told us, "Sure it does. Don't you see? I love *you* more and I love *you* more." This was her sense of fairness: No kid wants to hear that they are loved the *same* as their sister.[9]

I believe this story tells it all. It tells us about the tension between the need to be special and the idea that being special means, in a way, being unique. There is no logical way to reconcile these two ideas of being special and being unique. The paradoxical way of treating the "love more than" relation as if it can be used symmetrically is an extremely clever way of conveying the idea that you should resign yourself to the fact that you are special without being unique. What makes betrayal such a bitterly painful experience is that in cases where your uniqueness is endangered, as, for example, in cases of adultery, your sense of being special is battered. It is the fear of losing a meaningful thick relation and the fear of not being special that make betrayal so poignantly potent.

There is another notion of specialness that is highly germane to thick relations in extended groups such as nations, religious communities, and classes. The individuals who constitute such groups are not special as individuals, but they find the group very special, and they feel empowered and special by emanation from the halo of the group, as it were. The idea of the chosen people is very much at the source of the idea of group specialness: "It is not because you were more numerous than any other nation that the Lord cared for you and chose you" (Deuteronomy 7:7). The understanding of being special is inherent in the religious understanding of being chosen. The chooser is God. But then there are more worldly choosers—history, for one: for example, being chosen by history for a civilizing mission, or to liberate humanity. Nationalism is all about group specialness. There is no nation without a sense of specialness. On occasion it is a fusion of nationalism and religion: the nation is chosen to carry out a religious role, for example, being the best Christians.

If Jesus' suffering and Jewish suffering were signs of their being chosen and thereby being special, suffering nations and persecuted religious sects almost invariably adopt the idea of being special by virtue of being chosen for a higher calling. The idea of being chosen as the basis for being special charges the idea of specialness with the dangerously electrifying notion of being superior. For collective specialness, it is not enough to be special just in the eyes of its adherents. The collective's superior calling and mission should eventually be recognized by all. Moreover, being chosen is taken as having the right to rule over others in the sense in which the chosen messianic king has the universal right to rule over all others. In short, the idea of collective specialness, more often than not, goes hand in hand with ideas of superiority and domination, if not now, then in the future.

Betraying and Belonging

Betrayal is an erosion of the meaning of thick relations. I have already mentioned a whole list of features of thick relations that are candidates for impairing the meaning of thick relations. "Impairing" is a term Thomas Scanlon uses in conjunction with the meaning of human relationships.[10] For betrayal I reserve a stronger term: "erosion." Impairment can more easily be repaired.

I have already emphasized that it is the sense of belonging that betrayal erodes. Belonging as an answer to what is eroded is not an obvious answer. Yet it is a more helpful answer than trust. Belonging, by not being the obvious answer, calls for explanation. I can't stress enough the importance of the distinction between *belonging* and *achievement* to my distinction between thick and thin relations. Thick relations are oriented around belonging. This is the most important general feature of thick relations. It is this structural pillar that betrayal erodes, seriously endangering the whole structure of the relationship.

Belonging has, of course, two radically different senses: belonging as possession and belonging as "organic" relation and membership. The sense of organic relation between member and group, or part and whole, is orthogonal to the notion of possession. My flesh belongs to me in a different way than does the meat I buy from the butcher. I have an intrinsic relation of belonging to my flesh and an extrinsic one to the meat. My flesh belongs to me by the way I am, whereas the meat belongs to me by the way I interact with the world. I have my flesh in the way I have mass and not in the way I have weight. In a spaceship I may lose my weight but not my mass. The idea of intrinsic relation is metonymically extended in idioms such as "my own flesh and blood," referring to my kith and kin. Belonging in human relations is a metaphorical extension of the idea of an intrinsic relation. When Jesus says, "Whoever eats my flesh and drinks my blood remains in me, and I in them" (John 6:56), he gives a sacramental expression of how an extrinsic relation turns into an intrinsic relation. The mark of belonging as an intrinsic relation in a human relation is the irreplaceability of the thing that stands in the relation. This is not true of relations based on achievement. Irreplaceability admits of degrees, but as an ideal type, irreplaceability is a matter of all or nothing. By contrast, belonging as possession of property is based on the possibility of exchange (replacement). The book you bought can be replaced, but not the book you wrote. Your ownership of the book you bought is very different from your ownership of the book you wrote.

There were and are cultures in which marital relations were and are perceived as property relations. The husband owns his wife and has total control over his wife's relations with other males. Betrayal can come only from the wife's side and it is an infringement of the husband's property rights. The wife belongs to the husband as an asset. The wife's expected achievement is to bear children and especially male ones. Failing to bear children is a justified ground for replacement.

Ascribed Status and Belonging

Before I turn to the orientation of belonging—not in its possessive sense but in its bonding sense—there is a need, at some point, to distance our discussion from the talk about social status as couched in terms of *ascribed* status and *achieved* status.[11] There are in many societies disturbing connections between ascribed social status and relationships based on belonging. These disturbing connections should be mentioned, for they are at the core of the relation between morality and ethics. Ascribed status has very little to do with individuals' attainments or abilities and everything to do with facts of origin and birth, such as race, age, gender, family, and ethnic or caste affiliation. Ascribed status is based on involuntary or semi-voluntary attributes. Not all properties that feature in ascribed status manifest belonging relations.

But the connection is strong. It holds not only at the high end of the social ladder, for we find a sense of belonging among those who suffer from low ascription. Race, gender, and caste may serve as instruments for creating solidarity and belonging among people of low ascribed status, as demonstrated by "sisterhood" among feminists, or blacks referring to each other as "brother." True, some important ascribed status traits are not in general a manifestation of belonging relations, but some important traits are.

It is almost true by definition that only belonging relations serve to confer ascribed status, which is not true of traits that constitute achievement status. Important and rewarding as belonging relations are in our life, the relation between belonging and ascribed status can be rendered quite menacing by converting belonging into nepotism. Belonging fudges standards of accomplishment; as such, it is bad. The remedy requires that both orientations, belonging and achievement, must mutually constrain each other. Belonging without achievement is half blind, and achievement without belonging is humanly half empty.

Is a Betrayer More like a Murderer or More like a Liar?

The question we face is, which feature (or features) of a thick relation is the main feature that is eroded—indeed, shattered—by betrayal? The short answer is, belonging. At this point we are in the midst of the long answer. The first move in that direction was to discard the notion of belonging as *possession* and to support the notion of belonging as *bond*.

We still haven't paid sufficient attention to the gap between the act of betrayal and the actor as betrayer. Why is the gap between act and actor so important in assessing betrayal? In cases of betrayal, we move from assessing an act as betrayal to reevaluating the thick relation between the betrayer and the betrayed. If we think of betrayal in terms of breach of trust, then the inference from the breach is to the untrustworthiness of the betrayer: once a betrayer, always a betrayer. It is a poor inference, as inferences go. It is based on one instance: from one act to the character of the actor. The act is betrayal; hence, the actor is a betrayer.

By our account, an act of betrayal calls for reevaluating the nature of the *relation* between the betrayer and the betrayed. It is not a call to reassess the *character* of the actor, though it may be that too. But in reevaluating the nature of the relation—its thickness—we unavoidably move from the act to the actor, for a thick relationship is between individuals, not between actions. This is why it is important to elucidate the move from assessing the act to assessing the actor.

If you lie only once, you are not a liar. If you murder once, you are a murderer. I believe that the difference is that "liar" is usually used as a descriptive dispositional term in spite of the fact that lying has a strong normative ramification.

Murder is usually attributed normatively: one act of unlawful intentional killing is enough to make you a murderer. We may of course talk about a homicidal or murderous person, having in mind someone with dangerously violent tendencies, capable of killing for the slightest slight. Or we may talk of a serial murderer, referring to someone who has murdered more than three human beings, one at a time, with cooling-off periods in between. The killing in these cases turns one into a murderer in a dispositional sense, on top of the normative sense. But the term "murderer" used without qualification is normally understood normatively.

It seems that the normative use of "murderer," based only on one incident, is due to the seriousness of the offense: one act of murder is one too many. We don't take lying that seriously. We routinely tell lies in airport security checks: Was your luggage with you all the time? Sure. Did anyone give you anything to carry with you? No. Kant, who made a fetish of lying, required us to treat every lie with the utmost seriousness, but this is not the way most of us think about lying. Unimportant lies—"white lies," for example, which are meant to pluck us out of minor embarrassments—do not make one a liar.

What about a serious lie? Can a serious lie turn one into a liar? Colin Powell had a reputation for being an honorable man. This is perhaps why he was sent to brief the Security Council of the United Nations on February 5, 2003, saying that "an accumulation of facts and disturbing patterns of behavior . . . demonstrate that Saddam Hussein and his regime have made no effort to disarm" and, in fact, "are concealing their efforts to produce more weapons of mass destruction."[12] All of that was based on bogus evidence, which Powell marshaled before the Security Council to great effect. Powell later viewed his briefing as a blot on his reputation, and a blot it is. He denies, however, that he was consciously lying. He claims that he was misled by the intelligence community. But let us assume that he did lie, and let us further assume, as it is reasonable to assume in his case, that he hadn't lied in public before.

There is no question that his presumed lie is a serious one, with horrific consequences. The seriousness of the lie brought some people to call Colin Powell a liar, thereby transposing the term "liar" from its dispositional use to its normative use. And yet there are many who, in spite of their belief that Powell lied, hesitate to call him a liar. They wouldn't side with Iago in believing that "reputation is an idle and most false / imposition, oft got without merit and lost without / deserving" (*Othello*

II.iii.268–270). They believe that Powell deserves his reputation of honesty, but they also believe that he earned the blot on his reputation fair and square. What is the lesson learned from the story about Colin Powell? For some, the inference from act to actor is immediate: the act is lying and therefore the actor is a liar. For others, the inference from act to actor depends on one's overall reputation. If the overall moral reputation of, say, Tony Blair is not unblemished, he may suffer being called a liar by lying about Iraq. If Powell's reputation *is* unblemished, he can get away with not being called a liar. Lying, unlike murder, admits of degrees. The imputation of "liar" on the basis of acts of lying is not as automatic as in murder. Is betrayal like murder or like lying? Is a betrayer like a murderer or like a liar?

One act of treason is enough to turn the actor into a traitor. Treason, like murder, is taken seriously. "Betrayer" seems to vacillate between the dispositional use and the normative use, whereas "traitor" seems to be squarely within the normative use. "Traitor" is of course being used as a term of abuse, and it may very well be that this is its most common usage; but let us ignore its use as abuse.

The important inference is not between the act of betrayal and the betraying actor; rather, the main thrust should be the inference from the act of betrayal to reevaluate the thick relations between the betrayer and the betrayed. The reevaluation does of course reflect on the betrayer, but the focus should be the grossly compromised relation rather than the character of the betrayer.

Belonging and Significant Others

The expression "significant other" means an intimate partner of either gender. But "significant other" has an additional sense of being an individual who is important in one's life. "Important in one's life" is tricky. It may mean influential, or it may mean greatly valued. Our friends and family may be very influential in our life, but so are people from our reference group, including a reference group to which we do not belong but which we aspire to join. Thus professional peers may serve as a reference group, with immense influence on our behavior and thought, and yet they are in no way our significant others. Professional peers are colleagues, not friends. They may of course turn into friends also. Collegial relations may turn into thick relations without necessarily becoming intimate friendships. Working long hours together in the laboratory on a joint project may create an important bond with team spirit. If one member of the team cheats and cooks the results of a joint research project, it may very well be considered to be a betrayal of one's bonded associates. By contrast, breaking thin collegial relations by trashing the reputation of colleagues whom one barely knows is bad non-collegial behavior, but betrayal it is not.

Betraying the Relation

I have been giving priority to a human relation over the individuals standing in the relation. Being in a relation may affect the individuals standing in the relation differently. This holds true in cases such as friendship. I described friendship as individuals acting for the sake of their friendship. Still, doing something for one's friend may mean that the friend is the main beneficiary of the act, while the actor may suffer some cost. By changing the focus from the *relata* to the relation, we should be free from having to sort out whether acts of friendship are acts of altruism or acts of egoism. They are neither.

Betrayal in friendship affects the betrayer and the betrayed differently, but the betrayal is primarily a betrayal of the relationship. There are cases where the act of betrayal may be a move against the betrayed: for example, when the betrayer seeks retaliation for neglect, or feels resentment over being taken for granted. Yet, as I have already pointed out, betrayal in personal relations is seldom a move *against* an old friend but more usually a move *for* a third party, to the neglect of the old friend. There is a beautiful Israeli children's song that played a formative role in the upbringing of my generation. Danny the tiny toddler sings: "I gave Nurit a beautiful blue flower, I also gave her an apple, I gave her everything I had. Nurit ate the apple, tossed the flower on the ground, and went to play with another boy." Then Danny asks his mother in wonder why the tears form in his eyes and roll down his cheeks of themselves. We toddlers readily understood the scene and, sure enough, some of us were troubled by the question whether Nurit, the spoiled brat of the playground, betrayed Danny by taking the apple and going to play with another tot.

We all know people, ourselves included, who in moments of self-pity feel that if they love someone, it puts a burden on the loved one to reciprocate with love and friendship. An illusion is often created that a thick relation is established by the mere magic of loving someone, even without her knowing. The Dannys of such a story may feel betrayed when their Nurits go to play with someone else. Jealousy is understandable, but is the feeling of being betrayed so too? It seems that a reasonable requirement for a thick relation is that those who are supposed to be involved in the relation recognize themselves as being *in* the relation.

But this cannot be true as stated. Danny stands in a thick relation with his mother without necessarily knowing it. His mother stands in a *comprehending* relation to her toddler son. She has to

understand him and include him in her strong belonging relation, even if the child has little grasp of the relation. A comprehending relation is an asymmetrical relation. And so we seem
to be facing a conundrum: we feel that unilateral love does not
establish a thick relation if, as in the case of Dante's unilateral
love for Beatrice, the beloved is not even aware of being loved,
let alone reciprocating in kind, whereas no such recognition is
needed between Danny and his mother. In thick personal relations between adults of sound mind, mutual recognition of
being in a thick relation is needed to establish the thick relation. No such requirement is needed, however, in the case of
children or adults of unsound mind. The presumption is that
had they been of sound mind, they would have recognized that
they were in the relation (or not, as the case may be). It is a
problematic presumption. It may be misused in promoting un-
justified paternalism: intervention by the state or by individuals in the lives of other individuals against their will, based
on the claim that they are not in their right mind. One of the
things that make paternalism so annoying is the pretense of
agencies that do not, on the face of it, appear to have thick family
relations behaving as if they were in such relations by acting on
others' behalf.

But note that what we are concerned about here is not the right
to intervene in the lives of others, but a very different sort of
question: can thick relations be non-mutual? The answer is yes,
they can, in cases in which one party to the relation is not suffi-
ciently of sound adult mind to judge in what kind of relation he
is in and there is good reason to believe the counterfactual: that
had he been of sound mind, the relation would have been recognized by both parties as mutual.

Modularity

We normally lead our lives in a web of various thick relations: some thicker than others, some competing with others for our time, and some competing for our emotional resources. Some thick relations are in direct confrontation. Having a thick relation both with one's spouse and with one's lover is taken as a paradigmatic case of incompatibility. A recurrent psychological mechanism used by betrayers facing incompatible thick relations is to keep the two apart. They try hard to avoid the agonizing sense of incompatibility, much like avoiding bringing together positive and negative electrical terminals in a battery, which may explode once brought into contact. The rule is simple: never connect. Don't connect the relation to your spouse with the relation to your lover. The mechanism is modularity: each relation stands on its own.

For the modular person, having a lover and having a spouse doesn't seem to be a case of one at the expense of the other: neither of them is betrayed for the other. The two have nothing to do with each other, just as having a human partner and having a pet puppy do not compete. Betrayal is not perceived by the modular person as harming the betrayed. It is something totally unrelated. The betrayed feels that the betrayal was a move against her in favor of a third party. But modularity keeps the modular person secure in his feeling that nothing in what he does is at her expense. The question of incompatibility does arise for the betrayer, but only as a conventional social obstacle in forming a thick relation with the lover. It is a technical problem, such as keeping the relation secret, but it has nothing to do with real betrayal.

The betrayed may believe that she is constantly on the mind of her betrayer, but nothing is further from the truth. The betrayer tries hard not to think about the betrayed while he is with the lover module. He views the betrayed, if at all, as a complication to overcome, probably by cheating, but cheating is all there is to it: it doesn't seriously reflect his attitude toward the betrayed, or so he believes. Modularity, namely, the disconnecting of incompatible thick relations, should not be conflated with what psychologists call "dissociation": a disorder characterized by detachment from emotional experiences and from the world. The two are separate phenomena.

A constant theme in the literature, as it is in the reality of betrayal, is the shock of recognition by the unsuspecting deceived one. For the betrayed, quite often, the discovery of being betrayed is an earth-shattering experience. Yet there is nothing earth-shattering in mentioning this observation. The modularity model suggests that the modular betrayer—the betrayer who does not connect disturbingly incompatible thick relations—may experience a shock of recognition too. The betrayer discovers through the reaction of the betrayed that he has been a betrayer all along. He knew, of course, that what he was doing was regarded conventionally as betrayal, and he had to put much effort into hiding his affair from the betrayed. But this he thought a mere matter of social propriety, with no human or moral depth to it. After all, he still cherishes the betrayed, and nothing, he believes, is detracted from his old feelings and attachment to her by conducting an unrelated affair. The modular betrayer can be genuinely surprised to discover the shattering effect on his devastated old partner.

"Only connect the prose and the passion," advises Margaret in E. M. Forster's *Howards End*. It is exactly the prose and the passion in marital relations that the betrayer doesn't connect. He keeps the module of his prose disconnected from the module of his passion. He doesn't really think that his affair should affect the meaning of his thick relation to his old partner. The old relation is the prose, his daily bread, while his infatuation with the new lover is the passion, the cherry on the cake. Prose is prose and passion is passion and he can be attached to both without substituting one or the other. When "prose" complains about being deserted for the sake of "passion," he is surprised because he believes that "prose" is more important in his life than "passion," even if passion is less nagging and more fun. Prose is real life, whereas passion is taking short holidays from life.

Is modularity a recipe for self-deception—"bad faith"? Not quite. The story here, I believe, is more subtle. Self-deception means that we fool ourselves, and philosophers have been greatly worried about how this is possible. Who deceives whom in self-deception? All this is familiar ad nauseam, including the move of turning the self into a committee, in which one member of the committee cheats the other, which seems like saying that my left hand stole money from my right hand. Whatever our account of self-deception might be, modularity sets in motion a mechanism that is not unrelated to self-deception. It is our ability, when we are blamed for behaving badly, to give ourselves the benefit of the doubt in a way we never give to others. We recognize that our behavior may look bad to others, but only we know the full circumstances under which we acted. So it is not that we tell ourselves that we behaved well even though everyone else believes we didn't, but rather that we give ourselves the benefit of the doubt by an appeal to a privileged knowledge of our "inner feelings," to which only we, so to speak, have access. The modular betrayer knows well that to the betrayed and to bystanders his acts are acts of betrayal, but what do they know? He, and only he, knows his true states of mind, and in his mind he never meant to betray; indeed, he is very keen to go on with his old thick relation. It is on occasion the effect on the old partner that forces the modular betrayer to connect. And like connecting incompatible electrical charges, the result has explosive potential.

Shock of Recognition

Shakespeare made famous the words "Et tu, Brute?" (And you, Brutus?) This is the ultimate expression of the shock of betrayal of the least expecting person at the hands of the least expected person. There are various suggestions for the reading of Caesar's utterance: for example, as a curse, meaning, You too will suffer my fate and die a violent death. Yet the obvious reading of the saying in Shakespeare's *Julius Caesar* is as a shock of recognition: I have been betrayed by my nearest and dearest, by the least likely person to draw the dagger.

The shock is not Caesar's alone, for when Cassius asks, "Where is Antony?" he is answered, "Fled to his house amazed: / Men, wives and children stare, cry out and run / As it were doomsday" (III.i.106–108). If Antony is overwhelmed by the shock of great surprise at this "doomsday scenario," the same holds true for the people of Rome, who feel as though they were present at the End of Days spectacle. It is a spectacle viewed with an amalgam of terror, anguish, bewilderment, and a pang of awed deference to what is beyond them. The term "shock" conveys both an emotional reaction of dismay and sudden fright and an epistemic realization that the momentously unforeseeable is actually happening.

In bodily shock, the supply of oxygen, so vital to the organs, is choked off due to a blockage of the blood supply. Similarly, the physical sensation of the shock of betrayal is as if the blood had stopped flowing.

We are not really surprised to learn that people who have just been diagnosed with cancer are usually shaken to the core. To some, the diagnosis comes out of the blue: a routine medical checkup with no warning symptoms, then the discovery, and in no time one is exiled from the planet of the healthy to the planet of the seriously ill. But even for those who have reasons to suspect their health, the diagnosis is a shocker. A stage of expecting the worst yet hoping for the best may change abruptly when the test results with the final verdict arrive like a heavy blow. Why is there such a blow when the worst was expected and the hope for the best was unfounded? The answer, I believe, has to do with perspective. When we address our considered expectation about our health, it is our third-person perspective on ourselves that takes charge. However, our hopes, especially when unfounded, are an expression of our first-person perspective. The gap between the two perspectives leaves enough room for a shock wave.

We may find the triumph of hope over experience even among spouses who should have known better, such as those who fill the fourth or fifth slot of marriage in the life of a serial monogamist. She tells him that with him it will be different. Now, at last, she has found the love of her life, with whom she will stay forever and ever, which means roughly five years. His choice is to believe her or to believe induction; he opts to believe her. Reminding him later that "we told you so" is no good. This semi-farcical scene is a reminder that we do not lead our thick relations by induction, any more than the squirrel gathers nuts by induction (Ludwig Wittgenstein). The point, however, is that things that shock us from a first-person perspective shouldn't shock us from a third-person perspective. It was the advice of the Stoics that one should adopt a third-person perspective on one's own life to avoid disappointments, but this is indeed hard if we are not Stoic sages.

The Epistemic Rupture of Betrayal

There are obvious similarities between the shock of betrayal and the shock of cancer. The "it won't happen to me" attitude is only one such similarity. The shattering of the core of one's being is another one. But the shock of betrayal and the shock of cancer differ in an important way. The shock of cancer brings to the first-person perspective a sudden feeling of fear, fear of death. What nourishes the panic is the immediate leap to the worst-case scenario associated with cancer, namely, death after excruciating treatment. But even without the fear of immediate death, there is the justified fear that life won't be what it used to be, that things will only get worse in unknown and quite frightening ways. A third-person perspective might on occasion alleviate the panic by informing the anguished first-person perspective that the worst-case scenario is not the only scenario and that, for some types of cancer, the worst case is not even the most likely case. The shock of cancer comes from the fear of a distressing rupture in one's life, but it does not mean an epistemic rupture, whereas the revelation that one was horribly betrayed does seem to tear apart one's confidence that the world is what it seems to be. Being in a thick relation involves, for mentally sound participants, holding firm to the belief that others stand in the same thick relation as we. This is a foundational belief in one's life. If one doubts this belief, innumerable other important beliefs become shaky. If this belief turns out to be false, then one asks oneself: What do I know about anything else in my life? Thick relations are predicated on the assumption that what we see, with respect to our thick relations, is what there is, and suddenly—and the stress is on "suddenly"—this is not so.

My account of the sudden shock of betrayal ignores the crazily jealous husband who construes his wife's every smile as a threat of imminent betrayal, and the paranoid spy catcher who sees everyone as a spy: the more innocent one looks, the more likely one is to be a wolf in sheep's clothing. These types, when they eventually encounter true betrayal, feel vindicated: now that they have finally been betrayed, their worldview is confirmed, their constant agitation and restless suspicion abate, and they calm down. One way to address such obsessive behavior is to disqualify these possessed and possessive individuals from having thick relations. They are not really in a thick relation but in a sick relation, in which they tether possession to obsession. This, however, is too easy a way out. We should not by mere fiat conceptually disqualify possessive people from having thick relations. They too are part of the familiar repertoire out of which the rich drama of betrayal is made.

Past Orientation

Richard Rorty urges us to steer clear of the direction in which philosophy has traditionally been going. Instead of being immersed in the misguided project of epistemology, which rests on the misleading picture of a correspondence between our representations and the world, we should make a concerted edifying effort to cement human solidarity by basing it on a shared progressive future rather than on a tribal past. As I have already mentioned, Rorty's idea is that there is no need for the past in cementing thick relations of "solidarity"; all we need do is act toward the creation of a better future. Rorty's line concerns two issues: solidarity as a substitute for epistemology, and the role of the past in shaping thick human relations.[13]

Against Rorty, I claim that thick relations involve both epistemology and the past history of the relation. Betrayal touches on both. It creates a shock to one's set of basic beliefs, and it colors one's past relationship. The sense of belonging is the first fatality of betrayal; painting the past in dark colors is the second. Moreover, there is a close connection between solidarity (thick relations) and epistemology; they aren't antithetical, contrary to what Rorty would have us maintain.

Here is the connection. We lead our conscious life more by beliefs based on what we are told by others than by what we see with our own eyes. We rely more on testimony than on evidence. Some believe that testimony can ultimately be cashed in for direct evidence, much as signed checks in the market can in principle ultimately be cashed in for money. But whatever force "can in principle be cashed in" might have, one thing is clear: in our life we rarely "cash in" what we take on trust from the testimony of others. This does not mean that we are uncritical about what we are told. It only means that we check one testimony against other testimonies, rather than against the hard currency of direct evidence. For my purpose here, it is enough that to all intents and purposes we use testimonies as justification for a great many of our beliefs. We need the help of strangers in finding our way in a foreign country, and we find our way under the guidance of a strong presumption that when asking for a name of a street we get an honest answer. The presumption can be dropped if, for example, we are members of an occupying army asking our way of a hostile occupied population.

But we are particularly susceptible to testimony received from those with whom we stand in thick relations. The formative informants in our early life, and, for many of us, throughout life, are those with whom we stand in thick relations. Betrayal by a formative informant on whose testimony we heavily rely in the things we care most about not only smashes our relation to the betrayer as a reliable source of testimony but shakes our trust in testimony in general. This is part of the epistemic shock of betrayal: if the betrayer was able to fool us for so long, then there is nothing of importance on which we can rely anymore. The victim of betrayal feels that he made a fool of himself in being taken in for so long. The issue is not the proverbial cuckolded husband who made himself a public laughingstock in being the last to know. In making a fool of himself, I mean a fool in his own eyes. The result is not a healthy move from dogmatism to skepticism but a move from trusting to a mood of desperate disorientation.

On Not Wanting to Know

Edna Ullmann-Margalit raised the issue of the rationality of not wanting to know.[14] There is a strong Enlightenment assumption that when it comes to knowledge we should hold to the "pig principle" that more is better. When relevant information is available at no cost or at insignificantly low cost, it is always rational to use the total evidence available. The question is, is the rationality assumption right? Do you want to know, for example, that you inherited a mutation that indicates that you are very likely to develop a bad disease for which there is no cure, nor medication for temporary remission, nor treatment for slowing its development? It seems that there is nothing irrational about not wanting to know this bit of hopeless and helpless information.

What about not wanting to know whether you are betrayed? You encounter many signs that indicate that you are betrayed, but you (half-) consciously ignore them. You don't want to know. You have already convinced yourself that betrayal is a histrionic category good only for drama queens and kings. In real life it is a phase that doesn't indicate anything deep. You suspect that things are going wrong, but knowing it for sure would force you to take a stand, probably an overdramatic stand of making a scene, which you intensely hate and despise. It is better not to know, in the not unfounded hope that it is indeed a phase and will wither away. Betrayal, you may say, is not terminal illness. It is more like viral flu: do nothing and let it pass. You may go on to tell yourself that it is wrong to model life on literature. Betrayal is the stuff of literature, but when it is transposed to living human relations, it is a disaster. The act of betrayal was not meant to ruin your relationship, or, for that matter, its thickness. Don't be silly; you are not onstage, and you don't have to do any histrionic, if not hysteric, number. If you do, it may ruin your relationship, with catastrophic consequences. Better not to know. There is nothing irrational about not wanting to know this kind of disturbing stuff.

The main point here is the idea that betrayal has gone through a long course of overdramatization because of the hold art has on our lives. Life should be the model for art rather than art the model for life. Literature as a model for life accentuates the role of betrayal in real life way beyond reason. Betrayal is not art imitating life; it is life imitating art, much in the way that real people kiss like Hollywood rather than Hollywood kisses like real people. Betrayal has become a melodramatic kiss of death due to its presentation in art, but this is the wrong direction of fit: from fiction to fact.

I suggest taking the last remarks, with regard to not-wanting-to-know as corrective, not as credo but as useful reminders of the pitfall in overdramatizing betrayal.

Assessing Thick Relations

Ethics is supposed to guide our thick relations. It provides us with reasons to behave in certain ways with those we are in thick relations with. These ways of behavior depend on the nature of the thick relations: for each form of thick relation we uphold an ideal form of the relation. The ideal form provides us with ways of evaluating our existing relationships. The evaluation of thick relations has two tiers. Tier one is evaluating family relations and friendships by the ideals of such relations as conceived in the community. The ideals, needless to say, are greatly affected by culture and history. Against these ideals we assess tokens of actual thick relations. The second tier consists in evaluating other thick relations as extensions of the two paradigmatic thick relations of family and friends. On the second tier we have, first, to justify the type of thick relation we are interested in, and we do so by judging how similar it is to the ideal of family or friendship; only then do we judge the tokens of such an extended thick relation by reference to the ideal of its type. Ethics is to be regulated by advice rather than by orders. But it is strong advice, similar to "the doctor advised me to take antibiotics twice a day." This sense of the doctor's order or advice may take a weaker form, as in "the doctor advised me to take a vacation." My picture of ethical normativity is indeed based on a similarity to medical normativity, where the ideal is a healthy body. The advice is an instruction on how to achieve the ideal of being free from disease, given to people who care about their health.

Thick relations are habitually under the description of thick concepts (concepts that require continual interpretation). Thick relations, due to the fact that they are covered by thick concepts, are less amenable to being couched in terms of rules than thin concepts are. Morality, which regulates thin relations and is covered by thin concepts, is a proper domain for exceptionalness rules, but this is pretty dubious in the domain of ethics. Ethics uses the "divide and rule" strategy when there are no rules and the conceptual terrain is pretty unruly. "Divide and rule" means making constantly nuanced distinctions and comparisons.

Are thick relations subject to *Anna Karenina*'s principle of the kind "all happy families are alike"? In other words, are all good thick relations that approximate the ideal alike and all bad ones bad in their own way? A related question to the *Anna Karenina* line is: Are there countless ways to betray, but only one way to be loyal?

There is a picture here: the good is one and the bad is many. This is not a good picture. There are many admissible ideals. Only admissible ideals are ethical ideals. By admissible ideals I mean ideals that get a clean bill of health from morality. It is a necessary condition for an admissible ideal to pass the test of morality. Serving as an ethical ideal of thick human relations should pass morality constraints. However, more than one ideal for each type of relation may cross the benchmark set by morality. Not all happy families are alike. Does that mean ethical pluralism? Yes, it does. Morality is one; ethics is many.

The Four F-Models of Relations: Family, Friends, Firm, Feudal

My starting point in dealing with morality and ethics is human relations. Karl Marx stated, more generally, that human relations are the starting point for any account of human beings. However, he singled out production relations as the most important explanatory notion. His general point is that social relations take explanatory precedence over individual traits. For example, exploitation of a worker by an owner of the means of production should be explained by how the two stand in (capitalist) production relations, rather than by the stinginess and greediness of the owner or the meekness and servility of the worker.

Strange as it may sound, on many occasions our order of understanding is from relations first to properties second. For example, the relation "equal in height" may take precedence over the property "height."

In dealing with ethics and morality, it is a good idea to start with relationships. There are two human concerns that are important in our lives: concern with our relations to other humans in general and concern with our relations to particular humans and especially family and friends. The priority of relations over properties is inherent in the way I characterize the concern of ethics and the concern of morality. If morality were concerned with human virtues, which are character traits, then I would have started with properties rather than relations. However, I am primarily concerned not with virtues such as trustworthiness or truthfulness but rather with thick relations such as friendship.

Firms

Two *F*-words, "family" and "friends," provide us with paradigmatic cases of thick human relations.[15] Remember: betrayal, by our account, is an erosion of the meaning of a thick relation. This idea seems to face an immediate problem, indicated by another *F*-word, "firm," which stands in a contrastive relation to family and friends. By "firm" I mean a bureaucratic corporate enterprise that is oriented by achievement, such as maximizing profit. It is the achievement orientation of the firm (the ideal type of a firm) that contrasts with the orientation of belonging, which marks family and friend relationships. There are "in-between" institutions, such as family firms, which are a hybrid of family belonging and economic achievement, but the firms that serve as my models are impersonal corporations.

Cloak-and-dagger operations, involving intrigue and espionage, were in the past mainly directed at military and diplomatic secrets. But we won't be surprised if nowadays it is Silicon Valley with its precious industrial secrets, rather than the Pentagon, that is more of a target for intense espionage. Industrial espionage and military espionage have a great deal in common. They try, among other things, to recruit insiders to provide secret information. Bribery, blackmail, and fishing for employees with grudges or vulnerabilities are all pretty much routines of the trade, be it military or industrial. The fishing is for insiders, employees who are entrusted by their companies with industrial secrets of advanced technology. Related to insiders are deserters who abscond with industrial secrets and move to a rival company or establish one of their own. All of this is pretty much routine stuff in the economic world of today. Governments of the world are very much part of this business. There is nothing new in industrial espionage. The secret of Chinese porcelain drove the Islamic world as well as Europe crazy, because for centuries and centuries they couldn't produce the amazing porcelain that the Chinese could make; Europe needed a Jesuit priest spying on the Chinese production to reveal the secret. What is new is not the existence of industrial spying but the extent of it.

There is no question that there is something wrong with stealing information, as there is something wrong with the other kind of theft, and industrial espionage is stealing information. There is no question that an insider who helps in such theft is doing something that is morally wrong, in the sense in which insider collusion with bank robbers is doing something that is morally wrong.

But is the insider a traitor? Remember: being a traitor is not the only way to be bad. A worker providing competitors with vital industrial secrets may undermine the prospects of her fellow workers. This is indeed a betrayal, not of the firm but of fellow workers, in cases where the firm has created a thick solidarity relation among its workers.

It is interesting that the CIA and MI5, which try to muster the loyalty expected of associations based on thick relations, are respectively nicknamed "the Organization" and "the Firm," both highly bureaucratic labels. Bureaucratic organizations are not constituted of thick relations. The rationality of an ideal type of bureaucracy means that they are oriented toward achieving specialized ends by adopting the right means. This in any case is what Max Weber tells us. It is interesting that organized crime, which tries to emulate the corporate world, goes under the name of "family" or "clan" (from the ambiguous Italian term *cosca*, which puns on both "clan" and "artichoke," "clan" alluding to the thick bonds and "artichoke" to the tight, protective structure). It is also interesting to note that there is little truth in the popular impression that Mafia families are blood families.

So here is the puzzle. On the one hand, we have state espionage agencies, which are perceived in terms of the cold and calculating corporate world rather than in terms of the warm feelings of family and friends. On the other hand, in arrogating to themselves highly charged notions such as betrayal and loyalty and traitors and patriots, these organizations seem to succeed where the corporate world fails.

National intelligence agencies retain their hold on notions such as loyalty and betrayal because they are agencies that are perceived as protecting vital interests of the community. It is not the agency qua organization that musters the loyalty of its members, but rather its presumed role as guardian of the community. Thick relations are an attribute of the community. The organization may be cold, but it is in the service of something hot.

There is another possible explanation for treating the betrayal of, say, the Israeli intelligence agency Mossad (meaning "the Institution" in Hebrew) as a betrayal of thick relations, in spite of the bureaucratic label of the agency. It is not just a bureaucratic agency; it has the ethos of an elite fighting unit. Its agents operate under considerable risk, and they develop the spirit of camaraderie of an elite unit, with strong bonds to each other. Betraying the Mossad may mean betraying the lives of agents whom some of the people in the organization care about, above and beyond their usefulness to the organization. They are comrades in arms. Evening in and evening out, we may watch a recurrent plot unfold on the small screen: the agent who has lost her usefulness to the organization. The people at the top are willing to sacrifice her, only to be countered by a loyal comrade who exposes the betrayal and fights the bosses to the hilt. What these exasperating movies tell us is that intelligence agencies are caught between the two conflicting models of firm and friendship, with no idea of how to resolve the tension.

Affinity Scam

By "firm" I don't have in mind the traditional family business, which is built on a mixture of thick and thin relations: thick among the family that runs the business, and thin with many of its clients. But a firm may have assumed thick relations with some of its clients, who can be and on occasion are betrayed. The most glaring examples of such betrayal are conjured up by con men. I shall deal with three such egregious cases of financial betrayal that had to do with thick relations: the case of Charles Ponzi, the case of Bernard Madoff, and the bizzare case of Gregor MacGregor.

I am interested in con men for reasons I shall spell out shortly. I am not interested in con women—not because I am not interested in women, but because they have not been involved, as far as I know, in the kind of betrayal of trust in which men have been involved in the past. The kind of betrayal I am interested in is what I dub "betrayal of your people." A formidable female con artist under the assumed name of Helga de la Brache was able to procure a royal pension from the Swedish court by persuading it that she was the secret love child of King Gustav IV, but royalty does not fall under the formula of "betraying your people." So let me say more.

Johann Wolfgang von Goethe borrowed the term "elective affinities" *(Wahlverwandschaften)* from eighteenth-century chemistry to explain human bonding, the way chemistry explains the tendency of different substances to form chemical compounds. I shall use this pregnant metaphor of elective affinity for my notion of thick human relations. Family, friends, ethnic group, and religion are some of the elements that tend to form strong human bonds; in short, these are elective affinities. The point of switching metaphors from "thick relations" to "elective affinities" will soon, I hope, be clear.

Note that elective means choice, an optional conduct. Thick relations are not usually a matter of choice.

Betraying Your People

Bernard Madoff, or Bernie to his friends, who is responsible for one of the largest frauds in history, preyed predominantly upon his fellow Jews, with whom he had elective affinities, or so his fellow Jews believed. It turns out that there is nothing remarkable about this fact: many con men prey on their own people. The police have a telling term for it: "affinity scam." I don't know whether the police had Goethe in mind, or Weber for that matter, who borrowed the expression from Goethe. Yet the police use this felicitous expression to name a scam that undermines elective affinities, namely, a scam that on top of everything else betrays thick relations.

The obvious question is, why do the perpetrators prey on their people, of all people?

Willie Sutton was allegedly asked by a journalist why he robbed banks, to which he famously answered: "Because that is where the money is." Had Madoff been asked why he preyed on his people, he might easily have answered: Because that is where the trust is. Indeed, thick relations are possessed of something more valuable than confidence: they are endowed with trust.

We quite often use "confidence" and "trust" interchangeably, but there is a distinction to be drawn between them. Confidence requires that the one in whom you put your confidence be predictable, so as long as his interests and yours overlap he will serve your interests as well as his.[16] In trust there is an added element, which is that your interests weigh with the trusted one on their own account and not only as an instrument to promote his interests. There is trust and not only confidence in the cases I am about to describe.

Al Capone also had words of wisdom: "You can get much further with a kind word and a gun than you can with a kind word alone." But he was wrong. The story of some con men tells us that they got much further with their kind words than Capone ever got with his gun.

The Great Little Ponzi

The first is good old Carlo Ponzi, the well-groomed little crook—or, rather, the little man and big crook—who immortalized himself as the inventor of the scam that bears his name. The idea of the Ponzi scheme is that money handed over to the perpetrator is never invested in a legitimate venture that is meant to yield an honest profit. Instead, the investor, if lucky, is paid back with the money of subsequent investors, under the pretext that this money is a return on a legitimate investment.[17]

Ponzi was born in Italy and arrived in New York in 1893 at the age of fifteen. His business career started in 1919 in Boston. Ponzi noticed that letters at the time were sent with postal reply coupons that could be used to buy stamps for return mail. He also noticed that there were differences in the relative prices of those coupons: they could be bought cheap in countries with weak economies and sold dear in the United States. He promised his family and friends, including the local priest, that he could reap 100 percent profits on such investments by buying low and selling high. In fact, he tried out his idea of arbitrage on the coupons and made pitifully little money. But the story caught on with his near and dear, and they invested about $1,200 with him. To their amazement they were rewarded by Ponzi after three months with several hundred dollars in interest. The story of Ponzi's miraculous venture spread like wildfire, and in no time he was able to borrow $10 million from twenty thousand investors. Not all were "his people," but his springboard consisted of fellow Italian immigrants.

When heavy hints about Ponzi's monkey business started to circulate, Ponzi hired a journalist to shield him from nasty rumors; instead, the journalist discovered, within four days, the fraudulent nature of Ponzi's business. He went straight to the police. It wasn't the end of Ponzi: after serving several years in prison, he moved to Italy, only to be hired as a financial adviser for another charlatan, Benito Mussolini, even though Ponzi could hardly add.

Ponzi targeted mainly his people, Italian immigrants. Immigrants are particularly vulnerable to con artists: They have problems with the language. They are not always familiar with official financial institutions; moreover, they don't believe those institutions will work in their favor. They often want to stay under the radar of the tax authorities, preferring to be paid in cash by tax-dodging employers. Morality is not their priority; solidarity is. Immigrants strongly believe in ethnic ties. Ethnic ties are for them a natural extension of family ties, a guarantee of ethical ties. All these circumstances and more are the basis for many a Ponzi scheme.

Madoff and His Clients

In the case of Madoff, we discover once again the belief in ethnic ties as the foundation of trust relations, especially when ethnic ties go hand in hand with religious ties.[18] Madoff had as investors some hard-nosed individuals who could by no means be regarded as clueless newcomers. Avoiding the tax authorities was perhaps a motive among some of Madoff's investors too, but this cannot suffice as an explanation. So how come investors who knew a thing or two about the market believed in a scheme that would provide them with a 12–15 percent yield both in good times and in bad? Well, different people believe different things. Besides, cynicism is a reliable source of gullibility. If you believe that all horse races are rigged, then you believe that there is a sure bet, if you only know the secret deal. Between conspiracy theory and cynicism there is a connection.

But what has this to do with Madoff? Here is the connection. Shrewd investors do not believe that they can beat the market systematically, but they do believe that they can beat the market by having inside information about the firms in which they are investing. This is illegal. And so they invest with someone they believe has inside information. Being a shrewd investor, you can tell yourself: It is not I who gets the information, and the best policy for me is to not ask and to avoid being told. Instead, pretend that you believe that Madoff has no inside information, but rather insight illumination. He is a financial wizard, a genius with money. Madoff, you believe, may cheat, but he cheats the authorities, not *us,* his flesh and blood. This is my speculation about Madoff's sophisticated investors who belonged to "his people." Of course, not all Madoff's investors were Jews, but a disproportionate number were, and so his scam was an affinity scam.

But what story did Madoff tell himself? One way to deal with Madoff is to say that he was a cold, callous, calculating cynic who cared about nobody, including his close family. He used "his people" for his scheme and there is nothing more to say about it. I doubt that. More precisely, I doubt that that is all there is to it. Instead of being a cynic, he might just as well have believed that he stood in elective affinity with his people. While the scheme was running, his people felt happy and he kept them happy. They were very grateful to him and inflated his ego by viewing him as a financial genius. Then he told himself, If they go down, it is only because I go down. So we are both in the same boat. I didn't harm them any more than I harmed myself, and while I enjoyed the scheme, they too enjoyed it.

Selling Utopia

Ponzi and Madoff, by all accounts, are not terribly interesting individuals. They are interesting con men, but that's about it, and it seems that there is no need to go any deeper into their psyches. But another con man was far more interesting as a person, and he had a much more elaborate scheme. His name was Gregor MacGregor, and as the name suggests, he was a Scot. He preyed first and foremost on his fellow Scots. The time of the story is the second and third decades of the nineteenth century. MacGregor invented a country by the name of Poyais, on the Bay of Honduras, populated by dreamy, peace-loving, Gauguin-type natives, more than ready to serve new settlers from abroad. He, Sir Gregor MacGregor, was the Prince of Poyais.[19]

What lent credibility to his story was the fact—which he embellished quite effectively—that he had been a colonel in the wars of independence in South America. Moreover, there was already in Scotland a memory of a genuine effort to settle Scottish people on the Isthmus of Panama toward the end of the eighteenth century, the Darien scheme. MacGregor indeed capitalized on this memory by claiming that he was a descendant of a Darien settler.

MacGregor produced a guidebook of more than three hundred pages describing in great detail his promised land of Poyais. Anyone who is interested in utopian thinking should read this guidebook, since it strove to cater to the fantasies of real people in a surreal time.

MacGregor sold prospective settlers plots of lands as well as positions in his administration. More tragically, he organized five ships to carry the settlers to Poyais, only to drop them in the jungle; most lost not only their life savings but also their lives.

An astonishing fact about this sordid affair is that many of the survivors refused to believe that Sir MacGregor was a crook and, upon their rescue, signed a declaration of their belief in his innocence. They behaved like the proverbial believers in the gulags, who were of the opinion that had Comrade Stalin only known what was being perpetrated in his name, they would not be there.

In the days before information moved around the world at the speed of light, MacGregor could and did still go on peddling variations on his Poyais scheme. The only difference was that he had to move to Paris and his scheme stopped being an affinity scam. For those who care, let me tell you that he ended his life quite comfortably, receiving a pension from the Venezuelan government as an army colonel.

What is interesting in the stories of Ponzi, Madoff, and MacGregor is the scam. What is of interest to us is the affinity. People are cheated and are cheating others in the market all the time. Betraying is closely connected with cheating. It is not necessary to cheat in order to betray, but it helps. People who have been cheated are apt to describe their experience as betrayal. They feel the need for a strong term of condemnation, and "betrayal" comes in handy. But this is not a good use of the word. People who were cheated were abused, but that is not a good excuse to describe every case of cheating as betrayal. What makes the cases of Madoff and MacGregor fitting cases for the use of betrayal is the particular form of their cheating, namely, using and abusing the ethnic affinity between themselves and their victims—manipulating and exploiting the sense of thick relation. There is no moral difference between the case in which Madoff cheats a gentile and the case in which he cheats a Jewish acquaintance. But there is an ethical difference: on top of cheating, there is in an affinity scam a sense of betrayal.

Feudal Relations

I have already alluded to the possibility that the natural habitat of the idea of political betrayal is what I termed feudal morality: "feudal" in the sense that its best manifestation is what we take to be the feudal social relations in medieval Europe. But the notion of feudal here is not confined to Europe or to the medieval period. At the core of feudalism was the relation of lord to vassal (freeman). Loyalty and betrayal had to do with upholding or undermining this relation. It was understood as a personal relation. Feudal rule was personalized rule. On the local level it meant a manorial relation between a lord and his peasants. On a higher seigniorial level the personal relation was more of a fiction. The feudal political order was geographically so fragmented, and power so decentralized, that the focus on feudal personal relations should concentrate on what took place locally. Fragmentation and decentralization created a particular apprehension of loyalty and betrayal, especially with regard to non-local powers.

The stress is not so much on the word "personal" as on the idea that social relations are concrete. The contrast is to the abstract nature of modern social relations, which are mediated by intricate institutions, elaborate systems of laws, and a dense division of labor. Feudal personal relations do not mean close relations. The feudal lord, who inherited an estate due to some complicated family arrangement, might not have known the language of his tenants, or anything else about them. The basic feudal deal was protection for services. The top dog offered protection by his private army, and the underdogs offered their services as an exchange. This is admittedly a very crude characterization of the immensely varied phenomenon that goes under the title of feudalism. But the crudity doesn't hide the contours of the relations. They were more transparent than the relations that came after.

Historically, feudal relations incurred a huge investment in the maintenance of loyalty. It was a web of patronage, of being "another man's man," and, indeed, of making and taking homage. The political effort was to turn vassalage into the strongest glue, trumping any other human relation: "Vassals must help their lord against everyone—against their brothers, against their sons, against their fathers."[20] The hierarchical arrangement of feudal relations was as a matter of fact pretty chaotic and was definitely far removed from strict linear relations ("linear" in the way that the "greater than" relation orders numbers). It was not uncommon for a vassal to be a man of several masters. Homage to the lord was thereby weakened, and there was a constant search for a superglue that would produce the strongest fealty possible. For a while the liege played this role. Feudal relationships posed a challenge to family relationships. The former tried to supplant the latter as the strongest human bond, with the result that betrayal of one's lord was rendered the most damning depravity.

The ideal feudal relation is a relation based on belonging. It is this stress on belonging that made feudal social relations an obstacle to economic growth. The market economy shifted the orientation from belonging to achievement and freed the productive forces in the societies in which it took hold. The transition from feudal economy to market economy contributed to the development of companies with limited liabilities. One may say, metaphorically, that thick relations are partnerships of unlimited liabilities, whereas thin relations are partnerships of limited liabilities. The market economy made it clear that economic relations are based not on thick relations—family business—but in principle on anonymous shareholders, whose commitment should be proportional to their investment and to nothing else.

Family

There is a formidable progressive picture of the development of morality. The development of morality, in this picture, moves in ever-expanding concentric circles. The scope of morality moves from the particular (family, clan, tribe, ethnic group) and ends in the universal (humanity). By some accounts it should not stop there: the expanding circles, which graphically represent the scope of morality, should extend to animals or even to nature as a whole.

My picture of ethics, in distinction from morality, is of an ellipsis with two foci, family and friends, and the scope of the ellipsis includes those who stand in thick relations that are based on analogies to family relationships and friendships.

Historically, family relationships and friendships changed considerably, but not beyond recognition.

As for family, the idea that before the industrial revolution family took the form of the extended family, only to be contracted to the nuclear family due to capitalism, is more of an ideological myth than a reality. This myth harps on the theme that says that in the good old days the family was safe from atomism and alienation, evils that arose only later by division of labor.

But there is also a countermyth that harps on the liberating shift from the suffocating extended family to the nuclear family in which one hardly knows one's cousins.

The truth is that the nuclear family as an economic unit was known in England from the time shortly after the Black Plague. The nuclear family, or, by its other name, the conjugal family, is not a product of capitalism, though it is safe to say that it became more prevalent and important in the market economy.

The notion of the extended family has more ramifications than the glib account of the march from the extended family to the nuclear family suggests. Indeed, the Latin term *familia* meant household and not just family. What is relatively new is the idea that living together is confined only to family.

In all my examples I am referring only to European families, but of course families of different shapes and sizes are known everywhere. Yet their role in bringing up children, nurturing their development, and protecting them in time of sickness and in time of health is an invariant feature in all human arrangements that go under the label of "family."

The fact that the notion of family mutated and now includes different forms of extended families is at the core of the idea that by extension larger unities can imitate the family bond. And, at least historically, it probably provided the strongest bond. It may very well be the case that people in modern societies are more attached to their neighbors than to members of their extended family, whom they meet infrequently at depressing funerals and weary weddings, but even then they usually regard their conjugal family as providing a much stronger, if not necessarily pleasanter, bond than neighborhood fraternity.

The resiliency of the family arrangement is astonishing, given all the changes in all other human arrangements. It is no accident that it provides an object of comparison to so much else. It provides a powerful picture of human relations.

Picture

Throughout the discussion so far I have made extensive use of the term "picture," and I shall make more of it in the coming chapters. The danger is not in the use of the term but in its overuse. It calls for some elucidation. I borrow the term "picture" from Wittgenstein, and I hope that what I am about to say is in the spirit of his use.[21]

Pictures are metaphors, many of which are called dead metaphors, where the very expression "dead metaphor" is an example of a dead metaphor. The idea about pictures is that there are no dead metaphors, only hibernating ones, which may spring to life without warning and without necessarily being registered as metaphors. Metaphors are, in the language of Rudolf Carnap, a kind of transposed mode of speech, whereby we talk about domain A in terms of domain B, which stands in a certain relation to A. Domain B provides objects or events that serve as models for objects and events in A. But talking about A in terms that habitually refer to B, if used literally, is either false or nonsense. The language of B in its use to describe A presents a way of seeing

A in terms of B. Pictures make us notice some aspects of A through the lens of B, but it blinds us from seeing other aspects.

Take as an example the very idea of conception as an ability to understand or as a product of abstract thinking. We picture understanding in terms of conception as inception of pregnancy. It makes us think about thinking in terms of pregnancy. From here it is but a short step to thinking of the philosopher as a midwife trying to help others to draw out ideas, which are already there. These are "metaphors we live by"—in the apt title of George Lakoff and Mark Johnson's book—but they are rarely recognized as such. Wittgenstein was worried about pictures getting festive: they might run riot and nourish metaphysical illusions. I am less worried about metaphysics and more worried about the role pictures play in shaping social and political ideologies. Philosophical accounts of social ideologies should expose the formative metaphors, the pictures that nourish ideologies.

A picture has two typical features: it sounds both natural and necessary. By "necessary" I mean that it gives us the feeling of "How else can we think and talk?" Indeed, a sure sign that we are in the grip of a picture is when we do ask, "How else?" To get out of the grip of a picture is to be able to think of alternatives. This can be done by replacing one picture with another. A change of pictures involves a change in the questions we ask and the naturalness of our talk. Freud pictures our psychic life as a steam engine. With a steam engine it is natural to worry about energy, and in the case of the mind as an engine, we worry about psychic energy. Once we switch from picturing the mind as a steam engine to picturing the mind as a computer, questions about psychic energy lose their grip; energy has to do with huffing and puffing machines, not with computers.[22]

To wit, let me bring up a picture closer to home. We had a new pupil in our high school. He was brought up in an ultrareligious community and was very much an odd bird in our secular nest. At a certain point our teacher, a rather famous poet at the time and a rabid nationalist, told the newcomer that he had no national roots. To which the clever new boy retorted, "If God had wanted me to have roots, he would have created me a eucalyptus"; then he added, "I have a brain, not roots." This was my first philosophy lesson in the critique of pictures.

We usually judge trees by inspecting their fruit rather than by exposing their roots. This, I suppose, holds true also for the "tree of knowledge," namely, science. But philosophy is different in several respects. Critical philosophy, which is meant to unmask our deep illusions, demands that we expose our root metaphors as the source of our deep illusions. This painstaking task cannot in general be done on a wholesale basis. It should be addressed case by case. What I am suggesting here is that we inspect the role of family and friends as the domains that provide the pictures for thick human relations. The idea is not to hang people on their family tree but to see what in family relations suffer extension and what extensions go over the top.

Instead of a Summary: Betrayal Is an Ethical Notion

Betrayal is first and foremost an undermining of a thick relation. As such, the concept of betrayal is a concept that belongs predominantly to ethics, for ethics is a systematic concern with thick human relations, whereas morality is a systematic concern with thin human relations. There is nothing new in trying to recruit the two terms "ethics" and "morality"—whose sole difference is their etymology, "ethics" from the Greek and "morality" from the Latin—for two different tasks. What is new here is the way the difference in the use of the terms is marked. The semantic division of labor between ethics and morality points to the difference in our concerns with the people with whom we have special relations and the people with whom we have only tenuous relations in virtue of their being human beings. To describe our relations to strangers as a mere concern with human beings doesn't tell the whole story. It is hardly the case that strangers appear to us as bare human beings: they normally appear under descriptions such as "old," "female," "sick," and so forth. But we treat such titles as universal aspects of the human condition, and as such, they are covered by the idea of morality as the domain of our relations to humans in virtue of being humans, which includes universal aspects of their humanity. The humanity of others, especially under descriptions of human vulnerabilities, puts moral demands on us. Morality tells us how we must behave toward human beings. Our special relations to certain individuals and groups also put demands on us. We can escape cultivating our special relations, but we cannot escape having relations to other human beings. In that sense morality is forced on us; ethics is not. Morality is an outcome of our form of life as human beings; ethics is an outcome of our particular form of life, for example, of our being French as opposed to our being Vietnamese. We may call our human form of life our *natural* form of life and our particular form of life our *cultural* form of life.

Our natural form of life as human beings is marked by the fact that we see in other humans icons of ourselves. We are all created in the image of each other. Iconicity resonates with us. Iconicity is the basis for the feeling of our shared humanity, and the recognition of iconicity puts the demand on us that we should treat others as we would like to be treated by them. Yet with special forms of life, or within special forms of life, we find strong tendencies to deny our iconicity to all other human beings by making certain features, such as skin color, disqualifying features, thereby breaking the symmetry of our iconic relations. It thereby breaks our sense of shared humanity. Yet there is a tendency that pulls in the opposite direction. It denies the normative force that special forms of life should have in shaping the form and the content of our life. Only the universal human form of life should have relevant normative force on the way we must behave to others. The rest is tainted by nepotism.

Being human is the basis of morality. Iconicity is what brings others' humanity home. It makes us care even for the ones with no mind to speak of, the brain-damaged and their like; they are damaged, but they are like us in form if not in reason, and that is what counts. Saying that we were all created in the image of God is an ennobling way to talk about our iconicity to one another, but the whole point about iconicity is its elemental nature in our human form of life.

5

Treason

TREASON IS POLITICAL BETRAYAL. IT IS A VIOLATION OF one's allegiance to one's political community. It is a gross violation of one's allegiance to one's sovereign. Historically, the sovereign was a king or a king-like ruler. Treason as betrayal of the king played an important role in shaping the attitude toward treason. It turned it into the ultimate sin, something more criminal than murder. Treason is still a very grave offense in all states, but the horror of it seems to be on the wane. Does this mean that we are undergoing a reevaluation of treason?

Reevaluation

There are two types of reevaluation. A *strong* sense of reevaluation is when what was regarded as good is deemed bad, or what was regarded as bad is deemed good. A *weak* sense of reevaluation has to do with a change in the intensity of the value. We still view as positive what we took to be a positive value, but to a lesser degree. What used to be regarded as evil is deemed an ordinary vice—bad, but not terrible.

Adultery underwent a weak reevaluation. Did treason undergo a weak reevaluation too? We already met this question in dealing with the question "Why betrayal?" Here the gong calls for a second round.

One response to the question is: What we are encountering nowadays is not really a reevaluation of treason, but rather a change in circumstances. In time of war or in time of perceived existential danger, treason is taken seriously and is considered with the genuine horror it deserves. But in time of peace and security, it is perceived in a more dispassionate manner. To be sure, even in peacetime treason may be depicted in strong language weakly felt. In peacetime the attitude toward treason can best be captured by the cynical language of the Dual Monarchy of Austria-Hungary, in which nothing was taken seriously: treason is catastrophic but not serious.

It is not only danger that shapes our attitude toward treason. Settling scores with traitors after a bitter war is another occasion on which cries of "treason" reach the highest pitch. But in time of peace and calm, moral wrath tends to wax and wane.

There is no question that treason is perceived differently in time of crisis than in time of calm. Yet we should be reminded that uncovering a case of treason in time of prolonged peace, right out of the blue, can be pretty distressing, not unlike the distress of an unsuspecting spouse on discovering the infidelity of a longtime partner.

In any case, the claim is that a change in attitude toward treason does not necessarily reflect a strong or weak reevaluation of treason. It may just be a sign that a society is feeling relaxed about treason because it feels safe.

The question is about a reevaluation of *acts* of treason, but what about a reevaluation of *motives* for treason? Do they undergo reevaluation too?

Is committing treason for money judged less harshly today than committing treason for ideology? It seems that in many cases, unlike in the case of Judas's betrayal, people find it quite soothing to know that the act of treason is done for money or sex rather than for deep ideological reasons. It gives the society the assurance that what is at stake is nothing more than signs of general human frailty; to borrow a serviceable expression, "the flesh is weak," by which we acknowledge universal human weakness. If so, the members of the society can tell themselves there is nothing fundamentally wrong with their particular way of life.

How seriously the motives for treason are taken depends on how secure the society feels. Like acts of treason, motives for treason do not currently inspire horror or revulsion. This, again, should be taken not as a sign of reevaluation but as a sign of relaxation.

The fortune of appraising treason in the stock market of public ideas correlates with the ups and downs of two types of moral-political philosophy. One type is *security* philosophy, the main concern of which is how to *secure life*. The second type is *weal* philosophy, the main concern of which is how to *secure flourishing life*.

Weal philosophy takes for granted a situation in which there is very little danger to life and limb. Instead it addresses another question: What in (already secured) life counts as a flourishing life? For security philosophy, of which Hobbes's philosophy is a glaring example, life is at constant risk: a serious possibility of war looms large, and concern with a good life is deemed a luxury, while concern with a secure life is deemed a necessity. The thick notion of political betrayal goes naturally with security philosophy and much less so with weal philosophy. A shift from security philosophy to weal philosophy already involves a reevaluation of treason as the main form of political betrayal.

The Feudal Frame of Treason

The vexed question lingering unanswered throughout this study is whether we have inherited a feudal notion of treason that does not cohere with the rest of our modern ethical and moral notions. The worry is whether treason is just a relic of history. This in any case is a question I would like to address, not as a question in the history of ideas, but as a conceptual question masquerading, perhaps, as a historical question. I can hardly stress enough that my use of feudalism here is thoroughly anachronistic, if by feudalism we mean only what it meant in its eleventh-century European heyday. Feudalism in my use of the term is roughly a political order in which loyalty and betrayal, molded on personal relationships, are the constitutive notions. Feudalism in its medieval form is a clear example of such a political order.

One might object by saying that the feudal oath of loyalty is a mere contract of convenience, in which the suzerain provides protection and the vassals provide services. This, in many cases, was indeed the reality of feudal relations, but this is not the ethos behind it. I shall return to the gap between the reality and the ethos of feudal relations later, but for my present purpose it doesn't really matter whether Thomas Becket is the historical Archbishop of Canterbury or the Becket in T. S. Eliot's historically insightful play.

The case of Becket is indeed a good example of personal feudal relations. Moreover, Becket stands at various junctures of loyalty—dilemmas that are at the center of our discussion. His loyalty to God trumps his loyalty to the king, who also happens to be a close personal friend. Becket is a man of principles. But his principles are tested in a personal setup of concrete relations, including loyalty to the person of God.

"You are his servant, his tool, and his jack, / You wore his favours on your back, / You had your honours all from his hand; from him you had the power, the seal and the ring."[1] The speaker in Eliot's play *Murder in the Cathedral* is a knight who was sent to kill Becket and speak on behalf of the king. He addresses his words to Becket the priest and ends by accusing him of breaking his oath of loyalty and betraying the king: "Priest, you have spoken treachery and treason. / Priest! traitor, confirmed in malfeasance."[2] It is not just Becket's breaking of the oath of loyalty that constitutes treachery in the eyes of the knight; it is Becket's ingratitude for the favors and honors he received from the king that constitutes treason. Ingratitude is at the heart of the feudal notion of betrayal, and I shall address it shortly.

The knight has wrapped it all up in one utterance: betrayal, treachery, treason, and traitor, all conceived as personal relations. To which Thomas, in his defense, claims, "There is higher than I or the King."[3] But then he goes on to accuse Reginald, the knight who leads the murders, of being a traitor to Becket as his temporal vassal, and a traitor to him as his spiritual lord, and, above all, a traitor to God for desecrating the church. It is a conflict of personal loyalties, namely, of what trumps what in these semi-personal relations. There is a systematic ambiguity in the use of "personal relation" with respect to a feudal king. The ambiguity is along the lines of Ernst Kantorowicz's celebrated distinction between the king's two bodies: the earthly body, which has physical attributes and suffers death, and the spiritual body, which transcends the earthly one and never dies: "The king is dead, long live the king!"[4] So in speaking of a personal relation with the king, the question is: With which body of the king does one have the relation? Kantorowicz doesn't make the distinction between the king as a human individual and the crown as an abstract institution, which would seem the natural distinction to suggest. He talks of two bodies, of which the spiritual body of the king is a body perceived from a spiritual point of view. The point is that one can form a personal relation with such a spiritual body, whereas one cannot form a personal relation with an institution.

The social relations in feudalism are predominantly vertical, not relations among equals. Even the friendship between King Henry and Becket is not horizontal. It is this tension between a horizontal relation of friendship and a vertical relation of fealty to a king that Jean Anouilh's play *Becket* harps upon. The King addresses Becket's ghost:

> *King:* Did you love Gwendolen, Archbishop? Did you hate me that night when I said "I am the King" and took her from you? Perhaps that's what you never could forgive me for?
>
> *Becket:* I've forgotten.
>
> *King:* Yet we were like two brothers, weren't we—you and I?[5]

The answer to the king should be "Not really." Vertical relations saturate all feudal relations. This doesn't make them necessarily thinner, but it doesn't make them thicker either.

Betrayal as Ingratitude

"Blow, blow, thou winter wind / Thou art not so unkind / As man's ingratitude."[6] Shakespeare's song tells us that the frosty winter wind is not as bitterly cold as ingratitude. It is a way of saying that ingratitude is so bad that nothing can be compared to it, not even the biting winter wind.

At the basis of feudal ethics is the idea that betrayal in general and treason in particular are extreme acts of ingratitude. This claim covers a very wide spectrum of regimes and rulings, including, for example, biblical ideas of betrayal as ingratitude. It is a pretty strong claim. It implies that the underpinning of betrayal and treason is not transgression of a sacramental oath, though this too may be there, nor is it mere violation of the divine right of kings, though this too may be there, but it is first and foremost an act of ingratitude.

Again we need Shakespeare to convey it:

> For Brutus, as you know, was Caesar's angel.
> Judge, O you gods, how dearly Caesar loved him!
> This was the most unkindest cut of all:
> For, when the noble Caesar saw him stab,
> Ingratitude, more strong than traitors' arms,
> Quite vanquish'd him. Then burst his mighty heart.[7]

All these things took place, as Antony says, "whilst bloody treason flourished over us."[8]

Let me repeat: the leading idea of feudal relations, with regard to betrayal, is that it is an extreme form of ingratitude, and treason is its political manifestation. The Latin root *gratia* refers to favor, pleasing, and gift: ingratitude is their negation.

The Bible's attitude toward constitutive gratefulness is clear and rich. "In the beginning God created the heavens and the earth" (Genesis 1:1): this is the constitutive act of goodness, for which all creatures and all human beings should be *eternally* grateful, continuously grateful, without any interruption. To be eternally grateful means that one cannot discharge one's obligation to be grateful by repaying in kind, for the simple reason that one cannot in principle repay in kind. We should be grateful, not so much for the good that comes of being created but for our very existence.

The people of Israel owe God the added obligation of eternal gratefulness for delivering them from slavery in Egypt. Deliverance from the house of bondage is so momentous that the obligation to God should also be binding on the descendants of the people of Israel forever and ever.

The opening statement of the Ten Commandments is "I am the Lord your God who brought you out of Egypt, out of the land of slavery" (Exodus 20:2, Leviticus 26:17). The binding force of the commandments on the generation that was redeemed and on their descendants is the coercive benevolence of God. It is binding on all generations to come. The children of Israel have a special obligation to remember the exodus from Egypt, for it is this constitutive act of favor that is the basis for the special relation between God and his adopted children.

Of course, the children of Israel are not exempted from the obligation of gratitude to God that all humans have. "Is this how you repay the Lord, / you senseless, stupid people? / Is he not your father who formed you? Did he not make you and establish you?" (Deuteronomy 32:6). But then they have the added debt to God for being granted their freedom from slavery.

The foundation of general religious morality is gratefulness for the creation, whereas the basis of the special obligation of the Israelites is gratefulness for the redemption from the house of bondage. (Christianity added to creation the debt to God for sacrificing his son so as to redeem humanity from the fall of man.)

The unthankful people referred to in the quoted verse from the Hebrew Bible are labeled *nabal*. *Nabal* is translated in some contexts as "fool" and in others as "wicked," but in one important sense *nabal* means "ungrateful." The wicked fool is ungrateful.

The Hebrew Bible tells the story of David and Abigail, or rather David and the former husband of Abigail, whose name was Nabal. For all its pro-Davidic tendentiousness, the Hebrew Bible doesn't cover up the fact that David, before he became king, was an outlaw chieftain and extortionist. He asks Nabal for protection money: "Your shepherds have been with us lately and we didn't mistreat them: nothing of theirs was missing all the time they were in Carmel. Receive my men kindly, for this is an auspicious day with us, and give what you can to David your son and your servant" (1 Samuel 25:7–8). It is a story about extortion and protection. Nabal fatally believes that David's offer is an offer he can refuse. David summarizes the event thus: "It was a waste of time to protect this fellow's property. . . . He has repaid me evil for good." Abigail, who deserts her husband to become David's wife, says that her first husband lives up to his name. His name is Nabal and he is *nabal,* namely, an ungrateful miser.

Why do I bring up this biblical story, and at such great length?

The Bible is a good source for the idea of coercive benevolence: an act of benevolence that forces the beneficiary to be eternally in debt to the benefactor. We have already viewed two such acts, creation and exodus.

Parents giving life to their children is the model for God's creation. As already mentioned, giving someone life is not necessarily giving someone a good life, but creating something out of nothing creates obligation. This is "ontological" gratitude, for being given a life. Then there is "axiological" gratitude, for being given a free life. This is the case of the deliverance from slavery. But the most prevalent feudal notions of coercive benevolence are *protection* and *security.* The two are distinct. Security is providing defense from harms about to be done by others, whereas protection is providing defense from harms the protector might inflict if he does not get his extortionist due. The plain reading of the story of David and Nabal should be that of the story of a protection racket. However, the apologetic tradition finds it hard to stomach the idea that David was a mobster. It spins the story into a security story of David defending Nabal from the harm awaiting him from others. The ambiguity between protection and security typifies the coercive benevolence of feudal relations. And with it the ambiguous source of feudal morality vacillates between being guided by the model of the family and being guided by the model of the Mafia family.

The constitutive act in a feudal relationship, which carries with it coercive benevolence, is either providing security or extorting protection. The genius of feudalism is in elevating the protection racket by means of sacramental trappings. It is protection ritualized and routinized, yet a racket it is. When Jonathan Miller transformed the setting of Giuseppe Verdi's *Rigoletto* from the Duchy of Mantua into New York's Little Italy in the early fifties, it revealed how strikingly similar was the Gonzaga family, with all its pomp, to the Gambino Mafia family.

My triple jump in time and space between the outlaw David, the Duke of Mantua, and the Mafia family of Carlo Gambino may seem more than suspicious; it may seem a mockery. But the point I am making is a modest one. Obeying a sovereign out of gratitude or betraying a sovereign out of ingratitude is not just a matter of being grateful or ungrateful for a secure life, because it may easily be a forced gratitude imposed by an extortionist.

Security philosophy presents itself as dealing with security, but behind a security agent we often find lurking a protective blackmailer. The genealogy of the feudal ethics of gratitude is not pretty. Yet feudal ethics succeeded on many occasions in subli- mating and elevating the reality of brutal extortion into a fan- ciful fiction of valiant security.

How Bad Is It to Be Ungrateful?

Consider the strange question "What is so bad about treason?" It sounds like the question "What is so bad about badness?" Treason, after all, is perceived as the epitome of evil. Treason is helped by such obvious unwholesome features, including lying and deceit, that it is hard to see the point of the question "How bad is treason?"

But by tying ingratitude to betrayal and considering ingrati- tude as the main feature of political betrayal, we may very well ask, "How bad is it to be ungrateful?"

For the most part, we regard gratefulness and ungratefulness as a matter of etiquette rather than of ethics. It is prim and proper to write a thank-you note after being wined and dined. It is an act of appreciation and gratitude to one's host. Failing to do so is not nice, but by no means is it morally or ethically wrong.

You may say that this example is just too trivial to match the gratitude we ought to feel to the ones who gave us our life. If a thank-you note doesn't fit, try this for size. What do you owe to the surgeon who operated on you in an exceedingly difficult op- eration and gave you a new lease on life? You may donate money to the hospital, especially if you believe that it is the organization behind the doctor that contributed to the saving of your life. You may send your surgeon a nice gift in appreciation of her skillful work. But then you may well do less. In no way do you feel that you are under a lifelong obligation to your surgeon, let alone that your descendants should be under a lifelong obligation to the descendants of your surgeon.

Well, you may say, at least you have a lifelong obligation not to betray her in any way, for example, not to report her to the tax authority, which might get her into trouble. Indeed, it would be very unbecoming if, once you recovered from the surgery, you put on your seductive best to test your new zest for life and seduced the surgeon's partner.

There is something to say for the last caveat. There is asymmetry between the positive obligations and the negative obligations that gratitude imposes on us. Gratitude provides a reason not to betray, if not necessarily to obey. There is a difference between repaying good with bad and not repaying good with good.

The term "ungratefulness" is used here for "doing something bad in return for something good done for you," whereas the term "unthankfulness" is used for "not doing something good in return for something good done for you," namely, for being thankless.

Now let us separate two questions. One: What is our obligation to obey our lawful government? Two: What is our obligation not to betray our government by giving "aid and comfort" to its enemy?

I find the gratefulness argument, according to which one should obey the government and the laws of the state out of gratefulness, lacking in force. Plato in *Crito* (50d) uses the analogy according to which the laws of the polis (the city-state) are like parents. The laws demand loyalty out of gratitude, the way we owe gratitude to our parents.

Socrates was willing to pay with his life to keep this overstretched analogy alive. He didn't evade the law, although he could have. I wonder how many of us find the analogy between the law and parenthood plausible. Indeed, the contrast between law and love, which is one of Paul's main themes, gets its force precisely because we feel that the law cannot be a proper substitute for (parental) love. (Indeed, Crito himself already presented Socrates with the choice between law and love. He tells him bluntly that by not escaping from the city, Socrates is betraying his sons, whom he could raise and educate.)

Let us recapitulate our idea of the role of gratitude in feudal relations. Feudal relations are modeled on the eternal gratitude of children to their parents for being given life. The feudal lord is not a life giver but he is a life protector, as he proved in the constitutive act of protection that established the relation. Treason is conceived as a betrayal of eternal gratitude. Treason in its purest form is an act of siding with the enemy of the ruler, a ruler to whom the betrayer owes endless gratitude.

The epitome of thick relations is parent-child relationships, in which there is asymmetry in gratitude. The children owe gratitude to the parents but the parents don't owe gratitude to the children, even when they find raising children gratifying.

Gratitude-centered ethics, which makes gratitude to the benefactor the foundation of thick relations, may seem to us far removed from our modern sensibilities. But this is a bit deceptive. Think of the current attitude in many economically advanced countries toward immigrants. Immigrants in developed countries, whenever they complain, are accused by nativists of being ungrateful to the host country. They are reminded that they would have been much worse off had they stayed in their country of origin than they are now in their host country. Even when the immigrants become official citizens, their situation is compared not so much to the situation of other citizens as to what would have happened to them had they stayed in their home countries.

True, there is room for special gratitude toward the host country from people who received asylum in time of plight. But then immigrants are expected to be grateful, even if the host country should be grateful to them for doing the dirty jobs and paying for social services for the elderly population in the host country. Immigrants are perceived by many nativists as guest workers no matter how long they are in the country.

Guests

Gastarbeiter, "guest worker," was meant to be a benign word replacing the nasty Nazi category of *Fremdarbeiter,* "alien worker." Guest is a welcoming category, and from the standpoint of thick and thin relations it is an interesting category. Guests belong to a liminal category between those with whom we stand in thick relations and strangers with whom we stand in thin relations.

Guests stand between thick and thin. Indeed, it is the idea of strangers as guests that is our concern here. Here again the Bible is instructive. Lot is the nephew of Abraham. After his departure from Abraham he settles in Sodom. He hosts three guests. The wicked people of Sodom want to gang-rape them. Lot offers his daughters as a substitute, for one's guests trump everything once "they came under the shelter of my roof" (Genesis 19:8). Therefore, they deserve total protection. Hurting one's guests is the ultimate infringement of one's sovereignty, even if the guests are complete strangers.

For the people of Sodom, Lot is a newcomer: "The fellow has come and settled here as an alien, and does he now take it upon himself to judge us?" (Genesis 19:9). It is this story of gross mistreatment of guests that made Sodom an emblem of wickedness.

The ability to protect one's turf is the main sign of sovereignty; vulnerability is tantamount to lack of ability to protect one's turf. Being able to protect people under one's roof, including strangers, is a sign of sovereignty over one's household. It is not thick relations between host and guest that are infringed in Lot's case. It is his sovereignty over his household that is challenged. The guests, for their part, should be grateful for the host's hospitality.

Once again, in nation-states guest workers are perceived as guests. The expectation from them is that they should be eternally grateful for the favor of the host country. They are entitled to protection, but they should also know their place as guests. Their place is that of permanent strangers with some guest privileges. No matter how long they are in the country, their loyalty is always in question. In time of conflict between the host country and their country of origin they become instant suspects. The fear is that if the immigrants are not properly scrutinized, their ingratitude to the host country may turn into active support for the enemy.

This is admittedly a crude and gloomy account, but it is a painfully familiar one. It is partly a modern version of the role of gratefulness (or rather of ungratefulness) in dealing with immigrants as guests.

The Treason of the King

Feudalism, as a historical European phenomenon, was first undermined by the centralized absolute monarchies. The doctrine that fed the idea of absolute monarchy was the divine right of kings. The source of the king's authority was in being endowed with the uncontestable grace of God, namely, in receiving the gift of sovereignty from God. The king was accountable only to God, which means accountable to no other earthly authority. Among the true believers in this doctrine we can find Charles I in England and Louis XVI in France. The doctrine was meant to serve them well, but in their cases the doctrine went sour.

There was nothing new in the violent death of kings. We are still analyzing the gruesome skull of one of such king—Richard III—found beneath a parking lot; he reportedly lost his helmet in battle and suffered eleven wounds, nine to the head. But as Michael Walzer points out, the regicides of Charles (1649) and Louis (1793) were very different.[9] They were *legally* beheaded for treason. This is conceptually perplexing. The ideology of the monarchy was that only the monarch could call the shots on treason, for treason, by definition, was the betrayal of the monarch. The monarch could not conceptually betray himself, any more than he could measure his height by putting his hand on his head.

Thus the English and the French regicides dramatically changed the notion of treason. No one was exempt from suspicion of treason, including the head of state. Treason was conceived not as betraying the *king* but as betraying the *people* with whom the ruler was supposed to have thick relationships.

What People?

Here again we return to the issue of gratefulness and treason.

Consider a citizen who feels that she lives in an exploitative society, a society that should undergo radical transformation, namely, revolution, so as to abolish its exploitative structure.

Moreover, the ruling class is her enemy and those who oppose it are her friends. And not just friends, but an important instrument in bringing about the social change she deems necessary. She vehemently believes that the ruling class makes all the decisions as to what is lawful and who is the enemy. She does not accept their hegemonic labeling of "friends" and "foes." She feels that there is nothing to be grateful for and nobody to be grateful to, least of all to the government that currently rules the country. It is her revolutionary duty, she believes, to give "aid and comfort" to the "friends of the people" who are fighting the government, which serves only the ruling class. This line of thinking is familiar, at least to people of a certain age. It could, for example, be the argument used by the communist spy Lona Cohen, who, along with her husband, was an associate of both Julius Rosenberg and the Russian spy Rudolf Abel. This question can be generalized: Why should anyone feel grateful to a society he or she believes is grossly unjust?

Cohen was an American citizen. Abel was not. According to the gratefulness doctrine, she presumably should have felt grateful to the United States in a way in which Abel, a Russian citizen (who was born in England), should not have. He was a spy. She was a treasonous traitor by the mere fact that she was an American citizen. The assumption is that she stood in a different relation to her countrymen than he did. It doesn't matter that they both presumably acted from the same ideology, nor does it matter that she felt as alienated from her government as he was a stranger to it.

Abel was one of the most effective KGB spies ever to be captured.[10] The damage he inflicted on the U.S. military establishment was substantial. No matter what we think about the moral status of the organization that employed him, he was by no means a traitor, but rather a spy in the service of his country. What, then, distinguishes a traitor from a mere spy?

Is it merely an issue of citizenship? From the point of view of the law, this seems to be the case, although the case of William Joyce—the notorious "Lord Haw-Haw"—indicates that the law may vacillate on that. Joyce was not a legal citizen of Britain: he just pretended to be so that he could get a passport for traveling. But then all spies pretend to be citizens of the country they spy on, if it serves them well. In Joyce's case, however, there was an extension of the (legal) notion as to the scope of those who owe loyalty: it is not just citizens but also permanent residents. But our question is ethical, not legal. Who, if anyone, should feel grateful to his political community, with a strong obligation never to betray it? Well, the answer seems to be contained in the question: whoever belongs to the political community in question. But this answer with regard to the Red spies is a red herring.

Again, why was Morris Cohen, the husband of Lona Cohen and Abel's primary helper, who was born in the United States to parents who emigrated from Russia, branded a traitor? And why should not Abel, who spent many years in the United States and enjoyed what the country had to offer, be considered less grateful than Morris Cohen? It cannot be a matter of ideology, since it is very likely that Cohen was no less of a true believer in communism than Abel. We may of course switch the roles in the case of Abel and the Cohens and their respective allegiances to Britain. Abel was born in Newcastle upon Tyne and moved to Russia with his parents (ethnic Germans from Russia) when he was over eighteen years old, whereas the Cohens (under the alias of Peter and Helen Kroger) were serving as spies in Britain. So with respect to Britain Abel is a traitor whereas the Krogers were mere spies. The spy-traitor gambit doesn't change the general question: When should one be considered a spy and when a traitor?

Taking a cue from Plato's *Crito,* we may say that there was implicit acceptance of the commitment to be loyal. Staying in the country where one was born makes it one's country for better or for worse. But this, I believe, is a poor criterion for acceptance. For many people, leaving their country is not a life option. For one thing, one may have a life there, with lots of thick personal relations, commitments, joys of family and friends, or, for that matter, a deep attachment to nature. One may feel grateful to the creator for the natural beauty of America, or to the American sublime of the Hudson River school of painting, but no one should feel a debt of gratitude to the American people for the country's natural beauty, let alone to the American government. One may even feel indignant at the careless way various American agencies look after nature in the United States.

If the gratefulness doctrine is that we owe loyalty for the public goods we enjoy, then I don't see why an alien who is a permanent resident should be less grateful for the public goods than a citizen. By public goods, I mean not merely the conventional public goods, such as streetlights, but also lofty public goods such as culture, political tolerance, rule of law, and the like. What we regard as public goods for which one must be grateful makes no difference between citizen and resident, unless and until the citizens enjoy more privileges than the residents. So, again, why is one viewed as a traitor and the other merely as a spy?

The ideological traitor may believe that lofty public goods such as free speech are not really public goods but public evils that he should subvert rather than promote, but in so believing and doing he is not different from a foreign spy.

The difference between a spy and a traitor hinges on a particular notion of citizenship that I would dub primal citizenship. It is the notion of a citizen as part of a political community, whose members imagine themselves as standing in thick relations to each other; relations on which their distinct collective identity supervenes. A legal citizen in such society is presumed to be a "true citizen," namely someone who shares the primal notion of citizenship. A traitor is therefore someone who betrays his or her primal citizenship. The Cohens, by being genuine American legal citizens, were rightly presumed to be primal American citizens, a citizenship that they betrayed. This wasn't the case in the United Kingdom, where they were mistakenly presumed to be primal citizens by obtaining fake legal citizenship. On the primal account of citizenship, the Cohens were spies in the United Kingdom and traitors in the United States. Whereas Abel was a fake legal citizen in the United States, and hence he was there only a spy, not a traitor.

It seems that the idea of primal citizenship, as distinct from legal citizenship and citizenship as active engagement in political life, holds its sway more in closed societies then in open ones. While the strong sense of loyalty, which is implied by the idea of primal citizenship, should have gone the other way round.

Let me explain. Roughly, an *open* society is one in which you have the options of what Albert Hirschman calls "exit" and "voice."[11] The state doesn't hinder your ability to exit, namely, to emigrate: it doesn't stop you from leaving and doesn't decide for you where to go. The other option is your ability to raise your voice in protest and demand changes. In a *closed* state, exit and voice are quite inaccessible, and the real option for serious resistance is fight or flight. Needless to say, between the open society and the closed society there is a whole interval. Loyalty should be proportional to the accessibility of exit and voice. The more accessible they are, the more loyal you should be. But, ironically enough, it seems that as a matter of fact the attitude of ordinary people toward "disloyal" persons in closed societies is harsher than the attitude of the regime in closed societies, even more so than the attitude of ordinary people in open societies.

Gift

Making gratitude (ingratitude) the cornerstone of the ethical and the political order is based on the idea that life is a gift, whether from God or from one's parents. "Life as a gift" is a thoroughly religious attitude, where the heavenly gift is grace. But in humanistic ethics, an ethics that is grounded and justified only by appeal to human relations, the idea of being constantly reminded of the gratitude you owe for gifts you receive is not terribly appealing. There is a danger that "gift" has the sense of its meaning in German: poison.

Our concept of gift includes a strong element of giving something out of goodwill, gratis, without necessarily putting the other under an obligation to reciprocate. But grounding ethical and political obligation on coercive gratitude runs counter to this notion of gift. It echoes alien notions of gift, which emerged in gift societies. It raises the question of whether we want to live under the rule of gifts. Let me explain the question by a thought experiment.

Imagine a "potlatch society" that runs as follows: The society adopts and implements your ideal of distributive justice, whatever it is. The economy of that society is the most efficient market economy one can have.

According to you, it is an efficient and just society, if ever there was one. How does it work? Well, the successful producers voluntarily give all they accumulate to the less successful, and it is distributed according to your principles of distributive justice. But here is the catch: as a reward, the successful must receive high prestige, in proportion to their contribution. The society exerts tremendous social pressure on its needy members to express constantly their gratefulness for the magnanimity of the donors. After all, prestige is what keeps this society going. Glory rather than coercion is what makes the contributors work hard, what makes the economy thrive, and what makes the society just. It is a just and efficient society by definition: your definition.

Now here is my question: What is this potlatch society for you, a utopia or a dystopia? My reaction to the potlatch society is that I cannot make up my mind. True, the potlatch society is just and efficient by definition, but it suffers from one nauseating feature: the need to be grateful all the time. The feeling is that of the princess and the pea in Hans Christian Andersen's celebrated fairy tale: I dread the idea of enduring sleepless nights worrying about gratefulness. It is just a tiny pea, but enough to make us radically uneasy.

So even at its best, even living in a just society without coercion, it is not clear, at least not to me, that I would want to live in a gift society, in which I am constantly reminded of the need to be grateful. And if this is my attitude toward the best of all gift societies, no wonder that I am less than enthusiastic about opting for lesser forms of gift societies. Yet I can envisage an altogether different attitude toward my gift society: the attitude that gratefulness is a trifling price to pay for a just and efficient society, given the alternatives. What the last reaction is missing is the aim of taking seriously the requirement of the thought experiment, namely, to be truly grateful: just faking it won't work. We know of obsessively polite societies, in which each move is met with a thank-you. But meaningless polite gestures won't do in my thought experiment. You have to be truly grateful for the system to work. Now, I hope, you may start to get the full dreadfulness of it.

You may argue that my account is unfair in describing the reaction to the thought experiment from the side of those who receive and not from the side of those who give. This is true. But the problem remains even if you try to imagine what the giving end rather than the receiving end in such a society looks like. Being hemmed in by constantly grateful people telling you how great you are for contributing so much resembles the nauseating flattery that surrounds donors visiting the institution they support. It is a life of ribbon-cutting ceremonies.

I am not suggesting a tractate against gratitude. It is a tractate against a society based on gratitude, in which treason is viewed as an extreme manifestation of ingratitude.

Treason as a Political Weapon: The Case of Guy Fawkes

Treason is used as a political weapon for settling scores with rivals. Indeed, in the next section my dark voyage into treason as political betrayal will cross the U.S. Constitution as an effort to blunt treason as a political weapon in the hands of a monarch for use against political opponents.

The claim is not that accusations of treason in the past were always or in general baseless. The claim is that even in real cases of treason, treason—political betrayal—was used as a political weapon to hound political enemies who had very little to do with the treasonable act. As a reminder, let's turn to the celebrated case of Guy Fawkes: there was clearly treason in this case, but there was also political exploitation of the treason.

November 5, originally called Gunpowder Treason Day, later became known as Guy Fawkes Night (or Day).[12] The name Guy Fawkes became the name of an archvillain, though in the scheme of things Fawkes was secondary to Robert Catesby, the prime mover in a plot to assassinate King James I on November 5, 1605. It was Fawkes who was caught red-handed amidst barrels of gunpowder in the undercroft beneath the House of Lords. The idea was to blow up the House of Lords and with it the whole English establishment, lock, stock, and barrel. The aim was to replace James I and install the nine-year-old Princess Elizabeth as the Catholic queen of England.

The occasion was the opening of England's Parliament, with the expectation that everybody who was anybody in the realm would be present on that occasion. Guy Fawkes along with eight of the plotters was hanged, drawn, and quartered, the hideous fate of those who were charged with high treason.

To the treason plot of the Gunpowder Plot there is a subplot. There is no question that the co-conspirators wanted to restore the Catholic faith to England. There is a question whether the Catholic Church and especially the Jesuits in England (Henry Garnet, John Gerard, and Oswald Greenway) were part of the plot. There is no question that the plot was used as a massive excuse for further persecution of Catholics in England.

The Gunpowder Plot is an orgy of treason, betrayals, and loyalties: betrayal of king and country and loyalty to the old faith. On the one hand, we have the priests, who tried to shield the integrity of the institution of confession, and Guy Fawkes, who took the whole plot upon himself so as to safeguard his friends; on the other hand, we have the murderous plan to destroy hundreds of people.

My aim here is not to bask in gunpowder but to draw a historical analogy, a deep analogy, I believe, between the attitude toward the Catholic Church in England, in the light of the Gunpowder Plot, and the attitude toward communism and especially Soviet communism during the waves of Red scares in America.

Arthur Miller's *Crucible* and its film adaptation by Jean-Paul Sartre made famous the analogy between the McCarthyism of the fifties and the Salem witch trials at the end of the seventeenth century.[13] The idea of the witch-hunt was in the air in the fifties: Miller articulated and incarnated the idea. The snag in the witch-hunt analogy is that there never were any witches, yet there were communist spies. The Gunpowder Plot analogy is an apt one, since there is no question that there were Catholic conspirators, much as there were communist spies, but the treason in both cases was widely used to hound Catholics and ex-communists who had nothing to do with treason. It is treason as a weapon to hound and suppress ideological rivals that is at issue here.

The treason analogy between communism and Catholicism, I believe, cuts deep. The enemy helped by the traitors is an outside enemy, symbolized by a small location such as the Vatican or the Kremlin, but in fact it is a world-encompassing ideology with "secret agents," be they Jesuit priests or Comintern apparatchiks, who cross states borders and obey orders from the outside. Helping the enemy is the hallmark of treason, and rendering the Gunpowder Plot as the plot of the papists in the sense of people who take orders from the Pope was at the center of the witch-hunt directed against all Catholics in the realm.

Guy Fawkes today is nothing but a Halloween-style effigy. But for a long time November 5 wasn't just a day of treason but a Protestant "parade" stirring popular anti-papist feelings. Invoking the accusation of treason is a crude political and religious weapon. This doesn't mean that the accusation is always baseless; what it means is that the accusation is always a big stick that leaves no room for niceties and nuances.

But is the fact that Guy Fawkes Night turned from a story of a perfidious nightmare into a night of hilarious bonfires another sign that treason, like nostalgia, is not what it used to be? True, treason is still a very grave offense in all states, but the horror of it seems to be diminished. Is this, then, a sign that treason is undergoing a reevaluation?

Treason in the U.S. Constitution

The U.S. Constitution does not mention any crime apart from the gravest of all crimes: treason. But then the Constitution narrows the scope of treason more than any other definition up to that time: treason consists only in levying a war against the United States or giving aid and comfort to its enemy. More important, the betrayer is the only one who should die for the crime: "no Attainder of Treason shall work the Corruption of Blood."[14] The framers of the U.S. Constitution were keenly aware of the use and especially the political abuse of the British crown in ascribing treason to political rivals, thereby destroying them physically and ruining their families economically. The U.S. Constitution is an effort to blunt the destructive political weapon of treason; hence the narrow scope of the crime and the narrow scope of the punishment. Betrayal in the Constitution is not a matter of "personal relations." This should be contrasted with the British Act of Treason of 1351, with its stress on personal pronouns referring to the king: "levying a war against *him* and adhering to *his* enemies."

The framers of the Constitution could still feel firsthand the arbitrariness and the horror of "O monstrous traitor! I arrest thee, York, of capital treason 'gainst the King and crown" (*Henry VI, Part 2*, V.i).

The horror of treason, which had a great deal to do with the ghastly punishment of being "hanged, drawn, and quartered," which meant the gruesome spectacle of disemboweling, emasculating, beheading, and chopping the body into four pieces, is all curbed by the prohibition on cruel and unusual punishment.

All in all, I see Article III, Section 3 of the American Constitution not as a proof of the relevance of treason to current political concerns but as an effort to neutralize the old, bloody, horrific picture of treason. Indeed, very few people have been charged with treason in the United States. The Espionage and Sedition Acts of 1917–1918 are pretty harsh and were meant to deal with the concept of espionage, much as the Constitution had dealt with the concept of treason in the past. But we have already mentioned the difference between a spy and a traitor. Espionage and treason are conceptually different. Treason is ascribed to citizens who betray their fellow citizens, with whom they are presumed to stand in thick relation, whereas espionage is predominantly ascribed to foreigners, who do not fall under such a presumption. The relation between treason and betrayal is conceptual; the relation between espionage and betrayal is contingent.

The nativism of Old Europe and the idea that treason is an act of ingratitude didn't disappear in the New World.

Woodrow Wilson in his State of the Union Address of 1915 made a very telling comment regarding our concerns: "There are citizens of the United States, I blush to admit, born under other flags but welcomed under our generous naturalization laws to the full freedom and opportunity of America, who have poured the poison of disloyalty into the very arteries of our national life; who have sought to bring the authority and good name of our Government into contempt, to destroy our industries wherever they thought it effective for their vindictive purposes to strike at them, and to debase our politics to the uses of foreign intrigue."[15]

Wilson makes the feudal moral point that treachery is preeminently an expression of ingratitude: we extended our hospitality to foreigners and they met our generosity with vindictive purposes. For Wilson, to extend hospitality is to naturalize (we welcomed foreigners by a process of naturalization) and to naturalize is to adopt (the unnatural foreigners—"born under other flags"— became as natural as our biological children). Thick relations of blood were extended to them by the metaphor of the arteries, but instead of blood we got poison. The poison takes more than one form: hurting our industry, debasing our reputation, playing a role in foreign countries' intrigues.

The United States is a society based on civic nationalism, not on ethnic nationalism. But what is interesting in Wilson's address is how he appeals to thick relations in metaphors of belonging that are far more akin to the ethnic organic picture of thick relations than to the civic contractual one. Since the United States is not an ethnic nation, Wilson makes cunning use of the rhetorical trick of appealing to the nativists, who "adopted" the newcomers and whose generosity was betrayed. The model of naturalization is that of adoption. The adopted child owes as much to his parents as the naturally born child does.

What the harsh laws of 1917–1918 under their categories of sedition and espionage have in common with treason is that these categories gain their potency in time of war or fear of war. Thus the claim that treason has lost its grip on liberal societies has nothing to do with their being liberal and everything to do with the fact that these societies are leading a rather peaceful life. The minute these societies are put in danger—real or imagined—the grip of treachery in the guise of treason or espionage becomes tight.

Treason

Now that we have established the backdrop to the notion of treason, let us move to the core notion and the core cases of treason. The genus of treason is betrayal. The species is political betrayal.

What in a modern nation-state constitutes the political betrayal that is treason? Gratitude as such does not tell the whole story, though it may be an element in the story. The main attributes of the state as a political body are *sovereignty* and *territorial integrity*. Treason is an act that is seriously meant to undermine these two connected attributes. Helping an external enemy of the state to undermine the territorial integrity of the state and curb its sovereignty is the paradigm case of treason. In carrying out such an act one unglues one's relation to the members of the community, who constitute the state, for they are (ideally) the sovereign and the territory is (ideally) their home.

My way of dealing with treason is indirect. I proceed to deal with two celebrated cases of individuals who were accused of treason. These two cases highlight the relation between treason and thick relations in a modern state, in which the language of rights was supposed to have replaced the language of gifts and privileges. It was the French Revolution that stood for the shift from privileges to rights. The first case, the Dreyfus affair, can be viewed as an effort to undermine the outcome of the revolution in France. The second case is the case of Quisling.

Dreyfus Affair

When Émile Zola heard the details of the Dreyfus affair from Alfred Dreyfus's lawyer Louis Leblois, his first reaction was, "It's gripping!" but his exclamation didn't end there: "It's thrilling! It's horrible! It's a frightful drama! But it's drama on a grand scale."[16] And yet, notwithstanding all the exclamation marks, this exuberant comment is still an understatement. The Dreyfus affair brought about a cold civil war in France. The intensity of the animosity between the two camps, the Dreyfusards (supporters of Dreyfus) and the anti-Dreyfusards, was worthy of a bloody and protracted civil war. Instead of swords—though the sword of Captain Dreyfus was unduly broken in a ceremonial act of disgrace at the École Militaire—the main weapon was ink pens, used extensively by a new class, "the intellectuals." Every ingredient in the brew of betrayal can be found in the Dreyfus affair. Since intellectuals were intensely involved in the polemical warfare surrounding the affair, we have, apart from the brouhaha, a great many reflective thoughts and high-quality reactive attitudes.

In November 1894 a secret memorandum *(bordereau)* was picked out of a wastebasket by a French house cleaner working in the German embassy in Paris. The memorandum was addressed to the German military attaché. An inquiry led to half a dozen possible suspects, among them a French artillery captain on the General Staff, Alfred Dreyfus, who was an Alsatian Jew.

The head of the department, Jean Sandherr, also Alsatian, conveyed to the minister of war his unwarranted belief that Dreyfus was the chief suspect. Dreyfus was framed, and the prime mover in the framing was Major Hubert-Joseph Henry, who throughout the affair was responsible for supplying forged documents to incriminate Dreyfus. The hope, if not the belief, of the high command was that Dreyfus would hang himself, but when he stubbornly hung around, a military court unanimously decided that he was guilty of high treason. Dreyfus was sent to Devil's Island, a desert island as close to civilization as the dark side of the moon. When Sandherr was promoted to colonel in 1895, another Alsatian, Georges Picquart, was appointed to replace him. Then a new message was intercepted, the *petit bleu,* an incriminating message that pointed to its writer, Major Ferdinand Esterhazy, as a suspect. Indeed, it was Picquart who suspected that the writer of the *bordereau* and the writer of the *petit bleu* were one and the same, namely, Esterhazy, the descendant of a patrician bastard.

In revealing his discovery to his superiors, Picquart made a nuisance of himself. He was sent away, under all sorts of pretexts, to Tunisia. There was still another Alsatian in the fray, the vice president of the Senate, Auguste Scheurer-Kestner, and he is the one who eventually revealed to the public the name of Esterhazy as the traitor. I mention the string of Alsatians involved in the Dreyfus affair for a purpose, namely, of showing that Alsatians were on both sides of the divide between Dreyfusards and anti-Dreyfusards. Alsace, throughout its history, changed hands between Germany and France. Its character was ambiguous between French and German. Just twenty-three years before the Dreyfus affair the Prussian army had taken hold of Alsace and the region had come under direct rule of the kaiser. For Alsatians to be considered French, they had to be ultra-French by showing loyalty to France beyond the call of duty. If this was true for Alsatians, it was doubly so for Alsatian Jews. Indeed, part of the reason why Dreyfus looked so pathetic was that he tried too hard to be an exemplary Frenchman.

Even the great French patriot of the 1870 war, Scheurer-Kestner, once he had sided with Dreyfus, was turned in public opinion from a French patriot into a Kraut (the derogatory term for a German). It is interesting to note that during the annexation of Alsace to Germany, each individual in Alsace had to make a conscious choice whether to be German or French. Dreyfus sided with the French and moved to Paris, but his well-to-do family was on the other side of the divide. It didn't help.

The Dreyfus affair both expressed and contributed significantly to the ideology of the integral nation, as a reaction and rejection of the idea of a civic nation united by a constitution and not by blood and the cross. Dreyfus the Jew didn't belong to the integral nation. He was a stranger twice over: as a Jew and as an Alsatian. Father Vincent de Paul Bailly expressed his dark view of the matter: "Whereas Judas belonged to the people of God, being the apostle chosen by the Master, the Jewish officer did not belong to the French Nation."[17]

For national integralists, Dreyfus serving on the General Staff of the French army was like having a money changer in the temple. His guilt was ultimately not a legal matter but a metaphysical one, just like Judas's. The nation was glued by a combination of French ethnic nativism and Catholicism, and this glue could not stick to Dreyfus.

The contrast between the national integralists and the republican modernists was like the contrast between the Sacré-Cœur Basilica (built to repent for the sins of France, to which the clergy attributed the debacle of the 1870 war) and the modern Eiffel

Tower of the Paris Exposition of 1889, with their two different metaphysics and two different aesthetics. But it also presented a sharp contrast between ethics and morality. For the integralists there was only group ethics, their group's ethics, unconstrained by universal morality. When Hubert-Joseph Henry eventually admitted that he had forged documents in order to incriminate Dreyfus, the ultra-integralist Charles Maurras hailed his act as "patriotic forgery." No moral constraints should be put on the good of the nation—definitely not any in the form of a Jewish officer exposed to death on a rock in the Atlantic. Dreyfus didn't even belong to the nation, let alone to the good of the nation. Nothing external (read universal) should deter the nation. This is what the integralists drummed on throughout the affair, even after the issue of Dreyfus's innocence and Esterhazy's guilt became clear.

The keen interest in the Dreyfus affair was not confined to France, and so the French genuinely feared that the nations of Europe would boycott the Paris Exposition of 1900. A month before the exposition there was an effort to pass a bill that would provide amnesty to all involved in the Dreyfus affair.

The Dreyfus affair was an occasion for the integralists to advance their view that citizenship should be based on thick relations founded on ethnic, linguistic, and religious ties. Dreyfus was the negation of these ingredients of the *intégrisme* of thick political relations. He spoke French, but not quite: he had a bit of an Alsatian German accent. He belonged not to the *ecclesia* but to the *synagoga*, which is the opposite of the church. And, needless to say, he wasn't ethnically French.

National integralism doesn't view the Catholic Church as catholic in the sense of a universal church. It views it as a national church, an integral element of Frenchness. Treason was for the integralists an invitation to reevaluate their relations, not with Dreyfus only but with the Jews in general. You (Jews) don't belong—that was their verdict, and it would be tragically reaffirmed later in Drancy, the camp from which the Jews of France were deported to extermination camps.

Theodor Herzl, the founder of modern Zionism and a Viennese journalist at the time of the trial, inferred from the affair that Jewish assimilation—creating thick relations with their neighbors—was not an open option for Jews. They had no chance of being genuinely accepted. Herzl's line was a major premise of Zionist thought. Yet what calls for explanation is not the anti-Dreyfusard camp's attitude but rather that of the Dreyfusards. It was the Dreyfusards who won the battle along tortuous legal trenches, while being relentlessly bombarded by wild public opinion. Their version of the Republic, the idea of civic nationalism, prevailed—till the German panzers rolled into France.

Integral nationalism as a doctrine about the need for thick relations to gain true primal citizenship has another element that brings it even closer to fascism: the faith that the army is the depository of national honor. The French army during the Dreyfus affair was still a touchy thing. It was an army that had been badly defeated in the 1870 war. In the past, belonging to the army officer corps had required a touch of class, of the sort that the true villain in the Dreyfus affair, Esterhazy, had. Esterhazy, with his dueling scars, gambling debts, kept women, uncertain competence in battle, and certain incompetence in the gambling house, was replaced by Dreyfus: bourgeois, family man, serious, and competent, though a bit awkward.

Anti-Semitism was important, at the beginning of the affair, in putting the blame on Dreyfus for passing information to the enemy, but closing ranks so as to protect the army's reputation and honor was more of a motive in framing Dreyfus later on.

The idea was that the cream of the nation was an aristocratic officer corps, bonded together by the high ideal of defending the nation's honor. This idea had little to do with the reality of anything, but it had a great deal to do with a fantasy about everything. Treason and betrayal were ultimately judged not by their effect on national interests. The information passed to the Germans was trivial, to the point that some historians still believe that Esterhazy was a double agent handing the Germans chicken feed. Treason was primarily judged by its effect on the nation's morale and ethos. Avoiding embarrassment and public shame obviously played a role in the behavior of some of the key players in the affair, but saving the army's honor played even more of a role in the behavior of others of them.

Treason involves helping the enemy outside the borders. *Collaboration* involves helping an occupying enemy inside the borders. Quisling, a traitor par excellence, did both. I shall use his case to move from treason to collaboration.

Coda: Quisling and Hamsun

Quisling is an eponym—a personal name that becomes a general term—for designating a traitor. Who could be more of a paradigmatic traitor than Vidkun Quisling, whose very name is synonymous with treason?

Quisling, I maintain, is an ideal type of traitor, but in no way is he a typical traitor. For an ideal type, the relevant distinctive traits of the type are accentuated and hence become very salient. By contrast, the traits of a typical case are bland: they are normal in the sense of average, rather than in the sense of setting a norm.

Concepts that play a role in accounting for natural phenomena should be judged by their explanatory power in what is roughly a causal explanation of the phenomena. Concepts that play a role in accounting for human actions should be judged not only by their explanatory power but also by their elucidatory power in making us understand the meaning of the human action. Now, an ideal type is not, so to speak, just any theoretical construct. It is a construct with elucidatory power on top of explanatory power. An ideal type stands in an asymmetrical relation to other objects of the same type: we say "like father like son" but not "like son like father." An ideal type guides the creation of an equivalent class of typical objects (a class whose objects are informed by symmetric, transitive, and reflexive relations), but the ideal type itself is not one of the typical objects.

Quisling is an ideal type in more ways than just being chronologically the first of his type. Needless to say, an ideal type is not an ideal in the sense that it is a positive moral example, as the Quisling example makes amply clear. He was also the first to undertake a Nazi-backed putsch (in Norway in April 1940) and the first Nazi puppet ruler of the Second World War.[18]

His list of firsts is enough to secure him the emblematic notoriety that his name by now conveys. But it does not explain Margret Boveri's claims that "in a way" he was "the least typical of all the quislings."[19] The question remains, in what way?

His psychology is not the key to answering the question. To describe him as gloomy, taciturn, and a bit socially awkward won't do the trick. This has more to do with the stereotype of a Norwegian than with an atypical quisling. Besides, almost every serial killer goes under a similar description, and with him millions of others. If you add to it "peevish, morose, and proud," as some of his friends described him, you don't add much to his atypical personality, let alone explain the man. As for explaining the acts of betrayal of this man, something very typical happened to him: his promotion in the army was stuck, and a strong sense of injured merit took hold of him. But this has happened to so many other betrayers that there is nothing atypical about it. He was highly gifted and muddleheaded. The evidence for the first judgment (gifted) is his being the best student of his cohort in all domains of learning: math, languages, and history. The evidence for the second judgment (his muddleheadedness) is his crackpot, hazy theory of everything, which he labeled "Universism."

But then even outlandish megalomania is not atypical of betrayers. Yet Gisle Tangenes claims that Quisling's "megalomania stood out even by the standards of fascist usurpers." If he didn't play God, he at least played the king: he took up residence in the royal palace and ensconced himself on the throne. But this doesn't seem to amount to much. More convincing is a joke from the time of the occupation that Tangenes brings to illustrate Quisling's megalomania. Quisling is visiting a madhouse and announces, "I am Vidkun Quisling, Norway's greatest son since King Harald Fairhair." "Take it easy," says one of the patients; "that's how it began with me too."

Quisling was intensely hated by his fellow countrymen. But he had one very disturbing supporter, much admired by the Norwegians and by the literary world at large: Knut Hamsun, the Nobel laureate in literature in 1920 and indeed a great writer.[20] Hamsun was an eccentric, "green" Nazi sympathizer. By that I mean a supporter of Nazism in believing that it was the right ideology for saving nature from the evils of modern industrial life. The years he spent as a young man in the United States made Hamsun view the States as a rising evil empire that had to be stopped by all means. This motive of stopping an evil empire from doing its mischief he shared with another "spiritual" betrayer, Ezra Pound. Like Pound, he was declared mad against his will. To say that the men who produced such great works of art lost their sound judgment and went stark raving mad strikes one as an effort to defend and deflect great writing from wretched writers. After all, how else can we explain why anyone as sensitive and psychologically astute as Hamsun would suddenly become a Nazi sympathizer? Something terrible must have happened to the old man. He lost his mind, and therein the explanation lies. Madness is no justification, but it makes for a good excuse.

This cultural gambit of shielding the writing from the writer and then excusing the writer by declaring him mad is a bad gambit. It is like declaring mad anyone who commits suicide on the grounds that no one in her right mind would do such a thing. And how do we know that the person is not in her right mind? Well, the poor thing tried to commit suicide, didn't she? We need evidence for the madness of Pound and Hamsun that is independent of their collaboration and sympathy with the Fascists and the Nazis. The same holds for Quisling.

There are two fallacies involved in the attribution of madness here: the fallacy of character and the fallacy of culture. The first is the belief in stable human traits across a wide range of behavior, so that if someone behaved courageously in battle, he would also be courageous in the public civic sphere. Or more to the point, a writer who is as astute in his psychological observations as Hamsun cannot be politically obtuse.

It may very well have been the case that Hamsun and Pound were mad, but attributing madness to them was a way of protecting the great literature they had produced. By contrast, Quisling, a true

believer in Nazism, was judged sane by the court: beneath contempt, but sane all the same.

To regard Hamsun as sane is to confer dignity on Nazism. If a
great writer such as Hamsun had chosen knowingly, with all his
faculties intact, then there must be something to Nazism. This
train of thought is pretty tempting but wrong. There is no idea
so mad that you won't find some great writers adhering to it. Yet
holding a mad idea does not, in and of itself, make an individual
mad. Just think of arguably the greatest human mind, Isaac
Newton. He wasn't mad, but he held some pretty mad ideas about
the occult, the great tribulations, and the end of the world.

Going back to Quisling, the riddle is still with us as to what
makes him the emblem of a traitor and yet an atypical one. It is
partly, I believe, the syndrome of the good Lord and the devil,
namely, the total transformation from doing the noble thing to
doing the evil thing.

By "doing the noble thing," I mean his work with the humanitarian Fridtjof Nansen during the great famine in Ukraine and
Russia in the 1920s. Quisling was very good at what he did, and
what he did was good. And then in the thirties, he turned into
the monster his fellow countrymen remember him as. Shadows
were cast over his good deeds in Russia. He was depicted as a
serial betrayer for being a bigamist married to two Russian
women. But he married his first wife, a seventeen-year-old peasant
girl, as an act of charity to enable her to get a Norwegian passport.
Moreover, Nansen's testimony that he was "absolutely indispensable" attests to Quisling being a man working for the good.[21]

Quisling was indeed convicted of high treason, illegal amend-
ment of the constitution, and complicity with murder. Quisling's
line of defense seems to be typical of that used by other collaborationists: I did it for the good of the country, and I saved the

country from terrible bloodshed. The court wasn't impressed: "Even in the event that later happenings justify the assertion of the accused and prove his acts to have, in fact, been for the good of the country, he would not be free from the guilt of having committed treason."[22]

The reason: in time of war, to surrender a place or a fighting unit to the enemy is treason, irrespective of whether it saves lives. But is it? The court decided that legally it is treason. But my question is different: Is it morally treason—morally, not legally? We should distinguish between blaming the person and blaming the act—whether Quisling was a traitor or whether his acts were treachery—if he indeed saved lives from unnecessary death. The next chapter is about collaboration and this dilemma.

6

Collaboration

IT WAS PROBABLY MARSHAL PHILIPPE PÉTAIN WHO CAUSED the term "collaboration" to mean helping foreign occupiers. It was, however, his collaboration that gave "collaboration" a bad name. "Collaboration" had been a good word for cooperation, but because of Pétain and his ilk, it became a bad word for treacherous help to an occupying enemy.

My kernel question is this: When does collaboration amount to betrayal?

On the face of it, the bad connotations of "collaboration" are only in the eyes of the occupied, whereas the occupier looks kindly on the helpers, the collaborators. But on many occasions this is not the case. The occupier views the collaborator the way we view toilet paper: useful but disgustingly disposable. For many years, the slang term used by Israelis to refer to an Arab collaborator was the Yiddish word *shtinker,* whose rancid odor the English word "stinker" retains. There were many efforts in the Israeli security establishment to sanitize the term by referring to collaborators by good words. One such term, *meshatef peola,* which is close in meaning to "cooperator," was in no time tainted the way "collaborator" had been tainted in French. The trouble is the reality of collaboration, not the words. Even Adolf Hitler, the main beneficiary of French collaboration, stumbled when he had to pronounce the word *Kollaboration*.[1] A collaborator is a collaborator and by any other name still smells like a rat, almost regardless of perspective. I use the hedge "almost" advisedly. Collaboration is aiding and abetting the conqueror. But we quite often discover that the conqueror despises the collaborator, especially if the collaboration takes place for opportunistic reasons. Even in cases where collaboration is a product of deep identification with the conqueror, the conqueror quite often is baffled by the zeal of his ideological collaborator, much as old believers are baffled by the zeal of new converts. Furthermore, ideological collaborators are so intensely hated by the subjugated population that in many cases for the conqueror they become more of a liability than an asset.

Whose Perspective Should Decide?

The perspective of the occupier shouldn't dictate the answer to the question of when collaboration is betrayal. The question "Which perspective is the right perspective for assessing collaboration as betrayal?" should be answered before addressing the question "When does collaboration amount to betrayal?"

One worry about the right perspective is how to determine who speaks for the community when the political community is under oppressive occupation. For example, is it de Gaulle or is it Pétain? But whoever speaks for the community, it seems clear that it is for the community to decide what compromise with the occupier would be acceptable, and what would count as betrayal. For example, it is pretty clear to the Palestinians under Israeli occupation what kind of collaboration counts as betrayal: selling land in the occupied territories to Israeli Jews as well as informing on other Palestinians to the Israeli security forces. Surprisingly, however, working as a construction worker to help build Jewish settlements in the West Bank counts not as betrayal but as a necessity of life: not a good option, but an acceptable one.

Let's draw a distinction between three settings of collaboration: collaboration under *military occupation,* collaboration under *colonial rule,* and collaboration under *annexation.* Military occupation is temporary: territories under occupation may turn into territories under colonial rule, or into annexed territories, but military occupation is not supposed to determine the permanent nature of the occupation. I shall mainly concentrate on collaboration under occupation *during a war.* It is the clearest setting for collaboration as betrayal. But I shall start with collaboration under colonial rule.

The colonial setting is a setting of massive collaboration, but is it also a setting of collaboration as betrayal?

At the beginning of World War I about 85 percent of the globe was under colonial rule. By that I mean that C was colonized if it was governed by country A, whose center was somewhere else, and A's dominion over C was carried out by direct force or by coercive threats. The typical size of the colonized population relative to the colonial personnel (military and civilian) was overwhelmingly in favor of the colonized. This fact makes it clear that colonial rule could not be sustained without the massive assistance of the colonized population. Colonial regimes varied considerably in terms of how they were viewed by the indigenous population: were they viewed as an enemy or not? With respect to this question, the perspective of the colonized becomes tricky. For it seems that collaboration should be regarded as betrayal only after the colonized gained full awareness and were able to judge the colonists for the enemy they were, rather than taking them as their "natural" rulers.

Viewing the occupiers as an enemy doesn't necessarily mean that the occupier was viewed as such at the beginning of the occupation. The change in judgment from viewing the occupiers as patrons to viewing them as predators may evolve as the occupation goes on.

We must remember that colonialism was made possible by massive collaboration on the part of the local population. To view all collaboration with colonial rule as betrayal empties the idea of betrayal. If everything is betrayal, then nothing is betrayal.

Collaboration under annexation is even trickier than collaboration under colonialism with regard to the question whether collaboration is betrayal. The Anschluss (the political annexation) of Austria to Nazi Germany in March 1938 is a barefaced example.[2] True, Hitler didn't let the Austrian chancellor, Kurt von Schuschnigg, hold a referendum on the question of whether his country should be annexed to Germany or should remain independent, for fear that the Austrians might vote for an independent Austria. But then Hitler was not lying when he said that on the day of the annexation, March 12, he was welcomed by the Austrians as a liberator. The general impression at the time, and later, was that the Austrians were overjoyed at the Anschluss. The right-wing Austrian line at the end of the war that they were the first victims of Nazi Germany was met by many outside Austria as a detestable self-serving myth, and rightly so.

An occupying army is an enemy army if it is so regarded by a great majority of the occupied population. However, the population under occupation may be a diverse population, whereby the great majority of the occupied may look on the occupiers as an enemy, but some subgroups—ethnic or religious or ideological parties—may be favorably disposed toward the occupiers. They view the occupier as a friend rather than a foe. Well then, should we still insist that it is for the majority to determine the character of the occupier as an enemy? Should we also insist that it is for the majority to determine whether minority groups helping the occupier are traitorous collaborators?

I shall switch from the schematic to the specific: from talking in the abstract about majorities and minorities to talking about concrete collaboration with the German occupation of France. I do so not because it is the clearest case, but because it is the richest. Stanley Hoffman is right in describing collaboration in France as "infernally complicated," not because there was no collaboration in France—there was too much of it—but because the "too much" took on many shades and hues.[3] Indeed, France during the Second World War is as good a laboratory for investigating collaboration as Pasteur's laboratory was good for sorting out microbes: it had them all.

Voluntary and Involuntary Collaboration

Hoffmann introduced the distinction between *voluntary* and *involuntary* collaboration. I shall follow his terminology but not his distinction. For one thing, there is a need for more distinctions along the voluntary–involuntary axis. Involuntary collaboration is collaboration under coercion. One crucial distinction—not drawn by Hoffmann—is between coercion of *individuals* and coercion of *collectives*. There is a difference between a coercive threat directed to an individual qua individual, say, Pétain ("your signature or your life"), and a coercive threat directed to an individual as the representative of a collective, say, Pétain on behalf of France ("collaboration or Polonization," in Hoffmann's felicitous phrase). "Polonization" here means subjecting an enemy to direct brutal military rule of the kind the Nazis inflicted on Poland. Pétain faced the second kind of coercion: collective, not personal. Along the lines of this distinction, we should keep in mind the difference between keeping the territorial integrity of France and keeping the bodily integrity (life and limb) of an individual under duress.

We may further distinguish between coercing an individual as a person and coercing an individual as someone holding a certain role, say, the role of prime minister. Being coerced in a role takes place when a coercive threat to a collective is directed to an individual who is in a position to make a decision on behalf of the collective. Coercion can of course be directed both to the person ("your children or your signature") and to the role ("collaboration or Polonization").

Involuntary personal collaboration is not a case of collaboration, or at least not a clear case of collaboration. One can divulge useful information to an enemy by being credibly threatened with the murder of one's children, but it wouldn't be right to consider that person a collaborator. A clear case of a collaborator is an individual who willfully collaborates—free from personal coercion, but not necessarily free from role coercion. If I don't tar those who involuntarily help the enemy with the same brush as collaborators, it isn't because I want to imply that their acts are thereby justified. Coercion provides an excuse, but it doesn't necessarily provide a justification. Excuse means that what they did was wrong but that there were mitigating circumstances for doing it, whereas justification means that what they did was right, even if it doesn't look that way.

In separating involuntary collaboration on the individual level from involuntary collaboration on the collective level, I don't want to exclude important cases in which the two go together. One horrific case is the case of the *Judenräte,* the Jewish councils that the Nazi regime installed in many Jewish ghettoes. The Nazi policy was to use such councils to implement Nazi policy toward the Jews by compelling the councils to supply forced labor, make lists of those who were to be sent to the extermination camps, and help transport the victims to their death. There is no question that Jews in occupied Europe were brutally coerced by the Germans, both collectively and individually. One question with regard to the Jewish council members is whether they were coerced to serve in the *Judenräte.* Could one refuse without being severely punished? Another question is whether one could opt out of the council once he was there without being cruelly punished (it was invariably men who were members of these councils, never women, to my knowledge). It is not clear that there is a clear answer to these two questions. Isaiah Trunk's seminal work on the Jewish councils doesn't settle the issue.[4] For one thing, he tells us that there were many ways of forming the councils, ranging from places in which the Nazi commander nominated the head of the council, leaving the head to choose its members, to places where the prewar institution of the community council remained in place. It stands to reason that there were differences in the degree of individual coercion in these different methods of forming the councils. But whatever the differences were, the brutality was everywhere. Trunk tells us that Adam Czerniaków, head of the *Judenrat* in the Warsaw ghetto, by far the largest ghetto, was threatened by Hermann Höfle, the SS commander in charge of mass deportation to the death camps, that

Czerniaków's wife would be shot if the operation *(Aktion)* of transporting the victims wasn't successful. Adam Czerniaków eventually opted out of his role, not by stepping down but by swallowing cyanide.

After the war the term *Judenrat,* among Jews, was synonymous with treacherous collaboration, and being a member of the council meant being a collaborator. This was a cruel, uninformed wholesale judgment: some who served in the councils were saints, quite a few were villains, and most were normal people in an abnormal situation.

One thing is clear: there is no comparison between the horrendous coercion the members of the *Judenräte* went through and what Vichy officials faced. In Vichy, if one didn't collaborate, one had the option of leading a relatively normal personal life under the general privation of the occupation. For Jews, there was no such option. The pending threat to their lives was there all along. Some members of the *Judenräte* believed that by being on the council they postponed the danger to their family. There were others who believed that by collaborating with the Nazis and making the Jewish labor force indispensable to the Nazi war effort ("salvation by work") they postponed the fate of at least some Jews in the ghetto, with the reasonable hope that they would be rescued by the advancing Allies. This belief turned out to be wrong. It was based on an assumption about the rationality of Nazi Germany, namely, that it wouldn't destroy people it needed for its war effort. Well, the Nazis did just that.

Coercion involves a credible threat that makes the victim, with all the feasible options facing her, considerably worse off than she was before the threat. If the conqueror offers a confiscated house to a prospective informer in exchange for information, then it is an *offer* and not a coercive threat. The informer is presented with one option—having the house—which is better than what she had before. Morally repugnant as the offer is, she might think that she would be better off ratting and getting the house than otherwise. On the slippery slope of collaboration there is no hedge to break one's fall. One may start collaborating voluntarily, only to discover later that one is in the clutches of the conqueror and being coerced to stay in line.

The Dilemma of Collaboration

Collaboration takes place under occupation. Collaboration is not cooperation among equals. It is based on a deep asymmetry between the victorious conquerors and the defeated conquered. Conquerors have an interest in administrating the occupied territories with only a tiny fraction of their overall manpower. The Germans ruled over thirty-eight million Frenchmen with a tiny fraction of civilian administrators and policemen of their own. This interest of the conquerors to minimize their manpower in running the occupation can be fulfilled only with the massive collaboration of the subjugated population. But occupation with a "light touch" comes with a price for the occupier: leaving a measure of autonomy for the occupied. The occupier faces the dilemma of ruling by collaboration or ruling by Polonization. France was ruled with a mixture of direct rule over one-fifth of the country and indirect rule, through Vichy, over the other four-fifths. By contrast, there was little collaboration in Poland. Poland was never presented with the option of collaboration or Polonization: it was Polonization through and through. Poland was destined by Nazi rule eventually to become a living space for German settlers, with the Poles as their serfs. But the Nazi regime did present the French with a choice between collaboration and Polonization. The French opted for collaboration: not all the French and not all the time, but most of the French most of the time did accept collaboration.

Occupation is coercion, at least collective coercion. For the political community it seems that the coercive threat of collaboration or Polonization is nothing but the dilemma between the devil (Polonization) and the deep blue sea (collaboration), in the form of a loss of independence. Polonization is a naked and brutal loss of independence, whereas collaboration keeps a certain veneer of independence, but with the price of shameful, cowardly collaboration with the enemy. The choice between being brutalized and being besmirched constitutes a coercive threat, which is directed to the collective.

Pétain or de Gaulle?

Collaboration takes place under a continual coercive threat directed to the political community of the vanquished. Being under conquest is not the most propitious time to express public opinion. But what if it is clear to everybody that only a few are taking part in the active violent resistance to the occupation, and the appeal of the resistance is confined to a small segment of the population? The rest of the population cares about carrying on with their normal life in adverse circumstances. The general population, grudgingly but passively, is resigned to the idea of living under the occupation.

Note that the question refers to cases in which the population in general believes that it lives under occupation, and only a few are willing to resist.

This case differs from cases such as the Basque ETA or the Corsican Armata Corsa, wherein the general population doesn't ever believe that it lives under occupation in any literal sense. This doesn't mean that there are no grievances among the Basques or the Corsicans directed to Madrid or Paris, but grievances, even grave grievances, do not amount to occupation.

I have already posed the question of who better expressed public opinion in occupied France, Pétain or de Gaulle. This seemingly innocuous question is not well defined: it needs a time index. Its truth value varies with time. There is an overall sense that public opinion in occupied France at the beginning of the occupation overwhelmingly supported Pétain's collaboration.[5] The supporters believed that his collaborationist way was the only way for France to cut the losses of the defeat, as well as to avoid direct Nazi rule. At that time de Gaulle struck many as irrelevant or, worse, as an irritant. The attitude toward the options that the two represented changed as the war went on. The Nazis' direct involvement in the occupation became more and more readily seen and the retreat of the Wehrmacht on all fronts after 1942 became more and more evident. The contrast between Pétain and de Gaulle is not simply a contrast between collaboration and *internal* resistance. The resistance movement in France itself, the internal resistance, seemed on some occasions more of a literary genre than an effective rebellious undertaking. In measuring the resistance by how many Germans divisions were deployed to fight it, the French internal resistance doesn't look terribly significant. The French Free Army of de Gaulle, the *external* resistance, was quite impressive in numbers, though unimpressive in equipment; at its peak, toward the end of the war, it comprised 300,000 soldiers. It was of course a convenient myth after the war to depict France as a country divided into a majority of resisters and a minority of collaborators. The falsity of this myth was exposed to the general public on so many occasions, beginning perhaps with

Marcel Ophuls's documentary *Le Chagrin et la Pitié* (1971), that there is no point in mulling over it again. But if a majority of French people under occupation approved for a long stretch of time Pétain's policy of collaboration, then in what sense can we render the marshal and his followers' collaboration as betrayal?

Here is the problem: betrayal undermines thick relations, but if those with whom one is in thick relations under occupation, the Vichyists, don't consider their collaboration as betrayal, then who else is entitled to judge the collaboration as betrayal? More concretely, if indeed Pétain was supported by his fellow countrymen, in what sense did he betray them?

In the case of Vichy and Pétain there is the unmistakable evil act of rounding up and transporting the Jews of France to the death camps.[6] This wasn't only a terrible complicity in mass murder but also a betrayal of citizens of France, who were hounded by French police and handed over to the enemy. I shall come back to this dreadful affair later. But the charge of the collaboration of Vichy as betrayal goes beyond the fate of the Jews in France, and the question again is, on what grounds?

Betraying the General Will

Jean-Jacques Rousseau's notion of the general will seems to belong here.[7] His famous notion of the general will is distinct from the will of all, on the one hand, and from the universal will, on the other. And while Rousseau's position is distinct, it is also unclear.

What I am about to suggest is a timid variation on Rousseau's theme of the general will. Whatever Rousseau's "general will" amounts to, it should be pretty clear that occupation is not conducive to expression of the general will. The general will is the will of a political community cemented by thick relations of solidarity, deliberating from the point of view of their common good. The common good is constituted of concern with acts that promote the quality of the thick relations of the political community, free from the partial interests of its members.

The general will is expressed by reasons for action taken from the point of view of the common good, and only from that point of view. The general will is an associative notion different from the will of all, which is an aggregate notion combining the wills of all members of the body politic by presenting all their personal preferences from the point of view of their individual interests.

By the general will I don't mean a disembodied will, above and beyond the wills of individuals. It is a special kind of will in the sense of being sensitive to only one kind of reason. The universal will in distinction from the general will is a will sensitive to reasons that concern humanity at large. In the spirit of my distinction between thick and thin relations, we may call the general will a thick will, whereas the universal will is a thin will.

Theodor Herzl, founder of the Zionist movement, wrote his book *The State of the Jews* while living in Paris, surrounded by lively discussions about the general will. He was deeply troubled by the question of what right entitled him to speak on behalf of the Jews, advocating a Jewish state as a solution to their plight, without consulting their general will. For one thing, there was no way to consult the will of his dispersed nation. To overcome the issue of legitimacy, namely, to speak with authority on behalf of "his people," Herzl borrowed from Roman civil law the interesting idea of *negotiorum gestio* (business management).[8] The idea is that in cases where a principal is not in a position to be consulted, an agent may act on behalf of the principal's best interests without asking the principal. The agent is supposed to do it out of a sense of fraternity, and not for any personal gain. If you rush your unconscious friend to the hospital, you may decide on her behalf, without legally being her trustee, on various issues that concern her health. Herzl viewed his status vis-à-vis the Jewish people as their *gestor,* the one who runs their business while they are "unconscious," that is, not in a position to express their common good. One may view de Gaulle as a *gestor,* an agent of necessity, for "unconscious" France—France under Nazi occupation. As such, he is the one to best express its common good. The idea of an agent of necessity, incarnating the common good of a collective, is a risky one. It sounds like an invitation for individuals with delusions of grandeur and a savior complex to try to act on behalf of the people, telling them what is good for them. It should be no surprise that both Herzl and de Gaulle weren't above suspicion of an inflated sense of grandeur. Add to the fear of megalomania the fear that the general will is paving the way to "totalitarian democracy," and this may be enough to make you shy away from dealing with the explosive idea of the *volonté générale.* But with all these warnings in mind, the idea of the general will in one form or another is needed to address the question of who speaks for a people who are under occupation.

There is a third way, a third perspective, if you like. It is a perspective that Rousseau did indeed grapple with: the perspective of the universal will. It is a point of view taken from the angle of humanity at large. Republican France conflated the two senses of will: the general and the universal. Following the French Revolution, the French nation regarded itself as cemented by devotion to the mission of carrying out the universal will, whereby France represented the perspective of humanity at large, in contrast to any ethnic definition of the French people. Vichy was meant to undo this heritage of the French Revolution.

To strip the French Jews of their French citizenship was to betray France as a nation devoted to a universal mission. The collaborationist betrayal of the Jews of France should be counted as a betrayal of the heritage of the French Revolution according to which the sole justification for solidarity is citizenship on a universal basis. "Universal" here should be understood in a restricted sense: human beings who happened to live on French soil.

A Collaborationist Argument

If the Jews of France constituted a litmus test for France's collaboration with Germany, then it is a test that apologists of Pétain's collaboration may grab with both hands. Yes, they may say, there was the undeniably horrific and tragic reality of Drancy, the internment camp from which the Jews of France were deported to extermination camps between 1942 and 1944. Yes, there were 6,000 children among them. Yes, Vichy collaborationists played a shameful role in all of it. It is all true, but one should compare numbers: the fate of Jews in collaborationist countries was much better than their fate in non-collaborationist countries. In places in which the population opted for collaboration rather than Polonization, a greater percentage of Jews survived. In France, out of a Jewish population of 350,000 Jews before the war, only 77,000 were murdered, whereas in heroic Yugoslavia 60,000 Jews out of 78,000 were murdered. In collaborationist Belgium the ratio was 29,000 murdered Jews out of 66,000 who lived there before the war, whereas in neighboring Holland under direct Nazi rule 100,000 Jews were murdered out of 140,000. In short, collaborationism was better for the Jews. To be sure, no country collaborated with the Nazis for the sake of its Jews, but it seems that collaboration as a matter of fact was better for the Jews than Polonization.

The collaborationist denies that collaboration is a strictly competitive game in which one side's gain is exactly balanced by the other side's loss. Collaboration is nasty and humiliating, but the two sides, in spite of all the asymmetry between them, can gain from collaboration. Occupation means coercion, but coercion does not mean that the deal you are offered as the defeated side, namely, collaboration, is not better than no deal, which means brutal Polonization. Collaboration as daily normalization is the best one can do in such unfortunate circumstances. Those in charge who make the deal for their people should be regarded not as betrayers but as patriots who have the courage to choose the lesser evil in a very difficult situation.

A Resister's Argument

Note that we are dealing with *wholesale* collaboration, namely, collaboration on the level of state or statelike political entities: Vichy headed by Pétain is the paradigmatic example of wholesale collaboration. If wholesale collaboration is supported by the occupied population, we are back to the nagging question "In what sense, if any, is such collaboration betrayal?" One difficulty, mentioned already, is an epistemic one, namely, how do we know what people under occupation think about wholesale collaboration? The answer should be turned into a doctrine, the only honorable doctrine there is: only people who resist the occupation can speak with legitimacy, because they prove by their fearless resistance to be undeterred by the coercive force of the occupation. Resisters are either out of reach of the occupiers—de Gaulle in London—or free from fear. The free minority group can speak with authority for the whole group based on a counterfactual: their position is what the whole group would have expressed had they been able to express themselves freely. One shouldn't listen to the voices of the people under occupation, any more than one should listen to hostages expressing support for the demands of their captors. The assumption is that a shocked occupied population is not in a position to assess accurately who is a friend and who is a foe. True, resistance movements on many occasions are perceived as a threat to public safety, and the craving for normalcy in "the time of cholera" paints them as enemies of the people rather than the liberators they aspire to be. But this, the resister claims, is normal for abnormal times, and it shouldn't diminish the claim to represent the collective as a whole.

Betraying the Past

The effort to view betrayal as betrayal of the general will of the occupied population has a related move. Collaboration is betrayal of past generations. The idea is that the thick relations of a community under occupation go beyond its current population. It should include the community in the past. A contingent consensus in the current community under occupation may betray the people of the past. The long indictment of Pétain's collaborative treason was headed by three categories: *material, moral,* and *political.* Accepting a degrading collaboration between "victor and vanquished" went under the heading of the political, but the main thrust of the indictment went under the description of doing things that were "abhorrent to the Republic." This was taken as a moral category that included the effort by the collaborationists to undo the Republic and everything it stood for. By "abhorrent to the Republic" the indictment didn't mean that the

French people, at the time of the meeting between Hitler and Pétain in Montoire (1940), regarded with fright Pétain's act of submission to defeat. They looked with dismay at their defeat, but in no way did most of them view Pétain's act with abhorrence. The reference to the Republic in the expression "abhorrent to the Republic" didn't mean the Republic of 1940. It meant all past generations of the Republic. Thick relations can be relations with the dead as much as with the living. The Republic is the whole sausage (extended in time) and not a mere slice of it (a given point of time). Betrayal can go forward and backward in time. Anyone who speaks in the name of the past generations of France, so as to override the view of the living French generation of 1940, is bound to be charged with the arrogance of paternalism, the way one is charged for speaking in the name of the general will. The pressure is to view thick relations as relations confined to living creatures, and let the dead bury the dead.

Collaboration, especially with the Nazi regime, can be wretchedly wrong on many counts. It can be a rotten compromise, helping to sustain an inhuman regime, a regime based on cruelty and humiliation. Treachery is only one way to assess collaboration. Collaboration may be cursed, even without betraying thick relations. There is every reason to criticize Vichy morally without viewing it as treasonous to the French people. The French people were for Pétain at the beginning of the war; the French people were for de Gaulle at the end of the war. The shift in support from the beginning to the end tells you something about the French people, but not whether Pétain was a traitor. But the issue of betraying the past is still with us, and it has specific bite in the case of Pétain, for he seemed to be the best candidate to speak for the past.

Pétain: Betraying the Past

Perhaps no one believed in family and fatherland more than Marshal Pétain. Indeed, his "national revolution" under the collaborationist Vichy regime was based on the slogan "work, family, fatherland." Yet the hero of Verdun, the only general in the French army who was trusted by his soldiers not to waste their lives in useless assaults, was sentenced to death as a traitor on August 5, 1945 (only to have his sentence commuted by de Gaulle to life imprisonment).

Thick relations are based and cemented on shared history and shared memory. It is the shared history of the French people that Pétain debased and betrayed. What does it mean to betray the nation when the nation is conceived as a sausage (extended in time) and not as a nation in a particular slice of time, say, France in 1940? Pétain betrayed by trying to form a France that would eradicate the memory and the legacy of the French Revolution. It is the legacy of the French Revolution that Pétain betrayed. Pétain would have argued that he, more than anyone else, anchored his deeds in a shared past, a past distorted by the French Revolution, which created a homogenized and artificial France. So how can anyone accuse him, of all people, of betraying the shared past?

Every past is a mixed past, a blend of the noble and the nauseating. Being loyal to a shared past means more than taking the rough with the smooth. It means being committed to the best of the past. Thick ethical relations are good relations that depend on what in the shared past is picked as points of reference, points that are, to use a mathematical metaphor, fixed points. I shall address this telling metaphor of fixed points shortly. But first let me state that de Gaulle, himself coming from the same conservative background as Pétain, had the right historical sense of what in the history of France was worth conserving and, more important, what would count as betrayal. Pétain made the wrong ethical judgment on top of the wrong moral judgment by siding with a regime that was set on destroying the very idea of shared humanity. But Pétain betrayed also the people with whom he felt he shared strong thick relations by debasing the values of their shared past.

Betraying a Fixed Point

Objectivists believe that we objectively belong to certain groups. An objectivist may argue that subjective denials of such belonging are, in their benign form, expressions of lack of authenticity and false consciousness; in their malign form, they are outright betrayal and self-hate.

Identifying with what objectively destroys one's identity—be it by the gay person in the closet, the assimilated Jew, or the worker siding with the bosses—is an act of betrayal. Those who share the objectivist view may still disagree on which groups one objectively belongs to. Is it one's class? Is it one's nation? Is it one's religion? Is it any combination of these, say, Irish Catholic working class?

On this strong objective identity view, betrayal is, first and foremost, estrangement from one's very identity—namely, identification with something that objectively is not who one is. A full-fledged betrayal is identification with the enemy of the group to which one belongs objectively.

In this picture of objective identity, there is no room for genuine conversion. Conversion must be betrayal. Conversion doesn't mean only religious conversion; it includes any form of ideological conversion.

In conversion one gives up one's fixed point in life. Following a suggestion Sidney Morgenbesser made orally, "fixed point" means beliefs and actions that one holds invariant under all vicissitudes (transformations) that one may go through in life. In conversion, what one used to hold fast to ceases to be fixed. A fixed point is a point that is relevant to one's sense of self-identity. You may believe that you wouldn't eat spinach under any transformation, and indeed you do not eat spinach, but then eating spinach has very little to do with your sense of identity, unless you happen to be Popeye. But for a religious Muslim not to drink wine or for a religious Jew not to eat pork is a different matter: not drinking wine and not eating pork are fixed points. Taboos are fixed points.

The metaphor of the fixed point comes from mathematical topology. It is in topology that we find the celebrated fixed-point theorem, which roughly asserts that under certain constraints, if we map each point in a set onto another set, there is bound to be a point that is mapped onto itself. This means that the point remains invariant under the transformation of all the points in the set: it is a fixed point.

Ideologies that advocate strong identity postulate fixed points, which exist irrespective of their identification. The fixed-point metaphor is a subjectivist metaphor: it is what individuals actually hold as invariant in their life. Objectivists maintain that social identity is an objective thing, and so whether people recognize their identity or not doesn't determine what identity they should hold if they remain true to themselves. Objectivists switch metaphors from the metaphor of fixed points to the metaphor of roots. Thus, you may be told that at the root of your being you are a Jew, whether you accept it or deny it. Denial is taken as a form of inauthenticity, if not downright betrayal. The metaphor emerges from a metaphysical picture, according to which one's metaphysical identity over time is retained by having the same soul. My body may be utterly transformed, and so too my psychology, but I remain the same person because of my unchanging and unchangeable soul. From this picture it is but a small step to the picture of one's social identity as being dependent on having a certain type of soul, such as a Russian soul, a Russian Orthodox soul, and so on. The soul is your root whether you know it or not. Again, if you don't know your soul, it is because you lead an inauthentic life, not giving a sincere account to yourself as to who you *really* are. Selling one's soul to the devil is a betrayal of one's true self in order to gain outward success.

This is a bad picture, much in the way the picture in metaphysics of a disembodied soul is a bad picture, and a bad answer to the intriguing problem of personal identity. But it is an influential picture that affects, among other things, our notion of betrayal—making it a cosmic principle of one's betraying his or her true soul. We may turn back to the metaphor of the fixed point and combine the root with the fixed point. We may distinguish between two notions of fixed point: *personal* and *objective*. A personal notion means that one has a sense of having fixed points, such as beliefs, principles, and modes of action and interaction, so no matter what changes one may undergo in life, one would hold fast to these fixed points.

The objective notion is that, regardless of how the agent views it, there are fixed spiritual points, independent of her beliefs, attitudes, and style of action, that determine her identity. They are her reasons, in an objective sense ("external reasons"), even if she does not recognize them as her own reasons ("internal reasons").

In this view, betrayal and treason are objective categories, much like blood poisoning and tuberculosis.

Ideological Collaboration

Collaboration is association with one's enemies. The most obnoxious form of collaboration is betrayal by individuals or associations that share the ideology of the vanquishers. It is more disgusting than collaboration for personal gain, because the betrayal is not just helping the enemy but also providing an affirmation of the enemy's spiritual superiority, and not just the enemy's superiority in military might. Moreover, ideological identification with the enemy serves as a justification for the occupiers to hold on to their spoils.

If the enemy has the right ideology and our local rulers are in the wrong—ideologically, that is—then why not live under the occupiers' benign ideology, rather than under our dreadful ideology?

There are many forms of ideological identification that a collaborationist can take. Ideological identification may vary. In the case of France, it varied from explicit local Nazi parties to Mussolini-style fascist parties and ultraconservatives who didn't like Germany but viewed Nazi Germany as the last bastion against Bolshevism. The spectrum of ideological collaboration is wide: it runs from total identification in content and style to partial identification in content or partial imitation of style, be it style of organization or style of propaganda.

Collaborationism includes adoption of a *way of life*. The collaborator, in adopting in time of crisis the enemy's way of life, expresses lack of solidarity with her people. I was once told that upper-class women in Algeria started wearing the veil toward the end of the period of French colonial rule, even though they were well inside the orbit of French culture. The veil was their way of saying, "We are not collaborators."

Ideological collaborationism is contrasted quite naturally with *opportunistic* collaborationism, done for personal gain. But the contrast can be quite misleading: in collaborationism, opportunism and ideology can go hand in hand. Leaders of a marginal and despised ideological party who identify with the ideology of the enemy before or during the war may take the opportunity of the occupation to assume power under the aegis of the conquerors. There is no way for such a party to come to power on the strength of its own ideology, but now, with the help of the conquerors' bayonets, they can ascend to power.

Ideological collaborators view the occupation as a chance to settle scores with those who for years ignored and despised them. They reek of resentment. The proverbial "slave who becomes king" and proceeds to settle internal scores is particularly insufferable to the vanquished population. No wonder such obnoxious ideological collaborators become the most hated enemies of the people.

A Collaborator in the Court of History

A T AGE THIRTEEN, I WAS CALLED A TRAITOR. IN OUR Labor Zionist schools as well as in our youth movement we held annual mock trials of Josephus, the great Jewish historian of the first century CE. My school was one such. And I was cast as Josephus.

In court I was asked to identify myself: "Are you Josephus Flavius?" (His full name was in fact Titus Flavius Josephus, but this was not known to us at the time.) This seemingly innocuous question was actually a very loaded one. To our patriotic Hebrew ears, being called by a Roman name was already an ominous sign of selling out. I understood this instinctively. I pompously answered the court in the language of Josephus: "I am Yosef ben Matityahu of Hebrew descent, a priest from Jerusalem."[1]

What charges had I to face? Well, the obvious ones: desertion and dereliction of duty as commander of forces in the Galilee.

What was the background for this accusation?

Josephus was born in Jerusalem (37/38 CE) to a distinguished priestly family. At the age of twenty-six he was sent to Rome on a diplomatic mission. On his return from Rome, Josephus, who lacked military experience, was sent by the rebellious Jewish governing body to serve as the chief northern commander.[2] But as northern commander, he was accused of trying to find bridges to the Romans, and in the eyes of his many detractors he was already a suspect before the actual war even started. After all, bridges and traitors are the same, as the (once) bigoted Ian Paisley said, for they are trying to reach the other side.

So what is the story beyond this accusation?

When the Romans attacked the Jewish settlements in the Galilee so as to quell the revolt, Josephus was in Yodfat, the best-fortified city in the north. The siege of Yodfat lasted forty-seven days. On several occasions Josephus tried to persuade his fellow combatants to open the gate to the Romans so as to prevent the city's destruction, but they turned a deaf ear. After Yodfat fell into the hands of the Romans, Josephus and a few dozen of his fighters took shelter in a cave. Their hiding place was discovered by the Romans. Josephus's comrades refused to surrender and made a suicide pact. Josephus rigged the lottery that determined the order of the sequential killing so that he would be last, and then he capitulated.

Josephus was taken as a trophy by the Romans to be executed in Rome in the triumphal procession. He wriggled free of prison by prophesying to the Roman victor Vespasian that he was about to become emperor; after the death of Emperor Nero and his successor, Gala, the "oracle" gained currency and Josephus was released. He was at first free to go to Alexandria, but he later joined Titus, the son of Vespasian, in his siege of Jerusalem (68 CE). His role, as agitator, was to seduce the besieged to surrender.

Indeed, Josephus stood shoulder to shoulder with the Romans outside Jerusalem's walls, facing his fellow Jews, who were inside the walls and calling on them to lay down their arms.

There is nothing anachronistic in these charges. They were regarded as acts of betrayal then and are regarded as such now. It is even easier to imagine what the charges of desertion, defection, and collaboration meant in the reality of ancient walled cities than in our convoluted contemporary world.

Josephus settled in Rome as a protégé of the Flavian family. He was granted Roman citizenship as well as a sinecure from the emperor, and allowed to live in his mentor's palace. He led the life of a Roman dignitary and a scholar, but encountered intense hatred from his fellow Jews.

In my defense (as Josephus), I raised the analogy with the prophet Jeremiah when Jerusalem was likewise under siege (indeed, an analogy that was very much on Josephus's mind), only to be rebuffed by my classmate judges: How could I, as Josephus the traitor, compare myself to Jeremiah, the true prophet?[3]

Let us briefly review Jeremiah and his message.

Jeremiah preached total surrender to the ferocious foe, the Babylonian army of Nebuchadnezzar, while the city was under lethal siege. His defeatist call to give in grossly undermined the morale of the besieged. He thereby was giving the enemy, as the cliché has it, "aid and comfort."

Moreover, Jeremiah tried to escape from Jerusalem and was accused of trying to defect to the enemy camp. (He never denied that he tried to sneak out, but he did deny that he tried to defect to the enemy camp.)

What, then, is the difference between Josephus, so often reviled as a traitor, and Jeremiah, revered as a prophet?

The question is supposed to be answered by "the court of history." What is the court of history and what is its verdict?

The Court of History

Lately we hear so many deposed rulers appeal to history to be their judge. "History will judge me," said Hosni Mubarak. "History will have the final say," said George W. Bush. "History will judge us," said Tony Blair. And on it goes. If the expression "history will be the judge" makes any sense, it makes more than one sense. One sense is a metaphysical sense: history has a hidden purpose, and human actions should be judged by the way they promote (or hinder) the purpose of history. There are religious versions of this idea. But there are also semi-secular versions that purport to delineate what goes with history and what goes against it. What goes against history is thrown into the dustbin of history. Mubarak, Bush, and Blair also appeal to another sense of "history will be the judge": to be judged by history is to be vindicated in the eyes of future generations. By this account, history is not an impersonal agent; instead, the judgment of history is the judgment of future generations. The rationale is clear: many leaders were judged harshly by their contemporaries but were thought better of later on. Harry S. Truman is commonly brought as an example, though he is not a clear example for me. According to this picture, history is a court of appeals, wherein the verdict of the lower court, the judgment of the present, is bound to be overturned by an appeal to the court of the future. The court of future generations is a secular version of the Last Judgment, but with a twist: reward and punishment have to do with reputation rather than with resurrection.

Josephus held both notions of "history will be the judge." He perceived himself as a prophet, namely, as someone who has direct access to history in the metaphysical sense, believing that he would be vindicated by that kind of history. But he also appealed to future readers of his book in the belief that they would re-member him and approve of him. Oblivion is one sort of harsh historical judgment; infamy is another. According to the court-of-history picture, it is not the historian who is the judge, but rather the future readers of history.

Judges should be impartial. This does not mean that they are necessarily independent of the conventional wisdom of their time and society. Writing critical history is a radical project. The historians should be ready to submit the conventional wisdom of their society to unbending scrutiny. Judges can and usually do retain their conventional conception. The law is habitually con-servative: courts seldom, if ever, question the fundamentals of society. In the adversarial court's picture of history the best fit for the role of the judge is not the historian but the future readers. The historian merely argues before the judge. The historian, especially a national historian, is under pressure from his community to serve as a defense lawyer. His role is to defend "his people." The belief is that the national historian should present his people in the best possible light. The historian in this picture is not necessarily a liar, but he is a lawyer. A lawyer is not allowed to knowingly lie in court, but is entitled to blissful ignorance with respect to the guilt of his client. This is indeed what the historian as defense lawyer is supposed to do too.

In Defense of Your People

There are two kinds of defenses: defense of one's *creed* and defense of one's *people*. Josephus can be viewed as engaged in both. His book *Against Apion* provides a defense of Judaism. His *Antiquities of the Jews* is a defense of the Jewish people. In his great book *The Jewish War* he is in a double bind. He tries to defend the majority of Jews with the claim that the irrational revolt against the Romans was forced on them by a reckless minority of zealots. At the same time he tries to defend their enemy, the Roman Flavian dynasty. It is not easy to reconcile the conflict between the Jews and the Romans. Josephus manages it by putting all the blame for the destruction of Jerusalem squarely on the shoulders of the zealots, a minority among the Jews. He conveniently ignores the broad popular support for the revolt, including his own support in its early stages. He shamefully ignores the brutality of his masters, the Flavians.

In *The Jewish War,* one of the most important books of Jewish history, Josephus asks his readers to excuse him for giving vent to his hostile emotions toward the rebels. Expressing emotions is a deviation from the Greek canon of writing history. But more important, he asks them to forgive him for indulging in lamenting the destruction of his illustrious beloved city, Jerusalem. Lamentation over Jerusalem is strongly associated with Jeremiah. Indeed, the ancient name of the book known in the Jewish tradition under the name of Eikah was the Lamentations of Jeremiah.

The lament for a city is not a biblical invention, but it was most likely Jeremiah whom Josephus had in mind in his lament. We don't know who wrote the biblical Book of Lamentations, but few biblical scholars, if any, believe it was Jeremiah. Yet the tradition of ascribing the book to Jeremiah is just too good to be false, while the tradition mentioned in the Talmud (Bava Batra 15), according to which Jeremiah is also the author of the Books of Kings, is just too bad to be true. It is perhaps this tradition that made Josephus depict biblical prophets as historians who could successfully compete with the best of the Greek historians. By Josephus's account, there was a division of labor in writing Jewish history. Priests were in charge of writing ancient history, while prophets were in charge of writing contemporary history. Jeremiah was both a priest (descended from a deposed priestly family) and a prophet. Josephus too thought of himself as a priest (coming from a distinguished priestly family) and a man with an inspired message, a prophet of sorts. It would not be too far-fetched to ascribe to Josephus the thought that he and Jeremiah were each highly qualified for performing both jobs: writing ancient history as well as writing contemporary history. Be that as it may, Jeremiah is not a historian. For Josephus, it was Thucydides, not Jeremiah, who served as his model for writing. Jeremiah is not a historian, but he is a virtuoso of historical memory (for one thing, Jeremiah single-handedly fixed Rachel in Jewish memory as a sorrowful Mary-like mother of the Jews). The Bible itself is a book of *memory,* not a book of *history.* It is a memory of betrayal.

The prophets of the Bible are not historians; their concern is with idolatry, that is, with betrayal. They campaign against idolatry, a campaign that, according to Jeremiah, began with the exodus: "From the time your forefathers left Egypt until now, day after day, again and again, I sent you my servants and prophets" (Jeremiah 7:25). The kernel of idolatry is forgetfulness and ingratitude; hence, by combating forgetfulness, the prophets combat idolatry. They become, so to speak, the high priests of memory. Jeremiah is probably the best example. His appeal to history is not out of interest in human affairs as such, but for history as a source of obligations to God. Even the Books of Kings, the books that look like history, are in fact solely concerned with idolatry. Kings are judged only by their idolatrous practices: did they or did they not do "right in the eyes of God"? History in the Bible is one-dimensional: a fight against idolatry, which is a fight against betrayal of God.[4] The prophets of the Bible are constantly losing this battle. Idolatry goes on. But being a loser doesn't mean being unworldly. Jeremiah is a shrewd observer of the political scene. He spotted early on—right after the battle of Carchemish (605 or 607 BCE)—the shift in the balance of power in the Fertile Crescent. It was a shift in favor of Nebuchadnezzar's Babylon at the expense of Egypt and Assyria. Jeremiah was acutely aware of the implications of this shift for the future of Jerusalem.

But more important, the reality of power has a religious significance that is strongly tied to idolatry. The fear is that worshiping military and political power and especially a superpower is idolatry. The idea that power politics is idolatry was an ideology that had already found its place in the Bible and survived into Josephus's time. Indeed, Josephus describes a Galilean named Yehuda, a sectarian rabbi who incited the Jews to revolt against the Romans by arguing that it would be a disgrace to pay taxes to the Romans and to accept mortal rulers. God alone should be obeyed as the sole master. The idea was that only the direct rule of God, for which Josephus coined the term "theocracy," was acceptable. Any other kind of rule and ruler was idolatry. We find in the Bible powerful manifestations of this idea. Gideon turned down an offer to be king by famously answering: "I will not rule over you, and neither shall my son rule over you. The Lord shall rule over you" (Judges 8:23).

Jeremiah and Josephus rejected the idea that obeying a foreign ruler and turning Judea into a vassal state was idolatry. Both advocated accepting the yoke of foreign power: Babylon in Jeremiah's case, Rome in Josephus's case. Big powers were agents of God and not independent semi-deities. Resisting the reality of big powers could be an arrogant act of rebellion against God, rather than a religious act of zeal against idolatry.

Jeremiah is not a historian, so what role does he play in the court of history? He is both a prosecutor and a key witness. His charge is idolatry. Not idolatry as subjugation to a superpower, but idolatry as the sin of making something of no value into something of ultimate value. Idolatry means leading an illusory and morally sinful way of life. Forgetting God is the cause of it all. History for him is a set of reminders, and history will end when there is no idolatry and no need for reminders. He envisages the end of history. God will inscribe his presence in our hearts in such a way that forgetting God will no longer be possible. History as a history of idolatry will end by being replaced with an indelible covenant that will not be dependent on remembering favors from the past. This will be the end of the need for historical memory. It will be the end of history—the biblical kind of history.

Jeremiah is not only the prosecutor in the court of history; he is the witness of the destruction of Jerusalem. Rembrandt's celebrated painting of Jeremiah meditating on the destruction of the Temple amid the ruins makes Jeremiah's meditative pose, his head supported by his hand, a downcast expression of the destruction and not the attitude of a reporter.

Josephus, like Jeremiah and like his two great Greek models Thucydides and Polybius, was an eyewitness to the events he described. But unlike Jeremiah, he was not perceived as a moral witness to the destruction.

All three—Josephus, Thucydides, and Polybius—were suspects on account of their disloyalty to their people in time of war. Moreover, all of them were actors and not mere spectators in the events they described. Josephus was a witness from both sides of the war: from the Jewish side as a military commander and from the Roman side as a collaborating prisoner of war. All three viewed history first and foremost as present history and, moreover, as a set of events in which the historian has firsthand experience. This is rather different from the current view that regards present history as journalism and firsthand experience as a requisite for war correspondents. Yet Thucydides and Polybius were wary of accepting eyewitness reports, including their own. They believed that eyewitness reports should be cross-examined and tested by comparison to other reports. In their picture, the historian is a witness in the historical court of law: a trained observer and an expert witness who doesn't take all he sees at face value, but an observer nevertheless.

To be eligible to be a witness was in ancient courts a status. Reliability was closely tied to respectability. Women, for example, were not eligible to serve as witnesses in the biblical and Roman courts of law, or at least so Josephus claims. Being a biblical witness is far removed from being a detached observer. It is to be a warner, an admonisher. Indeed, Jeremiah took it upon himself to warn his people away from what he saw as coming upon them. So did Josephus. Yet Jeremiah, in spite of his defeatism during the siege, acquired in Jewish memory the status of a moral witness to the destruction of Jerusalem, while Josephus is regarded as an expert witness—but by no means a moral witness.[5] There is no moral weight to his testimony. So why is Josephus remembered so utterly differently from Jeremiah? I believe that part of the difference is explained by the different attitudes the two had toward power. Jeremiah is a true prophet in the profound sense of daring to speak truth to power, no matter what. Josephus was co-opted by power, if not corrupted by it. After all, Josephus was an official historian of the Flavian dynasty, tainted by his relation to power, while Jeremiah was willing to risk everything. He was the definitive sufferer. Josephus's relation to power should not disqualify him as a witness, but it does disqualify him as a moral witness, for a moral witness is never in service of the ruling power.

The Case of ben Zakkai

The rabbinic tradition tells the story that Yochanan ben Zakkai, a staunch opponent of the Jewish revolt against the Romans, was smuggled out of Jerusalem under siege in a coffin.[6] Once outside the city walls he was able to extract from the Roman commander, later to become Emperor Vespasian, the city of Yavne with its sages so as to be able to found a Jewish center of learning there. Moreover, he established there the rabbinic high court, the Sanhedrin. Even though ben Zakkai deserted his fellow Jews in the besieged city of Jerusalem and collaborated with the enemy, Vespasian, he was viewed very differently from his co-deserter Josephus. The importance of the rabbinic story is not in its historical accuracy. It isn't and cannot be true as told. It is a story about reevaluation of Jewish life by the rabbinic tradition. Ben Zakkai almost single-handedly shifted the emphasis in Jewish religious life from the centrality of the Temple and its rituals to a text-centered learning tradition.

Ben Zakkai didn't speak in the name of the rabbinic tradition; he created it. Sure enough, it was this tradition that later on vindicated him. But this still doesn't address the difference between ben Zakkai and Josephus. To describe Josephus as an ideological collaborator and ben Zakkai as the opposite is only half true. There was no ideology of the Romans that Josephus accepted. What he did accept from the Romans was a way of life, whereas ben Zakkai helped to shape a countering way of life, namely, the rabbinic way of life. Adopting the way of life of the enemy is a strong signal of a strong identification with the enemy and a blatant sign of alienation from one's "people." In talking about ideological collaborationism we once again see that we should include an "ideology," an adoption of a way of life. The collaborator, in adopting in time of crisis the enemy's way of life, expresses a lack of solidarity with his people. The meaning of the thick relation between an imitator of a style of life and his community is what is put in doubt in the case of Josephus, whereas the meaning of the thick relation between ben Zakkai and his community was never in doubt.

Here is the general point: betrayal and perception of betrayal have to do with *style* as much as they have to do with *content*. For style sends a strong signal of a thick relation, or the lack of it.

8

Apostasy

IDOLATRY IS THE BETRAYAL OF GOD. THE BETRAYAL TAKES the form of "whoring after strange gods." *Apostasy* is predominantly the betrayal of the religious community.

A formative picture used in the Hebrew Bible for elucidating idolatry is the relation between husband and wife: God the husband and Israel the wife. It is the exclusivity of the sexual relation that is metaphorically violated in the worship of strange gods. Idolatry is compared to sexual betrayal: jealous God is compared to a jealous husband, whereas idolatrous Israel is compared to a whoring wife. Indeed, the prophet Hosea was ordered to enact this metaphor. The Lord said to Hosea, "Go, get yourself a wife of whoredom and children of whoredom: for the land hath committed great whoredom, departing from the Lord" (Hosea 1:2). The biblical notion of jealousy in marital relations is what charges the picture of idolatry with power. Jealousy, and in particular the jealousy of God, is taken as a manifestation of his great care. Jealousy is the opposite of indifference. Unfaithfulness is whoring, an extreme violation of a thick relation.

The Israelites' obligation to God is formulated in the Bible not as an obligation in the service of a cause but as a personal obligation based on a kind of historical relation between God and his people. Idolatry is the betrayal of a thick relation with God. Strange gods are strangers; there is no history of relations with "gods who were strangers to them" (Deuteronomy 32:17).

The dialectic of the notion of idolatry as betrayal is a two-way street. We understand the idea of betraying God by having a familiar model of a marital relationship. In the other direction, we understand the idea of betraying a thick relation by making God an object of ultimate value, the only thing that deserves unreserved veneration and loyalty. Faithfulness to God becomes the model for the ultimate thick relation, and betrayal of God becomes the ultimate betrayal.

Humans, not God, are my concern here. Yet there is something important to learn about thick human relationships and their betrayal from the way in which the betrayal of God, idolatry, and the betrayal of religious friendship, apostasy, are accounted for in the religious literature.

Trumping the Family

Abraham, the great believer, was famously told by God to leave his father's house (Genesis 12:1). Even more famously, he was told by God to sacrifice his son Isaac as a burnt offering (Genesis 22:2). In the first case Abraham was ordered to dwell in the land that God would show him. In the other case it was to go to the mountain that God would tell him. In short, these were appeals to sever thick family relations for the sake of God. A relationship with God trumps all thick human relations, including that of a father to his most beloved son.

Jesus recruited his disciples from among the fishermen of the Sea of Galilee. There are three versions of what took place during the recruitment. By one stark account we learn that after recruiting the brothers Peter and Andrew, Jesus saw two more brothers, James and John, sons of Zebedee. They were on a boat with their father, mending nets. Jesus called them, "and they immediately left the boat and their father and followed him" (Matthew 4:22). In Mark's version (1:19–20), the two brothers left the father, but they left him with hired servants, which implies that they did not ruin him economically. In Luke's version the father is not mentioned at all. But the story in Matthew presents the naked choice in its cruelest form: following the call of Jesus means leaving the father to his own devices. The call of Jesus trumps the relation to the father.

Sartre was at a loss to say what trumps what: staying with an ailing mother or joining the resistance and fighting the Nazi occupation. But the sons of Zebedee were not at a loss. The immediacy of their response to the call leads me to believe that the whole point of the story is indeed to highlight the higher, trumping relations with God when earthly relations are in conflict with heavenly ones. This point is made very explicit in Jesus' saying "If a man comes to me and hates not his father and mother and wife and children and brethren and sisters, yea and his own life also, he cannot be my disciple" (Luke 14:26).

There are three ways to present the religious predicament. These three ways highlight secular predicaments as well.

(1) A conflict between concrete relations and abstract creed

(2) A conflict between two kinds of family relations, namely, earthly and heavenly family relations

(3) A conflict over primacy between two kinds of thick
relations, namely, family relations and friendship

One way of reading the story is as a conflict between a concrete
human relation and a great idea: between Zebedee, the flesh-and-
blood father, and belief in God. It is this clash between loyalty to a
cause and loyalty to personal relations that troubled E. M. Forster.
For him, the state rather than God is an embodiment of an abstract cause that calls for a creed. A friend is an embodiment of
concrete personal relations. Forster, like Dante, would set Brutus
in the lowest circle of hell, the place reserved for the worst sinners,
for betraying a friend for the sake of an abstract idea. The friend
is Caesar; the abstract idea is freedom. For Forster the *concrete*
takes precedence over the *abstract*. The proverbial and apocryphal
choice of Aristotle, "Plato is dear to me, but dearer still is the
truth," should, by Forster's account, be regarded as the wrong
choice. Plato is concrete; truth is abstract. And so it is in the choice
between Zebedee, the father, and God. Zebedee is concrete and
God is abstract. For Forster it does not matter whether the creed is
communion with God or with godless communism: both are abstract causes that shouldn't trump personal relations.

It is not easy to draw a distinction between abstract and concrete objects. On some readings of the distinction concrete objects are in space and time and can interact causally with each
other. Abstract objects such as numbers are neither in space nor
in time and cannot interact causally with each other. Abstract
objects are related by logical or conceptual relations. This poses
the obvious question of how we concrete human beings can grasp
abstract objects if they are causally inert. This question alludes
to deep metaphysics and deep epistemology, but not of the kind
that troubled E. M. Forster. He was troubled by the connotations

of the notion of the abstract as lifeless and bloodless, namely, lacking in feeling and vitality, lacking in fullness and richness, devoid of color and texture. For Forster, creed and cause were abstract in that pernicious sense, and hence loyalty to one's concrete friend should always trump creed and cause.

All these may be true in the abstract, but cause and creed stand for relations to concrete human beings who share the cause and uphold the creed. Cause and creed don't have the concreteness of blood and semen, but they may glue together flesh-and-blood human beings. England is not just an abstraction: it includes, as I already mentioned, E. M. Forster's aunt who raised him. Exposing England to the danger of the German Blitz was endangering Forster's concrete aunt and not merely the abstract principles of the Magna Carta.

The second way of thinking about the dilemma of Zebedee's two sons is to regard it as a choice between two families: the family in the flesh and the family in the spirit. In this understanding, there is a clash of loyalties: family relations are indeed the primary thick relations, but relations with the one in heaven should trump any relations on earth. In Christianity, the holy family trumps the earthly family. In Judaism, the heavenly father trumps the earthly father.

For Forster, personal relations are personal in the sense of face-to-face relations. His position, I take it, should hold true not just with respect to the imagined relation with God but to any relation with an imagined human community. The way I understand Forster's account, an abstract idea and an imagined relation cannot trump any personal, strictly face-to-face relation. Even if we think of the state not in terms of an abstract bureaucracy but in terms of an imagined community, we are not much better off, since the two are by his account abstract ideas.

But even the idea of being face-to-face in personal relations can be very tricky indeed—for example, facing one who has lost her mind.

Here a digression is in place. The philosopher Felicia Ackerman wrote a letter to the *New York Times* on December 26, 2001: "John Bayley admits that his wife, Ms. Murdoch, 'was extremely secretive.' But he justifies his cooperation with her biographers, saying, 'It was only after she was very ill, and after she died, that we thought that she wouldn't mind at all.' By that reasoning one can justify any betrayal of a dead or demented loved one. Does Mr. Bayley really think betrayal is acceptable provided that the betrayed can never find out about it?"

This letter raises very serious concerns with regard to betrayal. And in reference to the counterfactual on which Bayley rests his case, "she wouldn't mind at all," it should be understood that in the time that Iris Murdoch had a mind, she wouldn't have minded what might happen to her secrets once she lost her mind. This is rather intriguing since, as Ackerman points out, betrayal has very little to do with what the betrayed knows. An act of betrayal does not come to be such only when it is exposed and known to the betrayed. So why should it matter whether Murdoch has a mind that enables her to know? Face-to-face relations in the case of betrayal should not necessarily be relations confined to those who retain their faculties intact; they may even include relations to the dead, as, for example, in the case of ignoring a last important wish of the deceased.

The third way for Zebedee's sons to think about their predicament is to replace the family tie with a tie to a circle of friends. Indeed, this is the predicament that Jesus himself faced and resolved in a rather ruthless way. Jesus is standing with his disciples. His family is standing outside and would like to talk to him. Someone tells Jesus that his mother and brothers are waiting, wanting to talk to him. But here is Jesus' astounding retort: "Who is my mother? And who are my brethren? And he stretched forth his hand toward his disciples and said: Behold my mother and my brethren!" (Matthew 12:48). The controlling metaphor for thick relations is still family relations, and so the disciples are referred to as brothers. But the scene is such that Jesus' circle of friends is presented as a *surrogate* family. Friendship creates thick relations with a sort of surrogate family that is more meaningful than the original family.

The sons of Zebedee followed Jesus immediately. But Jesus addressed others. "Follow me," he said to one. But the response was different: "Let me first go and bury my father." To which Jesus responded, "Let the dead bury their dead" (Luke 9:59). The point he is making is that only forward-looking relations are compatible with the idea of establishing the kingdom of God. Familial relations are a paradigm of backward-looking relations. Those who are looking back do not fit in the kingdom of God (Luke 9:62). A comparable idea can be found in the most atheistic of movements. You can find it in Lenin's hope that the proletariat in Europe would cut their national, backward-looking, "reactionary" ties and join the war in the name of a new working-class solidarity and a future socialist kingdom come.

The Betrayal of Judas

Before we move too fast from Jesus' class of friends to the working class, let me tell you where all this is leading. It is leading to the paradigmatic story of betrayal, the betrayal of Judas. My claim is that familial relations provide the model that dominates the Hebrew Bible for thick relations. It is indeed replete with stories of betrayal in the family. Jacob cheats his twin brother out of his entitlement to be blessed by their father. And his sons sell their hated brother, Joseph, into slavery, thereby betraying Jacob in turn. David's family is in general a mess. It is a perfidious family indeed. But still, thick relations are first and foremost family relations. For Jesus' core circle of friends and disciples, an alternative model of thick relations is taking center stage: the model of friendship. I suggest viewing the betrayal of Judas within the frame of friendship, albeit friendship of an extraordinary kind.

Before we proceed with the betrayal of Judas we should address an act that is akin to betrayal: let us return to Peter's denial of Jesus. This story too should be set in the frame of friendship. The flesh is weak: even the truest of the disciples, the rock on which the church was founded, was incapable of being loyal enough. Peter was utterly confident that he would remain loyal to the master even if the rest of the disciples should fail. But we know all too well Jesus' answer to Peter's pledge of loyalty: "That this night, before the cock crows, thou shalt deny me thrice" (Matthew 26:34).

Denial is not betrayal in the strong sense of giving one up, through treachery, into the power of one's enemy. It is betrayal in the sense of disappointing an expectation of loyalty. To deny is to avoid an acknowledgment of belonging, to fail to show solidarity when solidarity is needed. It is abandonment by denying moral allegiance. Peter denied that he recognized Jesus and that he was one of the disciples who had been with Jesus. But whatever Peter's denial comes down to, it does not fall under the description of "one of you will betray me" (Matthew 26:17), which is reserved for the betrayal by Judas, the one who handed Jesus over to the enemy.

The question to ask about the story of the betrayal of Judas is "What is it in this story that impresses us as so deep and sinister?" For Wittgenstein, understanding what is deep and sinister in this kind of story is the essential part of what it is to understand the story, rather than the historical question about its origin. There are historical questions of great interest, such as whether the name Iscariot refers to the party of assassins among the Jewish Zealots known as the Sicarii (dagger men). But the answer to such a questions doesn't contribute to our understanding of the significance of the story.

One element that lends itself to the sinister character of Judas's betrayal is the kiss—more so, I would say, than the dipping of his fingers in the communal meal and then betraying those with whom he shared the meal. The kiss calls for proximity; it is a sign of supreme trust. Betrayal is a violation of thick trust. It is graphically depicted in Judas's story by turning the kiss from a sign of goodwill into a sign meant to identify Jesus and deliver him into the hands of the enemy: "And he that betrayed him had given them a token, saying, 'Whomsoever I shall kiss that same is he; take him, and lead him away safely.' And as soon as he was come, he goeth straightway to him and saith, 'Master, master!' and kissed him" (Mark 14:45–46). But Judas's sinister kiss of betrayal cannot lie just in the action.

In the Hebrew Bible there is a glaring example of kiss and kill that does not make the impression on us that Judas's kiss does; to understand the difference is to understand the significance of Judas's kiss. "And Joab said to Amasa, 'Art thou in health, my brother?' And Joab took Amasa by the beard with the right hand to kiss him. But Amasa took no heed to the sword that was in Joab's hand: so he smote him therewith in the fifth rib and shed out his bowels to the ground, and struck him not again and he died" (2 Samuel 20:9–10). This is a bloody story of gutting while kissing. Why is it that no one talks about the kiss of Joab but everyone talks about the kiss of Judas?

In the case of Joab and Amasa the relations are very much like Mafia relations. Amasa and Abner, members of the gang of King Saul, switch sides to King David's gang, to the chagrin of old loyalists such as Joab. The kiss of Joab is a ritualistic kiss, not a hug between intimates, as Giotto so wonderfully depicts in the case of Judas. True, the kiss of Judas is depicted by no less able a painter and Bible reader than Albrecht Dürer as a kiss of a vampire, but the force of the story is in the way Giotto understands it, namely, as a kiss given against the backdrop of assumed friendship. The treachery of the kiss is in the meaning of the kiss. The overt meaning is a kiss between two dear friends and not a kiss between two mobsters, while the covert meaning is a disciple handing his master over to the enemy.

These two elements—deceit and handing Jesus over to the enemy—are very prominent in Judas's story. By Judas's story I mean the overall impression formed by the various versions of the story. But then there is a third element, a motive that makes Judas an emblem of betrayal. It is money, the "thirty silver coins." I have already mentioned that betrayal for money constitutes the clearest form of betrayal in that it removes any ambiguity from it. Doing it for money is never considered a justification of betrayal, though it sometimes provides a good explanation. (In the case of Judas we don't know whether the thirty silver pieces amount to a "princely sum," as is said in Zechariah 11:13, or whether it is a meager sum, the sum paid as compensation for the death of a slave, as in Exodus 21:32.)

John's Gospel describes Judas as greedy and hypocritical. When Mary Magdalene uses a very costly perfume to anoint the feet of Jesus, it is Judas who raises the question of why this ointment is not sold and the money given to the poor (12:5). Good question. But not when the question comes from the one who, when he was entrusted with the money of Jesus' group, stole it. Such, in any case, is John's embellishment of embezzlement to Judas's story. To sum it up, the elements of the story are a base motive (money), a deceitful violation of faith (the kiss), and the handing over of a friend to the enemy. All are pronounced features of the story and pronounced features of betrayal. But the sinister impression of the story is not confined to these elements. It depends on one crucial element, the nature of the victim: "Judas, betrayest thou the Son of man with a kiss?" (Luke 22:48).

It is Jesus as the son of man, not as the son of God, whom Judas is perceived as betraying. Jesus is the perfectly good man, and in his role as a human being he is both a teacher and a friend. My claim is that Judas's betrayal is the betrayal of the ultimate friend. And that it was Jesus himself who understood the relations within his group as a model for thick human relations in general based on friendship: "This is my commandment, that ye love one another as I love you. Greater love hath no man than this, that a man lay down his life for his friends" (John 15:12–13). In the very act by which Judas hands Jesus over to the enemies, Jesus addresses him, "Friend, wherefore art thou come?" (Matthew 26:47). Thus Judas's betrayal, by my account, is first and foremost a betrayal of a beautiful friendship.

The saying "God gives us our relatives, but thank God we choose our friends" harps on the idea that we choose our friends, but our relatives are forced upon us. We are free to choose our friends and we are free to betray them. We are not free to choose our siblings, yet we are free to betray them—metaphysically free, not morally free. I have already mentioned the fishermen's immediate response to the call of Jesus. The immediacy of their response gives the impression that they respond out of some kind of necessity, as if they were saying, We shall follow you. We cannot do otherwise. This strong sense of "we cannot do otherwise" is of course not the metaphysical sense of necessity. It is not even psychological necessity in the sense in which compulsion is. It is psychological necessity in the sense of inescapable mission and submission, with no sense of choice: all alternatives do not seem like real options of life.

The story of how the friendship in Jesus' circle was formed gives the impression that the disciples established their friendship with a sense of burning necessity. But if the friendship was founded on such necessity, Peter's denials, let alone the betrayal by Judas, should have been ruled out as options of life, at least for this group of friends. And although Judas's betrayal is the paradigmatic betrayal motivated by the basest of motives—money—the feeling is that Judas's act of betrayal (as well as Peter's act of denial) is conceived not as a free act but rather as an instrument for fulfilling an ominous prophecy.

It is interesting to note that two people who were very much involved in a case of the alleged betrayal by Dreyfus, Charles Peguy and Bernard Lazare, addressed the issue of Judas's betrayal. The first was a romantic Catholic and the second was a romantic Jew, both with a keen interest in the fate of the damned. They saw Judas as a man who had deliberately chosen his mission of being damned in order to fulfill a fateful prophecy. So it is a free choice to become a betrayer, but only if the cause is to make divine prophecy come true.[1]

In the popular imagination, Judas's betrayal is not confined to the betrayal of just one man; it was also the betrayal of the other eleven friends as well, "the team," if you like. The sports section of the *Independent on Sunday* on November 18, 2001, has a photo of Spurs (Tottenham) fans holding posters with one word: "Judas." The Judas is Sol Campbell, who defected to archrival Arsenal. On his first return to White Hart Lane (the Spurs stadium) with his new and hated club, cries of "Judas" could be heard. For some years Campbell was like the club's famous emblem of the rooster, the symbol of the Spurs. But then he switched to a club that was willing to offer him more money and a better chance to play in prestigious games in Europe. These are legitimate ends for any professional footballer. This was clear even to the Spurs fans. Yet the sense of betrayal comes from the fact that the fans of a football team believe that they are in thick relations with the team. A mere commercial contract between a player and a team does not express the bond that the fans feel with a particular team. They are caught between two models of relations that they do not know how to reconcile. On the one hand, they regard a professional player as someone who is entitled to pursue his own interests, say, money and professional ambition. And so they assume thin relations between the player and the club. On the other hand, they believe that the relations with the team should be very thick indeed and the players should feel thick relations with the team and with the fans as much as the fans feel them. To be a fan is to take the rough with the smooth, and the rough—a losing streak, for example—can be hard to take. Read the marvelous account of what it takes to be a fan in Nick Hornby's *Fever Pitch* (ironically, he is a fan of the club to which Campbell defected), and you can see how thick such relations are, at least from the fans' perspective.[2] No wonder that they expressed their sense of having been betrayed by invoking the metaphor of Judas.

Sol Campbell is black. I don't know how much of the fans' anger at him was fueled by the idea that he should be under a special obligation to be grateful for the chance the club gave him to advance in life. It is conceivable that being black in the case of Campbell intensified the sense of betrayal in the same way in which the phonetic association between "Judas" and "Jew" may have intensified Judas's betrayal.

What does the story of Judas's betrayal come down to? Judas is not by any means an ordinary apostate, namely, someone who abandoned his religious faith. In my understanding of the story, there is a shift in the paradigm of thick relations from family to friendship. Judas's betrayal is not a betrayal for a cause but a Forsterian betrayal of a friendship. In claiming that there is a shift from family to friends, what I mean is a shift from regarding family relations as the best of human relations to treating them as merely second-best: a group of friends is better, especially when judged by its comparative advantages in serving God. Since most ordinary people cannot live up to the ideal best that comprises a life of total dedication to God amid friends (such as we find exemplified in monastic life), they should pursue the second-best goal of leading a wholesome family life.

True, the family metaphor for thick relations is just too powerful to give up, and the group of friends is addressed as brothers, but with the idea that the circle of friends is the true surrogate family.

The shift from family to friends is a shift in the notion of ultimate betrayal. It consists of betraying friendships formed in the service of God. That is the apostasy of Judas.

Not only Jesus had friends. As I already mentioned, Job had friends too. Job believes that his friends betrayed him: "My brothers betrayed me like a torrent, / Like the watercourse of the torrents that run dry" (Job 6:15). By "brothers" he refers to his friends. The verb he uses is *bagdu,* which literally means "they betrayed." The question is, what does the betrayal of his friends consist of? They took the side of God and denounced Job in the name of a conventional justification of God's justice. But what does this have to do with betrayal? It is not quite clear what the friends of Job are accused of. Are they accused of being smug and insincere in uttering their boringly conventional piety while speaking on God's behalf? Or are they sincere but accused of being wrong in understanding God's will?

I tend to opt for insincerity rather than misunderstanding. The point of God's answer to Job's protest is to let Job know that he did not get it right either, the "it" being divine justice. But at least Job was sincere. One necessary condition in forming a surrogate family of friends is *sincerity.* Betrayal among friends is *insincerity.*

The Apostasy of Brother Daniel

The amazing story of Oswald Rufeisen, a Jew who became a Carmelite monk, has more direct relation to the standard understanding of apostasy than the case of Judas. He was a Second World War hero who showed incredible courage in saving fellow Jews while serving in Nazi police uniform. In short, he was an apostate who remained loyal to his former religious community, an oxymoron worth understanding.

The story of Rufeisen, better known in Israel as Brother Daniel or Father Daniel (depending on whether he is taken as a monk or a priest), is strikingly told by Nechama Tec.[3] Rufeisen fled with his brother Arieh from the advancing Nazi army in Poland. He was caught and escaped, twice, before ending up in the small Belarusian town of Mir, known in Jewish history for its famous yeshiva (a school of high rabbinic learning). Being fluent in German, he posed as a Pole of German extraction and became an interpreter to the Nazi police officer in charge of Mir. He was trusted and liked by his superior and had a good chance of surviving the war under his German cover. But he decided to help his fellow Jews.

He smuggled arms to the underground, helped release Jews who had been arrested, and provided useful information about the various plans of extermination. He took daily risks. Rufeisen was exposed and placed under arrest by his German commander, who had treated him well and felt bitterly betrayed by him. Rufeisen escaped from prison and sought refuge at a nearby convent. He was taken in by the nuns and, while staying with them, underwent a religious conversion and received baptism. By his account he tried to make sense of the plight of the Jews and started viewing the Jews as Christ among the nations: the way Jesus suffered for humanity, the Jews were suffering for the nations. This made him view himself as a Christian Jew. When it became dangerous for him to remain at the convent, and in order to make the point that he had converted not to secure shelter but out of true conviction, he fled to the forests to join the partisans. There was tremendous risk involved in his escape, but he survived.

At the end of the war he joined the Carmelite order and, regarding himself as a Zionist, asked his superior in the church if he could be stationed in Israel. His brother and his family already lived there. While in Israel he appealed to the Israeli authorities to become a citizen under the Law of Return, which grants every Jew who wishes to settle in Israel the right of automatic citizenship. His case was brought to the Supreme Court of Israel, which had to decide whether an apostate is a Jew. They decided against him. Curiously, the court, in giving its criterion for who is a Jew, reverted to what "an ordinary simple Jew" thinks about who is a Jew. And, on behalf of the simple Jew, the court ruled that an apostate is not a Jew. What is curious about this ruling is that it is not the dominant view in Jewish rabbinic law, which holds that "though he is a sinner, he is still an Israelite." There is no question that among ordinary Jews, someone who becomes an apostate, without being coerced to do so, is a betrayer, not just of the faith but of the Jewish people.

In the Jewish imagination before it was dimmed by secularism, for a Jew to wear the garb of a Catholic monk was a real horror. Yet Brother Daniel's case is very confusing indeed. He passed the ultimate test of loyalty to his people. None of his friends and family disavowed him. On the contrary, they remained fiercely loyal to him; they might even have sensed a quality of saintliness in him. Yet they believed that he had betrayed the faith that many of them, being secular Jews, did not observe. They actually found it easier to understand Gustav Mahler's conversion in order to become a conductor in Vienna than to understand the conversion of Brother Daniel.

Let me repeat the point I have already made with regard to the ideological betrayer: converting out of sincere conviction is more of a betrayal of the faith than doing it for money or status or career is. It involves conferring moral worth on the adopted faith. This is the dialectic of betrayal. Betraying family, friends, or the nation for money is, on the one hand, the clearest, most unambiguous case of betrayal. Betraying a faith, a creed, out of conviction is, on the other hand, worse than doing it for money.

The Two Projects

In my book *The Ethics of Memory* I made a distinction between two projects that, for lack of better terms, I called the Jewish project and the Christian project.[4] The Jewish project keeps the two-tiered distinction between ethics and morality, between what you owe to your own people and what you owe to humanity and human beings in general. Only at the End of Days does the distinction become blurred and ethics prevail. The Christian project is committed to creating a universal community of the faithful guided by the ethics of thick relations (by love). Jesus and his disciples should be viewed as a model for a community of the faithful that supersedes conventional thick relations, and even the thickest of all relations, family relations.

But the community of the faithful around Jesus is indeed a community based on shared faith. It is faith that serves as antecedent to the forging of friendship and not friendship that happens to have a shared belief. Apostasy, being a rejection of the belief of the faithful, which is the bond of the friendship, dissolves and betrays the human friendship and forfeits the allegiance to God. Faith and friendship on this model are so inextricably intertwined that rejecting the faith is betraying the friendship.

In the case of Judas, it is not clear what belief he betrayed. Is he the carnal Jew who preferred worldly joy, symbolized by money, to the life of the spirit advocated by the one whom he betrayed? Betraying Jesus and betraying the faith are in this picture one and the same thing.

It is against this background of making friendship conditional on a shared committed belief in a cause that I understand E. M. Forster's proclamation "I hate the idea of causes." He laments that personal relations without a cause are regarded as "bourgeois luxuries, as products of a time of fair weather," as something that we cannot afford, the world being the way it is. Friendship trumps faith, according to Forster. That faith trumps friendship is, I believe, the belief of the New Testament.

The dilemma between family and friends in creed may be ascribed to Islam as much as to Christianity. The idea is that the *umma*—the universal Islamic body politic—supersedes all former family, clannish, and tribal allegiances. In the Quran, the sura Al-Mujadilah (The Debate) 58.22 says: "Thou wilt not find folk who believe in Allah and the Last Day loving those who oppose Allah and His messenger, even though they may be their fathers or their sons or their brethren or their clan."

The clash in Islam is between the ideal of a community of faith and tribal solidarity *(asabiyya)*. The model for the Islamic community is the community around the Prophet and his companions *(shababah)*, which includes not just the Prophet's family but also his friends. The category of the companions includes all who stood in face-to-face relations with the Prophet, were free from lying, and died as Muslims.

The case of Brother Daniel severs the Gordian knot between faith and community perceived as extended family. Unlike other converts, he remained extremely loyal to his family, friends, and people. The problem that he poses is whether the Jews are a community of faith or whether they are predominantly a community of thick relations and shared history that happens to have a shared faith but is not constituted by the faith.

Let me explain. We associate the Stradivari family with its top-notch violins. That is what the family is known for. But the identity of the Stradivari family is not dependent on its producing Strads. Its sons and daughter could have picked up other professions and still belonged to the family. The Jewish people's relation to the Jewish faith, in this view, is like that of the Stradivari family to its violins.

Brother Daniel raised the question for the Jews of whether he was their "brother" in virtue of his family or the "other" in virtue of his new faith. Most modern Jews lost their faith without for a moment losing their sense of being Jews. They are like the Stradivari family members who stopped producing string instruments but did not stop being Stradivari. Some people in the family might have thought that those who did not enter the family business betrayed the family heritage. But even they, I suppose, did not reach the point of expelling the renegades from the family. In this view, thick community relations among Jews are not predicated on creed. But if that is the case, why did the predominantly secular Supreme Court of Israel decide not to recognize Brother Daniel as a Jew? I believe that it is mainly because becoming a Catholic monk has among Jews the association of selling out to a historical enemy of the Jewish people. For Brother Daniel to wear the Carmelite frock is at least as bad as Sol Campbell wearing the Arsenal uniform.

To repeat, the notion of betrayal makes *full* sense only in the context of thick relations. The paradigms that shape our notion of thick relations are family and friends. I tried to argue that the Jewish paradigm is family and the Christian paradigm is friendship. Family implies unconditional belonging. Friendship based on faith is conditional on faith: no faith, no friendship.

The Jewish story as it relates to the confusing case of Brother
Daniel is more complicated than viewing it as a mere family
business. The rabbinic definition of a Jew is anyone who was born
to a mother who is a Jew. (There is an added clause of becoming
a Jew by conversion, but let us leave it aside.) The definition looks
circular. It defines a Jew by using a Jew in the very definition. But
it is a perfectly good definition—this type is used extensively in
arithmetic and is called a recursive definition. A Jew is anyone
who was born to a mother who is a Jew, who in turn was born to
a mother who is a Jew, and so on. We go back until we get to the
first woman who is postulated to be a Jew without her mother
being a Jew. Now, who is this Ur-mother of the Jews? By the
popular account it is Sarah, "our mother," as she is called, the
wife of the founder of the faith. This is based on an unconditional
everlasting covenant, according to which God promised Abraham
"to be God to you and to your descendants after you" (Genesis
17:7). The other candidates are the mothers who attended the covenant on Mount Sinai, which is a conditional covenant: you are a
member of the Jewish people if you fulfill God's commandments.
But what if you renounce the commandments, as is clearly the
case with an apostate? The conditional covenant at Sinai makes it
sound as if creed, or at least the commandments, were built into
the identity of the Jews. It is not just family ties but also creed that
define who is a Jew.

The last caveat points out how things are more complicated for
Jews with respect to the relation between creed and belonging, but
it also introduces a new element to our discussion on betrayal: the
idea of the covenant. The covenant is not a mere contract but a
sanctified contract confirmed by an oath, sacrifice, or other ritualistic gestures. And the way the covenant between God and his

people is formulated in the Bible is similar to the way that was used by kings in the ancient Near East. It starts with the history of the relations between the parties to the covenant and ends with promises if the covenant is obeyed and terrible threats if it is not.

With the covenant we are back to what we referred to as feudal relations. God is not just the father who trumps all other relations and obligations; he is the king and the father in the double role of ultimate father and ultimate king. Betrayal of God is a double betrayal. I have already stressed the point that feudal relations, especially those that are codified by an oath of loyalty and protection between suzerain and vassal, are very susceptible to the fear of betrayal. Feudal relations are ritualistically presented as very thick relations, the betrayal of which is a real horror. This horror is epitomized in betraying the fusion of king and father. What the king adds to the father is the demand for undivided loyalty to one's sovereign.

The main challenge to anyone who believes in the project of ethics, and in the importance and viability of the notion of betrayal, is to disentangle the notion of betrayal from its feudal underpinnings. Having a grasp on apostasy and idolatry is a good start for grasping the feudal-religious underpinnings of betrayal.

9

Class Betrayal

I REMEMBER THE DAY. IT WAS JUNE 18, 1970, THE DAY OF THE United Kingdom's general election. I was standing at a desolate bus stop in Oxford, on my way to friends with a TV set to watch the World Cup. A ruddy-faced toff Tory arrived, sporting a top hat and a beaming carnation.

He had an aura of Merry England, and he ingratiated himself in a friendly manner. I made it clear to him that he should not waste his limited canvassing time on me, since I was a foreigner who was not entitled to vote. "Well," he said disarmingly, "since I have nothing better to do, let me ask you: if you had a chance to vote, how would you vote?"

"Labour," I said, adding, "Of course."

He stared at me, genuinely puzzled, and said, "But why would you betray your class?"

I was stung and stunned. I had been raised in the labor movement, believing that I belonged to the working class. We sang solidarity songs in our Hebrew labor movement school at the time this Tory was going around the mulberry bush, and to betray our class meant to be a scab, to be a knobstick, to cross the picket line. And here I was being confronted by a man who assumed that anyone associated with the Oxford gown rather than with Oxford the town belonged to *his* class.

No one believed on that day that Edward Heath and the Tories would win the election, least of all the canvasser. But since he was so nice and, in spite of his aura, he looked so vulnerable, I tried to cheer him up. "Well, you may still win," I said without conviction. "Look, a few days ago I was watching the soccer match between England and Germany in a local pub. England was leading 2–0 but cruelly lost to Germany in the last minutes. The working-class kids were so down in the mouth that they won't have the energy to vote, and you may win." Little did I suspect that something else was brewing in my working class.

Working-class people in great numbers voted the Tories into power on that day. They were responding, belatedly, not to England's soccer defeat but to Enoch Powell's "Rivers of Blood" speech on the dangers to Britain of immigration. Powell echoed the Sibyl's words in the *Aeneid*: "I see wars, terrible wars, and the Tiber foaming with blood."[1] Millions of working-class people saw blood and were so bloody angry at their Labour government's liberal immigration policy that they voted for the Tories. I felt that Powell's Labourites, like Le Pen's socialists later in France, betrayed their class in not showing solidarity with the immigrants. But Powell ex-Labourites, like Le Pen ex-socialists, had a very different perception. They felt that the traditional parties of the working class had betrayed *them* by not defending them from the immigrants, with whom they hadn't felt the slightest sense of solidarity.

Betraying from Above and from Below

One can betray his class from *above* by being above and siding with the lower classes, or one can betray one's class from *below* by being below and siding with the upper classes. In assuming that I had decided to side with a class that was lower than the one I belonged to, the canvasser in Oxford accused me of betraying my class from above. He didn't specify what my betrayal consisted of, but I guess that what he meant was that I was betraying my personal interests in trusting a party of a lower class. By his account, I would pay more income tax with Labour in power than people like me would pay under the Tories. He most likely thought that I was betraying my personal best interests. The way I understood him was that he questioned my rationality, not my morality.

But he might have meant something else: betrayal from above means undermining the legitimate claim of the upper class to govern. The upper classes perceive themselves as the natural rulers, born to govern, free of the fickle nature of the multitude. They stand for continuity (often called "heritage"), stability, long experience; in short, they stand for tradition, the tested wisdom of generations.

In their view, the lower classes—the masses, the mob, not to say the chavs—are inherently unsuited to govern, guided as they are by irresponsible demagogues and contemptible populists. There is no safety in numbers, only recklessness. Cato, rightly, hurled this accusation against Catiline; Edmund Burke, wrongly, hurled it against Mirabeau and Sieyès; and many Boston Brahmins treated Franklin Delano Roosevelt in the same manner. *Traitor to His Class* is indeed the title of a recent biography of FDR.[2] It means betraying one's class from above, eroding its claim to rule, by joining forces with "the common people." Even Kim Philby, the archtraitor of Britain in the twentieth century, is perceived by some as having betrayed his class, who trusted him with the most classified secrets of the realm, more than as having betrayed his nation.

I am interested in the idea of betraying one's class from below, namely, betraying working-class solidarity. The question I am interested in is: What does one betray, if anything, by not siding with the working class? The idea I am about to examine is that working-class solidarity is an *enabling condition* for bringing about a just society. Therefore, betraying working-class solidarity is betraying the cause of justice. Justice stands for a particular form of human relations: the right form. Therefore, betraying the cause of justice is betraying human relations rather than betraying an abstract idea.

There are two famous stories about Zhou Enlai. One story has it that the uncouth Nikita Khrushchev, who envied Zhou's worldliness, tried to snub him by saying, "It's interesting, isn't it? I'm of working-class origin, while you were born to a family of landlords." To which Zhou's quick retort was, "Yes, and we each betrayed our class." The other is that when Zhou was asked whether the French Revolution was a good thing, he famously answered, "It is too early to tell."

I would like to combine these stories by looking at betrayal and justice in the light of the French Revolution.

Back to the Revolutionary Triangle

The starting point of this book was the triangle of *liberté, égalité, fraternité.* I stated that the revolutionary triangle set the agenda for much of the political thinking since the revolution. I complained, however, that a great deal of effort in political thought is devoted to explaining the twin notions of liberty and equality, and that the neglected side of the revolutionary triangle is the side of fraternity, or, in the workers' language, solidarity. "Fraternity" is a much more elusive term than either "liberty" or "equality." Fraternity as a brotherly attitude toward people who are not literally brothers strikes many as a metaphorical term that cannot be couched in literal terms.

There is, however, something else that deters thinkers from dealing with fraternity: the fact that it smacks of moral kitsch. Kitsch attracts activists and propagandists, but it deters serious thinking. Kitsch, in my eyes, is not just an expression of bad taste. It is a term that should be applied to morality as well as art. Sentimentality is what is wrong with kitsch. But what is wrong with sentimentality? The answer is that it distorts reality to enable us to indulge our feelings. Talking about strangers as brothers is such a distortion. Making the Other (with a capital O) the definitive brother is kitsch.

To indulge in "brotherly love" is not to be in love with strangers. It is to be in love with our phony love of strangers. It is a second-order emotion, an emotion toward another real or affected emotion.

Kitsch solidarity, as expressed in the old leftist "smiling brotherhood" marches toward the blissful future, was quite annoying. However, it had one crucial advantage over the culture of victimhood that replaced it: the workers were not passive victims but active creators of human civilization. Solidarity is an expression of pride and not of simple misery.

Ralph Chaplin in his touching "Solidarity Forever" says it all:

> It is we who plowed the prairies; built the cities
>   where they trade;
> Dug the mines and built the workshops, endless miles
>   of railroad laid;
> Now we stand outcast and starving midst the wonders
>   we have made;
> But the union makes us strong.[3]

Fraternity: A Family Business

"Fraternity," like the French *fraternité,* is rooted in *frater* (brother) and *fraternus* (brotherly). It evokes a metaphor of family relations: relations between brothers. The revolutionary idea of *fraternité* was meant to be extended to all humans so as to view humanity as an extended family: the family of man. Relations between brothers are basically horizontal relations: relations between equals. Revolutionary fraternity is in competition with another political family metaphor: paternalism, which is the government of a father over his children. It is a thoroughly vertical relation of authority and hierarchy. "Paternalism" is a relatively new term, coined in the second half of the nineteenth century, but viewing the king as father and his subjects as children has been with us from time immemorial. Paternalism is based on the idea that the ruler, the metaphorical father, knows what is good for his subjects, his metaphorical children, better than they do. Fraternity differs from paternalism and in a way is a rejection of paternalism. "We," the metaphorical brothers, will help you as long as you are loyal to the family.

Solidarity does not invoke and does not connote family relations. Its etymology is quite different, and if we trace it to its Roman root, it has to do with the joint debt of a group whose members are liable for themselves and each other *(in solidum)*. Fraternity and solidarity are in the grip of two different pictures: fraternity is modeled on family relations, solidarity on a strong partnership with joint and several liability for a debt.

Nationalism is in the grip of the family picture. It makes us think about the nation in terms of an extended family: lineal descent from common ancestors. Class solidarity is not conceived in family terms. When it matters, I shall use "fraternity" for national solidarity and reserve "solidarity" for what is predominantly class solidarity.

Let me hasten to add that the secular left has no monopoly on the use of the term "solidarity." The term has an extensive use in Catholic writings, including conservative Catholic writings. A society, by the Catholic account, is in solidarity to the extent that its members view their mutual dependence on each other as being derived from their dependence on God. It is no wonder that the famous movement in Poland that helped to bring down communism was called Solidarność, for it catered to both types of audience, Catholic and communist (or rather, ex-communist).

Class and Nation

Nationalism is a huge exercise in matching a nation (ethnic group) to a territory to create a state. This exercise is fraught with a familiar problem: usually there is more than one nation (that is, "people") inhabiting a given territory, and thus the nation-state's cohesiveness seems to be threatened by a plurality of nations in a given territory. Another threat to the nation-state is class division and with it class conflict. When there is overlap between a class and an ethnic group that doesn't belong to the dominant ethnic group of the nation-state, the class becomes more akin to a caste.

I am interested in the tension between the demand for solidarity with the class and the demand for fraternity with the nation. Betraying one's class and betraying one's nation are very much in line with my concern. Though cohesiveness is a concern of every society struggling to stay a society, I am interested here in only two types of society: the class and the nation, each embedded in a state.

Historically, two ideologies competed for primacy of loyalty and solidarity: nationalism, with "nation first" its mild form and "nation only" its extreme form, and socialism, with "working class first" its mild form and "working class only" its extreme form. Social democrats, under tremendous strain, were eager to keep both loyalties: to the nation and to the class. We shall later see at what price.

Liberals glued society by means of the social contract: a contract between rational, self-interested individuals. The question for the liberals was and still is whether the contract is good enough to hold society together—is it enough of a glue? The "lawyerly" contract seems lacking in the kind of emotional potency that would make members of a society willing to make the kind of sacrifices sometimes needed to shield their society.

Solidarity: Fate and Destiny

In a famous Jewish homiletic book, *Kol Dodi Dofek,* Joseph Soloveitchik makes a useful distinction between two modes of existence: *fate* and *destiny.*[4] Fate is an inert mode of human existence in which an individual or a group is a passive object affected by outside forces—usually adverse ones. Destiny is an active mode of human existence in which an individual or a group tries to shape its life in the face of forces acting on it. Destiny has the meaning of calling or vocation, in contrast to the fatalism of fate. Fate is thrust on the individual or the group; destiny involves choice. Based on this distinction, Soloveitchik introduces two types of sacramental covenants: the covenant of fate, based on shared suffering, and the covenant of destiny, based on a common calling.

I shall not here go into his theology and the meaning of these two types of covenants in Jewish life. What I would like to do is discuss fate and destiny as two elements in solidarity relations.

Solidarity is a necessary condition for turning a covenant of fate into a covenant of destiny. By fate I mean common misfortune. Instead of two covenants, we may talk of two solidarities: solidarity of fate and solidarity of destiny. Solidarity of fate tends to stress victimhood and belongs very much to the culture of victimization; solidarity of destiny tends to be based on responsibility as a historical agent and on pride.

Solidarity of fate consists of allegiance to those who share the common fate. Solidarity of destiny consists of allegiance to a common cause. In the case of solidarity of destiny, it seems as if human relations are bedimmed and the allegiance seems to be an allegiance to a cause. But the cause only helps in forming solidarity: solidarity is predominantly a relation between human beings.

Fate and destiny form two different orientations in time: fate is oriented toward the past, destiny toward the future. Solidarity of fate creates a community of memory, whereas solidarity of destiny creates movement and collective action. When fate and destiny are united and solidarity is a combined force of memory and action, solidarity is in full force.

Solidarity, be it solidarity of fate or of destiny, covers a whole gamut of human emotions. It may begin with mild sympathy, then move to thoroughly intense sympathy involved with moral support, and end with total alignment with a group, which includes readiness for personal sacrifice for the sake of solidifying the relationships in the group.

But solidarity is more than a heap of emotions; it is an entire life stance toward people and ideals.

Solidarity with the Sufferers

The Bible gives us a very telling story about solidarity; it has to do with Moses' first act as an adult.

"One day after Moses was grown up, he went out to his kinsmen and observed their labors. When he saw an Egyptian strike one of his fellow Hebrews, he looked this way and that, and, seeing no one about, he struck the Egyptian down and hid his body in the sand" (Exodus 2:11–12).

Bible commentators throughout the ages have wondered about the nature of Moses' act. What was his justification for killing someone, without trial, for merely hitting someone else? This is one worry. Another worry has to do with the nature of the solidarity that Moses showed in his act. The idea is that, having being raised in the Egyptian court as an Egyptian prince, Moses could easily have sided with the oppressors, but instead he opted to stand with the oppressed. Did he stand by the oppressed out of a sense of justice, because they were oppressed, or did he side with them because they were "his people," though in plight?

To translate this into my lingo: Was Moses motivated by morality (siding with the oppressed, whoever they were, because they were oppressed), or was he motivated by ethics (siding with the oppressed because they happened to be his people)?

In both cases oppression plays a role in Moses' sense of solidarity. Was oppression sufficient for Moses to take a stand (morality), or was that oppression merely necessary, while it was the fact that they were his people that made it sufficient for him to side with the oppressed (ethics)?

In the New Testament we have two conflicting accounts. Acts (7:23) gives the ethical interpretation of Moses' act of vengeance. But Paul (Hebrews 11:24) understands Moses' act very differently. Moses, according to Paul, acts out of faith, not out of solidarity. It is out of faith that he decides to stand with the sufferers. But he stands with the sufferers because they are the people of God: "By faith Moses, when he had grown up, refused to be called a son of Pharaoh's daughter, preferring hardship with God's people rather than enjoying the transient pleasure of sin."

It is because they are the people of God that they are his people, and not because they are his people that they are the people of God. Paul refuses to view Moses as being caught in the dichotomy between ethics and morality.

Let us return to Julian Tuwim, discussed in Chapter 4. Following the Nazi occupation of Poland in 1939, Tuwim immigrated first to France, then to Brazil, and finally to New York in 1942. In April 1944 he published one of the most moving expressions of solidarity with his fellow Jews. "We Polish Jews" was its title.[5] Tuwim was the first to be aware that, coming from him, the title was puzzling. He starts by describing how much of a Pole he is. Being Polish, for him, is on the level of breathing, something you don't need to give an account for. "Good, but then if a Pole why then 'we Jews'?" he asks. His answer is "blood." Not in the racist sense of Jewish blood, endowed with magical, spiritual, and transcendental properties. It is blood in the literal sense of the blood in the veins, the kind of blood that is a matter for medics, not for mythomaniacs.

His solidarity with his fellow Jews (he was born to an assimilated Jewish family from Lodz) was because the Nazis were pouring the blood of the Jews from their veins. But is that all there is to it?

Blood plays a dual role in Tuwim's expression of solidarity. It is the blood from the Jews' veins, but it is also the blood relations that Tuwim had with his fellow Jews. Blood relations are not a property of blood. They are a mode of human relations, based on extended family ties. Had it been only a matter of solidarity with people whose blood was being poured from their veins, any of the great Polish poets might have written "We Polish Jews" using the "we" of solidarity as a metaphorical device, in the sense in which, *mutatis mutandis,* John F. Kennedy's celebrated *Ich bin ein Berliner* is metaphorical.

Tuwim meant his "we" of solidarity to be taken literally: I am related to Jews by blood relations and by suffering (the blood from the veins), and it is time for me to express both my belonging to the suffering people and that they are suffering. He is saying, I am in solidarity with Polish Jews both ethically and morally.

The hard part for him is to explain in what sense he is ethically related to the Jews, given his personal history of total assimilation into Polish culture. In a moment of utmost plight he wanted to give meaning to his blood relations with the Jews without accepting the notion of Jewish blood, or any other adjectival blood. Tuwim in his use of the "we" of solidarity entered into ethical as well as moral relations with his fellow Jews.

The examples of Moses and Tuwim raise the issue of the kind of relation one should have with people who are deeply wronged. Solidarity has a great deal to do with camaraderie among people who are wronged or among people who were wronged in the past and still remember—as a community of memory—the wrong done to them. Being wronged is a moral category. Does it mean that morality must be a constitutive part of solidarity?

Being wronged is not a defining feature of solidarity. Immigrants from the old country to the New World may feel a bond of solidarity, expressed in mutual help and reciprocal affection, even if their particular group hasn't been particularly discriminated against in the new country. The very first immigrants from Norway to the United States (1825) suffered from persecution—mainly as Quakers—both in the old country and to some extent in the New World, but the main bulk of immigration from Norway had no history of suffering from discrimination on either side of the Atlantic. Yet their cohesiveness along lines of origin was kept for a long time, especially in places such as Minnesota.

However, solidarity is best tested in facing wrong. The moral dimension is not a necessary condition for solidarity, but it is a necessary condition for being a core case of solidarity.

Back to the question about Moses: Was Moses bonded with the Hebrews because they were oppressed, or was it because he was bonded to the Hebrews by family ties that he attended to their plight?

The question has a psychological twist. The bond with kith and kin is what makes us attuned to their moral plight, rather than their moral plight being what creates our human bond. But the question also has a normative reading, namely, morality is what should dictate solidarity, even if in the psychological order of things the reverse is true (solidarity comes in time and in motivation before morality).

Solidarity, in contrast to mere sympathy, is a demanding relation: it calls for commitment and readiness to pay a significant personal cost. This is why solidarity is tested by siding with a wronged group, and this is why the core cases of solidarity are those with a moral dimension to them. Siding with nice Norwegians in Minnesota is pretty much costless; siding with Mexican immigrants in Arizona is costly.

There are groups of people whom we habitually depict as victims of wrong behavior. Aristocrats and kings are not among that lot. Yet aristocrats may have class solidarity, based on the sense of being wronged and not just on the basis of family ties and common privileges. I shall come to this later in dealing with the French Revolution. But let me mention here a famous play at the beginning of the last century, *The Scarlet Pimpernel*.[6] It is a play about a secret society of twenty English aristocrats led by the Scarlet Pimpernel, dedicated to saving their fellow aristocrats from the fate of the guillotine. Their class solidarity is unquestioned and unquestionable, but so is their conviction that their fellow aristocrats are being subjected to unspeakable, morally shameful treatment. The Scarlet Pimpernel and his secret society are viewed by the audience as acting in the belief that their fellow aristocrats are being denigrated and murdered by kangaroo courts.

Choosing the Cause of Solidarity

There are too many groups that are wronged in the world, and wronged in many different ways. Is there a principled way of choosing our solidarities and commitments, or is such choosing a mere matter of taste? I may have a taste for Byzantine art and

be seriously engaged with such art, yet have no taste whatsoever for Israeli art, even though I am an Israeli. Can I have in
the same vein a taste for Darfur, showing great solidarity with
Darfur, whatever it takes, but no taste for the poor in my own
society?

Solidarity may express itself in vicarious action—say, contributing to Oxfam—but core cases of solidarity are composed of
direct action: strikes, demonstrations, and picket lines, if not
actual fighting.

We may distinguish between *soft* solidarity and *hard* solidarity. The distinction is based on commitment, risk, and the
direct action involved. Soft solidarity is manifested mainly by
showing solidarity; hard solidarity, by *acts* of solidarity.

We are very constrained by how many commitments of hard
solidarity we can make, and we are limited even in our soft
solidarities. Given what we can realistically expect from human
beings, hard solidarity seems on many occasions to demand
something that goes way beyond the call of duty.

In concentrating on core cases of solidarity, such as solidarity
with groups that feel morally wronged currently or historically,
we can point out a tension that is built into the very idea of solidarity. It is the tension between being a *passive* victim due to a
trait that is the basis for the wrong done to the group (most sa-
liently skin color) and being an *active* agent in resisting the wrong
done to the group. We are active, partly or fully, by taking pride
in the stigma that caused the wrong done to the group. The answer to the tension is solidarity: it provides the social chemistry
that transforms passive victims of despair into hopeful agents capable of collective action.

For Marx, the basis for workers' pride should be the fact
that they are the creators of the civilized world. Indeed, being

exploited is what detracts from their ability to view themselves as creators. Nature and work are the sole source of everything valuable. The workers are the demiurge that shapes nature and turns it into civilization. Marx's analysis is concentrated on the producers and not on the consumers, on the supply side and not on the demand side. His social criticism is very unlike the cultural criticism of our society as a consumer society. Consumerism isn't Marx's concern. Production highlights the role of the workers in the role of creators.

I have already stressed the role in Abrahamic religions of gratefulness to God the Creator as the source of all obligations. Obligations are anchored in a sense of gratefulness. Marx endowed the workers with the role of creator: not the Creator ex nihilo, as in religious thought, but the creator as shaper, imprinting forms on nature so as to create civilization. This may lead us to suspect Marx of deifying human beings qua workers, of endowing them not just with pride but with hubris. But this is another matter.

Victimhood may bring another move: elevation of the suffering, dignifying, if not deifying, the suffering of the group with the status of the suffering God. The Poles and the Irish modeled the history of their suffering on the suffering of Christ among the nations. The whole nation goes along Via Dolorosa, and each tragic event in the life of the nation is just another station on the way to the cross. Suffering as a sign of being a chosen nation is very much at the center of the Jewish experience. Olympic Games for suffering nations to settle which of them suffers most are very much in the spirit of the culture of victimization that followed decolonization. Suffering is regarded as a badge of honor.

But for the Grace of God

The demand for solidarity from all those who bear the same stigma, which should go beyond the requirement of goodwill from anyone else, calls for serious justification. One argument is an argument against free riders. She, the bearer of the stigma, is the one who is going to enjoy the beneficial outcome of the struggle of solidarity, without contributing to the effort.

Solidarity is an instrument to overcome the effect of free riding. This is all too commonplace to expand on, yet true enough to mention.

Less banal is the direct appeal to solidarity on the ground that "it could have happened to you." Even if you can escape its fate by disguising the stigma, you should not do so since you better understand how it feels to be a bearer of this particular stigma. It is in the name of this unique understanding that you should shoulder the burden with those who are forced to face it.

The English reformer John Bradford (1510–1555) is known for his saying "There but for the grace of God goes John Bradford," which is the source of the idiom "There but for the grace of God go I."[7] Bradford uttered this famous sentence while waiting in the Tower of London for his execution when he saw someone else being led to the gallows. (It is an echo of 1 Corinthians 15:10: "But by the grace of God I am what I am.") The idea is clear: Once I realize that it could be me in place of the victim, it should have a special moral pull on me. In the same spirit but in a different context, the maverick Trotskyite Max Shachtman debated the meaning of socialism with the man who used to be the leader of the Communist Party in the United States, Earl Browder. At a certain point in the debate Shachtman listed leaders of communist parties who had been murdered on Joseph Stalin's orders;

then, mentioning that Browder too was a leader of a communist party, he ended by saying: "There but for an accident of geography stands a corpse!"[8] The same thing could have happened to you. And this near miss should be a good reason for you to feel solidarity with the victims.

Authenticity and Solidarity

Not honorably bearing a social stigma is a sign of an inauthentic life. Being inauthentic is a bad thing. But what kind of bad is it? One answer is that it is self-betrayal. But self-betrayal, by my account, is neither an issue of morality nor an issue of ethics.

Authenticity is acting out a metaphor: that we are the authors of our lives. Life, in this view, is an art form. One should be judged by the quality of the way one scripts one's life. To be an authentic author of one's life is to write one's life freely, according to one's inner feelings and needs rather than the dictates of one's society. To bear one's social stigma honorably is to lead a life of solidarity with the fellow bearers of the stigma.

Let us imagine an individual with the same life story and the same racial profile that President Barack Obama had before he made his decision to become a black community activist. Instead of adopting his father's last name, he adopts his white mother's last name, Dunham, thus becoming Barack Dunham.

Dunham opts to be a white man on the strength of his identification with his white mother and his ambiguous looks. Dunham might argue that receiving the dictates of society and admitting that black is a relevant label to one's life is a sign of inauthenticity, saying, "I don't want to belong to the ritual of false pride that 'black is beautiful.' Black, as such, is neither beautiful nor ugly, and neither is white. I don't want to lead my life under a stigma and I don't want to lead my life under a reevaluation of the stigma, turning the trait of being black into a good thing. I want black to be irrelevant to my life and I wish it were irrelevant to the lives of others, but to the extent that it is nastily relevant, I don't want to be its victim, if I can help it. I am willing to take my share of the responsibility along with everyone else in the society for removing the destructive and malicious effects of the stigma, but I don't see why I should bear the burden of solidarity in a way you white people are exempted from doing."

The counterclaim—claim more than argument—goes like this: To reduce blackness to skin color is to trivialize what is at stake. Living with a stigma creates a whole form of life. The idea of authenticity, like solidarity, has force only if there is a willingness to pay a personal price in trying times. Both solidarity and authenticity go hand in hand with the idea of being tested in extreme experiences: war, plague, exile, revolutionary struggle, and, most important, facing death. Indeed, active solidarity in a struggle is the litmus test for authenticity. Failing to join the struggle on the ground that it is costly, being estranged from the people with whom you are expected to be in thick relations— these are expressions of inauthenticity. They involve lack of solidarity when it matters most.

I think that in the background of the demand for solidarity manifested as awareness of an authentic life is the expectation that a black person, for example, will be in thick relations with his fellow blacks by sharing a common meaningful fate, which is responsible for creating a meaningful form of life. But what if he does not feel like standing in thick relations with what we regard as his fellow blacks, and resents the litmus test for solidarity that is thrust on him? Is he more obligated to stand in a demanding relation of solidarity than any other person in the society? Does the mere fact of social expectations to show special solidarity carry any moral or ethical force?

From a moral point of view, those who bear the stigma, actually or potentially, are not more obligated to show solidarity than anyone else. If noblesse obliges, stigma does not. From an ethical point of view the answer is almost a tautology: if you are black and feel the hold of thick relations with your fellow blacks, then you should show special solidarity when it matters. That is what having thick relations demands.

What about the reverse relation? You belong to a group that systematically and seriously wrongs another group. You are thickly related to the perpetrators, and negatively thickly related to the downtrodden. The enmity between the two groups goes back a long time, to the point where the two sides are intimate enemies. You want to right the wrong, but you feel utterly ineffective among your people. Should you desert your people and join your historical enemy in an act of solidarity, in the hope that you can be of help there? How far can you go in siding with the other side? In short, should you betray your ethical relations with your people out of a moral consideration that your people are in the wrong?

Meursault, the protagonist of Albert Camus's celebrated novel *The Stranger,* is indifferent to his mother and to his mother's death, and he murders a man. He transgresses both ethics (his relation to his mother) and morality (his relation to his fellow man). The distinct feeling is that he receives capital punishment for violating ethics more than for violating morality, which is a surprising twist given that murder is the ultimate crime.

Camus's own personal dilemma during the Algerian war was a tough one: should he side with "his people," the Pieds-Noirs, the community with which he had thick relations, epitomized by the fact that his mother belonged to it, or should he side with the indigenous Muslim population? The Pied-Noir label is misleading: it lumps together owners of grand colonial estates—clear cases of exploiters—and the lower class. This lowly class of Pieds-Noirs consisted of struggling people like Camus's family. They were technically French nationals, descendants of many nations, natives of Algeria, with only a tenuous relation to metropolitan France. For Camus the standard move of turning every colonist into a colonialist was already a suspicious move. He definitely didn't think of his mother as a colonialist.

There are those for whom the issue is clear-cut: one should shake off the yoke of one's community, if it is in the wrong, and side with the oppressed. Camus had strong reservations about what the Front de Libération Nationale (FLN) stood for. He didn't share Sartre's political analysis. But let us assume for the sake of argument that the two agreed on the politics. What should Camus have done in terms of solidarity? With whom should his commitment have lain in this bitter and violent struggle?

Put schematically, what should we do, in terms of solidarity, if we are caught in a bitter conflict between "our people," the ones with whom we have long-standing thick relations, and "them," with whom we have negative thick relations or no relations at all, yet we believe that our people are morally in the wrong in the way we treat "them"?

I think that we should make a crucial distinction between two cases: in one case the conflict is *violent,* and in the other the conflict is *nonviolent.*

Siding on moral grounds with the party that is wronged, even against your own people, when their struggle is nonviolent is justified. Siding with the other party when they are violently attacking your people can be justified only in extreme cases. I mentioned in Chapter 2 that Willy Brandt did the right thing in joining the Norwegian army to fight the German occupation. But fighting Nazism is like fighting nothing else. In a time of nonviolent struggle morality should be the guide to solidarity, but in a time of violence directed against your people, especially if your side didn't initiate the violence, ethics should prevail. You should still fight in your society against the evil it commits, but you should not participate in the violent acts of the other side against your people. That is what ethics demands.

As Camus famously overstated, "I believe in justice, but I will defend my mother first." His mother was among the Pieds-Noirs. He could not side with the FLN, and rightly so, for the FLN threatened his mother. But then he knew all too well that he shouldn't side with the Organisation de l'Armée Secrète, the vicious paramilitary organization during the Algerian War, either.[9]

Solidarity and Violence

Freud gave an original account of original sin: an account of the birth of morality and religion. Once upon a time, humanity consisted of a single group dominated by an alpha male who controlled all the females and expelled all his potential rival sons from his harem. The expelled band of brothers joined forces and one day killed their father, whom they feared and admired, loved and hated. To atone for this act they commemorated the father by making him their totem, shrouded in a set of taboos.[10]

Morality came after the killing of the alpha male, but the raw feeling of Oedipal ambivalence toward him was there innately. The bond between the brothers—fraternity and with it the emergence of embryonic morality by the set of taboos—was an outcome of primeval violence. The commemoration of this act took the form of communion. Sharing food—the symbolic flesh of the totemic father—cemented humanity as a fraternity. These primeval young Turks who killed the sultan and shared his harem were able not only to compete but also to cooperate. Humanity is based on both: cooperation and competition.

Sartre coined the expression *fraternité-terreur*. It is not an oxymoron, in Sartre's use, but an indissoluble compound.[11] Terror, for Sartre, was part and parcel of political fraternity.

Three strictures should be added right away. First, I use the language of the past ("was"), since Sartre seems to have changed his views on fraternity, judging by his conversations with his disciple at the time, Benny Lévy.[12]

Second, my tentative language ("seems to") is related to Sartre's position that fraternity, though a fundamental notion, eludes a precise account, partly because it is so fundamental: there's nothing better in terms of which this notion can be accounted for.

Third, the expression "political fraternity" is contrasted with primary fraternity—the kind that obtains for a family or a tribe, where "fraternity" is taken literally. Political fraternity is already being used in an extended sense.

There is a third sense of fraternity on which Sartre wanted to build universal human relations, the half-mythic, half-literal sense in which we human beings are all descendants of one primordial couple, the mythic Adam and Eve or the quite literal original couple living way back in Africa from whom the human species emerged. We all, as it were, sprang from one womb. This common source, like the one family relations are based on, should be the source for establishing what is in my lingo a universal ethics of the "family of man."

In Freud, violence and fraternity have to do with family romance. In Sartre, violence and fraternity are in the realm of politics: the realm of conflicts, interests, and competition over scarce resources.

How is the inextricable relation between violence and fraternity established, according to Sartre—or, more cautiously, according to one possible reading of Sartre? In a revolutionary act of uprising against the old order, there is an ecstatic moment of a true and pure experience of solidarity among the rebels. This sense of solidarity fuses the rebels into one political body. This is a revelatory moment that cannot last long. The revolution turns from poetry into prose, from a true experience of solidarity into a bunch of clichés about fraternity, uninspired and unpersuasive.

The revolutionary élan cools off and the revolution, which depends on a strong sense of fraternity, is dissolved. The revolutionaries face a question: How should they revive the revolutionary impulse and save the revolution?

To save the impulse of the revolution, the revolutionaries perform a semi-sacred oath of blood *(le serment)*, with each comrade swearing on his life that he should be killed before he betrays his comrades and with them the revolution. In Sartre's revolutionary oath, the idea of the political is the internal distinction between loyalists and traitors. Each is capable in principle of being both. This is, in short, the revolutionary fraternity cemented by an oath and by terror. The advantage of such an oath is that as long as the society lives, there will always be a supply of traitors to feed to the revolutionary furnace—unlike external foes, who may come to be in short supply as the revolution gains ground.

This constant tension between loyalty and betrayal in the revolutionary group keeps the revolution from disintegrating. This is a terrifying vision of revolutionary fraternity, which no infatuation with violence can hide.

Internal terror does not cement fraternity but dissolves it. The internal terror of Joseph Stalin's and Mao Zedong's reigns was meant to stoke revolutionary zeal. Whatever else the terror did, it destroyed the solidarity of civil society and atomized the general population.

Terror and fear are a centrifugal force of disintegration rather than a centripetal force of solidarity. To be sure, solidarity can hold among perpetrators of crime, much as it can hold among victims of crime, but the ambiguous posture of being both perpetrator and victim, like Georges Danton or Nikolai Bukharin, produces terror without fraternity.

Georges Lefebvre, the great historian of the French Revolution, disagrees.[13] The majority of the French people, he argues, passively favored the revolution and objected to the foreign invasion of France, but they lacked discipline and a sense of cooperation and they had no sense of the new French state. It was the terror, he believes, that forced them to act in concert and created their sense of national solidarity.

There is confusion here. Solidarity brings about collective action out of a sense of fraternity. Terror can bring about collective action out of fear. Terror can serve as a means to collective action in the absence of solidarity. But it is wrong to view terror as an ingredient of solidarity. Terror apologetics, be they of the French Revolution, the Bolshevik Revolution, or both, make terror and solidarity complementarities.

Lefebvre may be understood as saying that terror was used as a negative instrument to muster collective action, and once the nation was in place as an outcome of the revolution, terror was replaced by national solidarity as a positive instrument. Even if true, Lefebvre's line does not support the fraternity-terror compound in which terror is an ingredient of solidarity. At best, he describes the replacement of terror by solidarity, but by no means their coextensive existence.

Hippolyte Taine had his own unique take on fraternity-terror, saying that a revolution is like a drunken party: first there is joy and a mushy sense of fraternity, and then it turns nasty, deteriorating into irrational violence.[14]

It is easy to lose sight of what we are dealing with here. We are not asking whether violence against outsiders contributes to a sense of solidarity in a group. Frantz Fanon, for example, may be right that colonized people may feel empowered by their violence against the colonizers and because of that gain solidarity. Our worry here is of a different kind.[15] It is the relation between solidarity and violence that is directed inward. Inwardly directed terror is the enemy of solidarity rather than its element.

The contrast we pose is between solidarity and terror, but then the question is, terror against whom? Well, terror against traitors. The idea is that the cult of revolutionary solidarity is the cult of revolutionary Moloch. This cult constantly needs a supply of traitors, and this need is not just a psychological by-product of revolutionary paranoia; it actually belongs to the logic of the revolution. Traitors (mostly imaginary ones) are grist for the revolutionary mill. Violence is a by-product of the need for traitors, rather than traitors being a by-product of the need for violence so as to keep up the revolutionary élan.

More on Solidarity and Justice

Justice raises two separate sets of questions. One: What is a just society and what procedure may in *principle* yield a just society? Two: Given that we have a notion of a just society, then we come to the question of its *implementation:* how do we bring about a just society in real terms?

John Rawls made a famous suggestion in answer to the first question. His procedure is to negotiate a system of fair social cooperation over time. The negotiation takes place in a given society among free and equal individuals who disregard their specific personal attributes.[16]

The first set of questions is about justice *in vitro,* and the second set of questions is about justice *in vivo.* I am interested in justice in vivo, namely, in the implementation of justice, given a shared notion of justice, a notion that hits the right balance between freedom and equality.

Justice in vivo is partial justice among individuals who are somewhat free and somewhat equal, and who know full well who they are and take it into account in their deliberations. These individuals are not indifferent to justice, but they are subject to other needs and considerations. Their sense of justice is not a burning force to make them act seriously to bring about justice in general. For one thing, some powerful members among them enjoy the current unjust arrangements in society (the status quo), which works well for them. In describing the members of the society as being somewhat free, I mean that many of them are free to choose to whom they sell their work, but they are also unfree in that they have to sell it to someone. Being a worker is being forced to sell your work; otherwise you cannot make a living. Being a psychological workaholic does not make you a worker unless you have to work to earn a living. Being somewhat equal means being equal legally, as a citizen or a resident, but not necessarily equal socially or economically. These are conditions that hold in economically advanced societies; in other societies, we hardly encounter even this imperfect situation.

My questions about justice in vivo concern the conditions for bringing about a just society, and especially the role of social solidarity as a key condition.

I assume that a sense of justice as fairness is evenly distributed in the society and that it does not reside with a particular group of people who have innately more of a sense of justice than others, be they the workers, the students, the educated middle class, or the enlightened bureaucrats. A sense of justice, I assume, is not in and of itself enough to motivate people to bring about justice. This assumption can be questioned in some special circumstances, such as those that brought about the abolition of slavery. It was people who were motivated solely by a sense of justice that brought about the abolition of slavery.

But in general, for justice to be implemented, a sense of justice is not enough of a motivating force. On top of the general motivation for justice, we expect to find another motive: the prospect of being significantly better off in a just society.

It looks as if the workers as a group are the ones who have the most to gain from a just society. Again, there is no assumption here that the workers are endowed with special moral virtues. The only assumption is that they have a personal stake in justice, which the upper classes, privileged by the status quo, don't have. We may of course argue that the jobless poor have an even higher personal stake in justice than the workers, but then, unlike the workers, the jobless poor are not a group that is capable of sustained collective action.

The debate or rather the struggle over national health insurance in the United States is a case in point. At a certain point in time most Americans believed, according to the polls, that national health insurance should be reformed and that leaving millions with no health insurance was unjust. Yet most Americans said at the time that they were satisfied with the health insurance they had and that they were worried they would personally be worse off under the new scheme. There is tension between this pair of numbers: tension between the majority on the side of justice and the majority on the side of a status quo that is advantageous to some. It seems that a sense of justice as a motivating force may not be strong enough to override the forces for retaining the status quo.

Most advanced countries have some form of national health insurance. It is only the United States that lacks it. In all those countries national health insurance was brought about by worker-related organizations: unions, workers' parties, or other political parties that competed with the workers' parties for the support of the workers.

The idea so far is that a sustained structural change in society that would establish a society guided by justice calls for powerful social forces for change, and that they can hardly be expected to be brought about by politics as usual.

The worry is that the changes that have taken place in advanced capitalism have diminished the force of the traditional working class to the point of social impotence. Counting on the working class as an active force to bring about a just society because of its special stake in such a society is an exercise in futility. In the legal tender for a class that will carry out the struggle for a just society, there are no bidders.

It may very well be the case that politics as usual—based on constant compromises among various groups with different stakes in the status quo and different stakes in change—leaves the arena with not enough forces to bring about a just society.

The idea that only social forces such as social classes can bring about significant change has been with us from the beginning of the deep debates about the nature of the mother of all revolutions: the French Revolution. By one influential account, that of François Furet, there was no social revolution in France that brought the capitalist bourgeoisie to power, for there were no capitalists in France at the time of the revolution. The destruction of feudalism was a process carried out by the centralist monarchy and not by capitalists. The elite that carried out the events of 1789 consisted of a lot of people who betrayed their class: nobles, clerics, and high bourgeoisie (not capitalist bourgeoisie). Had the forces of 1789 acted on their own, they might have achieved a compromise, not unlike the one that was struck during the Glorious Revolution in England. But the joining of the masses with the political struggle derailed the revolution from such a likely course. It created a rift between the representative legislatures and members of revolutionary clubs who claimed to be "the people" by acting on behalf of the general will. Three sets of events happened in tandem, each having its own character, and to lump them all together under the portmanteau title of "the French Revolution" is more misleading than enlightening. The three events are the insurrection of the petite bourgeoisie in the cities, the tribulations of the peasants in the country, and the political events in Versailles. All in all, the French Revolution, by this account, was a political revolution, with republicanism as its main outcome. It was not a social revolution that brought about capitalism as a replacement for feudalism.

On the other side of the debate, Jacobin Marxists of various stripes claim that it was capitalism that was brought about by the French Revolution, though it was not an immediate outcome but a process that took about a hundred years.

The relevance of this debate is in raising the issue of whether major constitutive social changes are an outcome of politics or whether radical social changes are an outcome of collective action brought about by the direct action of a social class.

We are interested in the conditions for bringing about a just society. For that the relevant controversy is whether political activity can bring about a radical shift from the status quo toward a just society or whether what is needed is collective action that is carried out by a social class whose interests reside in a radical deviation from the status quo.

If there is a need for a social class in order to form a just society, and if the only candidate for such a class is the working class, then, given the dramatic changes in the scope and the formation of the working class in economically advanced societies, the working class is not up to its historical role of bringing about a just society. If it is indeed the case in advanced economies that the social conditions for bringing about a just society do not exist, then betraying the working class is in no way tantamount to betraying those who yearn for social justice in society. The working class is objectively not up to the role of bringing about justice.

The working class as a class is thoroughly weakened. It has been deserted by the professionals and the skilled; these white-collar groups deserted the blue-collar workers for fear of being déclassé. The workers express lack of solidarity with immigrants, who could enlarge the working-class base. Instead, they stress their national solidarity as insurance against being déclassé. I can go on and enumerate more reasons for the strong sense that the traditional working class has lost its clout as a major social force. There are of course workers in the traditional sense of workers, but they are proportionally few; moreover, they are less important economically and less organized.

Moreover, there is a deep division between workers who are *insiders* and workers who are *outsiders*.[17] The insiders enjoy secure jobs and care, politically, about the conditions that keep their jobs secure. Social democratic parties tend to represent the insiders, since historically they are much better organized, and the trade unions act mainly on their behalf. The outsiders struggle with their unstable income. Nativists constitute the main bulk of the insiders, immigrants the largest part of the outsiders. Lack of solidarity between these two groups is due partly to conflicting interests and partly to ethnic overlap between nativists and insiders, on the one hand, and immigrants and outsiders, on the other.

The terms "solidarity" and "working class" may strike many not only as nostalgia verging on kitsch but also as utterly anachronistic and irrelevant for describing the social and economic reality of advanced postindustrial societies of today. The accusation of anachronism has two senses: one descriptive, one normative. In the descriptive sense of anachronism, the working class has lost its grip in advanced societies, which are no longer organized around machine production. Machine production of the past had a particular type of workplace and working class, which was the breeding ground of the reformist left. But we are living in the advanced information-based economies of today, which have dismembered the organized working class as we knew it. Hence to talk about solidarity with the working class is nothing but nostalgic talk unchecked by reality.

In the not so remote day in which the Tory canvasser approached me at the bus stop, the reality of classes in the greater Oxford area was still very visible. More than twenty thousand worked in the huge Morris Motors plant in Cowley, the bastion of the conscious working class. Today there are about four thousand workers there—and, mind you, it is the largest employer industry in Oxfordshire.

In any case, the talk about the working class in advanced society being a class that potentially may subvert the status quo is, if not nostalgic, then at least deceptive, given that the insiders among the workers have a stake in retaining the status quo.

There is, however, an opposing observation. It indicates something different. It tells us that in searching for a working class in economically advanced societies as an agent of change, we are looking in the wrong direction. We ignore the rise of their numbers in rapidly developing countries such as India and Brazil. The appeal to the working class in emerging markets is not an appeal to the vague notion of cosmopolitanism.

Solidarity determines the extent to which a society is a candidate for establishing just institutions and a just constitution. Had humanity at large been able to form a solidarity group, then the extent of a just society would have been the whole of humanity. But as Michael Walzer says, there is no politics in cosmopolitics, only a metaphor, and humanity at large is not a political unit with enough of a sense of solidarity.

Solidarity is not a cosmopolitan notion but an international one, and so is justice. The word "universal" in contrast to "particular" blurs an important distinction about solidarity and justice, namely, the distinction between universal in the *cosmopolitan* sense and universal in the *international* sense, the latter comprising of a variety of particular solidarities.

Promoting Justice or Fighting Injustice

Justice needs more than a sense of justice in order to be implemented. But if justice is a "faint passion," injustice is a pretty powerful one; moreover, injustice nurtures a strong sense of solidarity.

The claim is that a sense of justice is a faint passion, unlike being incensed with injustice, which is full of passion. It is not justice that hurts us into action, but injustice.

Solidarity as a force in the service of morality is first and foremost a force in the service of a negative politics of fighting injustice, rather than a candidate for fighting for justice. Indeed, the abolition of slavery was fed by a strong negative sense of injustice rather than by a positive sense of justice.

There is a moral asymmetry between resisting injustice and pursuing justice: the former is both more urgent and more important. But there is on top of that an immense psychological asymmetry. Fighting injustice is much more concrete than pursuing justice based on abstract principles: abstract principles do not make people fight for justice any more than they make martyrs sing in the flames. Thus, for example, progressive taxation is a positive principle of justice, but it is a highly abstract principle for most of us. How many of us know our tax bracket or how much we are taxed in comparison to others? By contrast, the glaring injustice of tax exemption for the nobles and the clerics, and putting the whole burden of taxation on the third estate, was strong enough to stir revolution in France.

So where does all this leave us? Here is the grand scheme: gross injustice is a powerful force for creating a sense of solidarity, especially among those who suffer directly from the injustice. In creating an organized solidarity group that is capable of collective action, what starts out as a group motivated to counter injustice may turn into a group motivated enough to pursue positive justice, or, rather, motivated enough to pursue more justice. The idea is that a chain of action can be created by fighting injustice, which may in turn create a solidarity group that might bring about justice.

10

A World without Betrayal

BETRAYAL CAN BE REGARDED AS A TELLING SYMPTOM OF a great human malaise: the lack of transparency in human relationships. Jean Starobinski made a formidable case for the claim that the main thread weaving Rousseau's thoughts into an organic whole is the ideal of *total transparency* in human relations.[1] Loss of transparency is the fall of man. In the state of nature there was transparency. It is civilization, with its artificiality, that is responsible for our downfall, by turning immediate uncluttered human relations into mediated relations, entangled in simulation and pretense. The gap between social reality and appearance is a by-product of artificial decorum. It puts heavy makeup on genuine human relations. Betrayal is only one symptom of the disease; hypocrisy and secrets are even more salient symptoms—but the full scope of nontransparent syndromes can fill Pandora's box. The bitter medicine to the malaise of opacity is total sincerity. Healthy human relationships must be totally transparent.

There are two separate complaints about lack of transparent human relationships. The distinction is between lack of transparency

in human relationships and lack of transparency *of* human relationships. Holding back vital information from you, my friend,
means lack of transparency *in* our relationship. Whereas viewing
a human relationship through fetishistic properties of objects is
lack of transparency *of* the relationship. This happens, for example, when my relations to the producers of my sports shoes
are obstructed by my sheer interest in the quality of the shoes:
the working conditions of the ones who produce my shoes are
masked by the elasticity of the shoes' soles.

Rousseau was worried about transparency in relationships;
Marx, about transparency of relationships.[2] Betrayal stands at a
sensitive juncture between lack of transparency in relationships
and lack of transparency of relationships. Fear of betrayal creates
a yearning for total transparency. The fear is accompanied by a
strong desire for an unfailing test that can tell the sheep of
true friends from the goats of false ones. The yearning for
transparency is the yearning for a world without the possibility of betrayal.

It is Theseus who cries out: "To know each friend whether he
be true or false; all men should have two voices, one the voice of
honesty, expediency's the other, so would honesty confute its
knavish opposite, and then we could not be deceived."[3] And it
is Medea who laments: "O Zeus, why did you give men certain
ways to recognize false gold, when there's no mark, no token on
the human body, to indicate which men are worthless."[4]

As we can see, the desire to peep into the inner thoughts of
others is as old as the hills. The next best thing is to wish on
others a Pinocchio sort of nose that becomes longer whenever
they tell a lie, an overt lie detector.

It is not the opaqueness of our skull that secures our "inner"
thoughts. If our skull were transparent, we wouldn't know

any more than we do now about others' inner thoughts. We don't think thoughts in our head the way we digest food in our stomach.

Wittgenstein famously dismissed the importance of the distinction between the *outer* and the *inner* in accounting for our mental life. The inner is tied to the outer conceptually: there is no inner without the outer.

However, we can keep our thoughts to ourselves. This fact is of great moment. To be sure, there are those who cannot resist sharing their thoughts with others, and under torture all of us may reveal our thoughts. Yet again, the Stoic idea of our capacity to retreat to our "inner citadel" by keeping our inner thoughts to ourselves is vitally important, no matter how it fares metaphysically.[5] Even the Stoics, with their stress on the inner, recognized that our thoughts are influenced by what comes to us from the outside. But they insisted that we are free to affirm or deny the truth of any thought we entertain, without sharing it with others. Our inner citadel is thus free no matter what our outer situation is, whether we are kings like Marcus Aurelius or slaves like Epictetus. We are radically free in our inner life. It is this lack of transparency, "the opaque skull," that is responsible for our freedom to think for ourselves. The Stoics believed that this is the most important sense of freedom. If the price of our inner freedom is the undesirable by-products of betrayal and hypocrisy, so be it.

In Greek tragedies we find an irresistible yearning to penetrate the inner citadel. This yearning is driven by fear of betrayal. But there is another urge for transparency: disgust with hypocrisy.

Hypocrisy is an ordinary vice. Betrayal is not. Nevertheless, hypocrisy is a source of an odd anxiety, making some thinkers impute to it extraordinary importance. Hannah Arendt is one of them: "The hypocrite's crime is that he bears false witness against himself. What makes it so plausible to assume that hypocrisy is the vice of vices is that integrity can indeed exist under the cover of all other vices except this one. Only crime and the criminal, it is true, confront us with the perplexity of radical evil; but only the hypocrite is really rotten to the core."[6]

This passage strikes me as a misplaced hyperbole. Rebecca West seems more judicious in saying that "because hypocrisy stinks in the nostrils one is likely to rate it as a more powerful agent for destruction than it is."[7]

The way I understand West's remark is that hypocrisy vitiates our aesthetic sensibility on top of our moral sensitivity. We find it disgusting. It is because we find it disgusting that we give hypocrisy such misplaced weight. Arendt captures the adolescent sensibility with regard to hypocrisy: revulsion of hypocrisy seems to be strong in adolescents and tends to wear out as one grows older, partly through practice and partly by realizing that some measure of hypocrisy is a necessary by-product of civilized life.

More important, hypocrisy greatly troubles world religions. There is a whiff of paradox here, since religions can always appeal to an omniscient God who has total access to our inner citadel. It is like the air of paradox surrounding the religious institution of confession (in private). What can the sinner tell God that he doesn't know?

Some religions grant permission for dissimulation in emergency situations, on the assumption that God can see to the heart. According to the Islamic doctrine of *taqiyya,* mostly advocated by Shia Islam, one is allowed to deny the faith in time of danger, as long as the believer keeps the true faith in his inner thoughts.

Horror of betrayal and disgust with hypocrisy are the two reasons mentioned so far for the craving for total transparency in society. There is, however, a third reason, one that is related to betrayal and hypocrisy: a strong aversion to secrets. The feeling is that secrets are cancerous cells metastasizing in the most delicate tissues of human relations. Secrets exclude people who are not in the loop of information. Secrets establish social one-upmanship for those in the loop over those out of the loop, and as such, secrets may turn ugly.

Bernard Williams, in his review of Sissela Bok's book *Secrets*, claims that the British are obsessively interested in secrecy, which is not unlike attachment to pornography. The intense interest in the Cambridge spies, he believes, has very little to do with what secrets they revealed and everything to do with their own sexual secrecy as an expression of the hidden life of the ruling class, who keep the rest of society from their "secret gardens."[8]

I wonder if he is right. It seems to me that it was their access to real military and political secrets that made their "secret gardens" an object of fascination. Take away the cold war and hot war secrets from the Cambridge spies and there is little to their story in comparison, say, to the sex and gardens of Vita Sackville-West and her upper-crust lot.[9] Surely, few care today about the content of the secrets that Kim Philby passed to the Soviets. More people may still be interested in whether, in passing information to the Soviets, Philby betrayed agents who lost their lives because of him. Admittedly, the content is passé, but not the fact that he handed over top secrets to the Soviets.

Purification from betrayal, hypocrisy, and pernicious secrecy are the reasons for the belief that sunlight is the best disinfectant. It is hard to explain the wide recognition that Edward Snowden received (the *Guardian*'s Person of the Year 2013, Whistleblower Prize 2013, Sam Adams Award 2013, among others) without viewing it as protest, mainly of the young, against the secretive society as incarnated by the National Security Agency. It manifests the yearning for a totally transparent society.

Transparent Society as Dystopia

A Dutch-windows society is a society in which no curtains are drawn and everything is for anyone to see. There is nothing to hide; even the prostitutes in the red-light district are behind see-through glass. But do we need curtains—metaphorical curtains, that is? I guess that the non-metaphorical transparent Dutch-windows attitude has its origin in a Dutch Reformed–Puritan streak of having nothing to hide as a necessary condition for gaining purity of heart. We may indeed find the ideal of transparency most strongly advocated in Scandinavia and the Netherlands, where there are secular remnants of the Puritan doctrine.

The puritanical idea that wearing makeup is a form of deceit belongs to this family of sensibilities. Cosmetics are a cowardly camouflage for not facing the truth. It is interesting to note that the root of the Hebrew words for "dye" and for "hypocrisy" is the same: *ts.v.a.* The general idea is that truth is unadorned: it is the naked truth we should be after. Covering the truth is camouflaging reality with intent to deceive. Indeed, in Hebrew *b.g.d* serves as the root for the words for both "cloth covering" and "betrayal," while the root *m.a.l* serves for both "gown" (priestly gown in particular) and "violation of religious endowment or taboo for secular profit," and in modern Hebrew it is used for "embezzlement."

The puritanical idea of purity of heart goes hand in hand with purity of language. There is a strict prohibition on lewd and offensive language. We can find remnants of the puritanical obsession with clean language in what goes under the doctrine of political correctness. Political correctness is linguistic etiquette that requires a great deal of restraint in one's expression. The irony is not in the need for restraint in expressing one's feelings in public; the irony is that it is exercised by people who put so much weight on the value of sincerity in expressing inner feelings.

In a very revealing essay, "Concealment and Exposure," Thomas Nagel writes: "Concealment includes not only secrecy and deception but also reticence and lack of acknowledgment. There is much more going on inside us all the time than we are willing to express, and civilization would be impossible if we could all read each other's minds."[10] The fantasy of total transparency is of a destructive nature: it means the end of civilization as we know it. I believe Nagel is right. But then a question can be asked: Does it hold true for all forms of possible civilizations, or does it hold true only for civilization as we know it?

Total Exposure

It is not clear what it means to be subjected to total exposure. Does it mean that we should be compulsive talkers, bombarding one another with an uncensored report on the goings-on in our inner life? This requires a Tristram Shandy kind of life, in which it takes a year of writing to cover one day of our life (which is possible only if we live an infinite number of years).

Being the finite creatures that we are means that even as a fantasy, pouring out our soul calls for selection. Selection means holding back thoughts. It means keeping hidden thoughts.

But why not leave the selection to the listeners? Total transparency would then mean providing any relevant information promptly when it is demanded by outsiders, including any strangers who happen to be sniffing around, all in the name of their "right to know." This seems to be a wretched idea on the face of it, but at least it gives some substance to the fantasy of a totally transparent society. But then the metaphysical possibility of total transparency is not terribly interesting, in being so removed from real life.

The civilization that is incompatible with radical (as distinct from total) transparency is bourgeois civilization, for at its center is the idea of privacy. Privacy is an immense human achievement. To give up on privacy and on sharp separation between public and private life is to give up on the kind of civilization that enables it. This is what is at stake.

The detractors of bourgeois society say that privacy should be a license to leave people *alone,* to mind one's own business, but that in fact it is a recipe to leave people *lonely,* out of indifference.

But bourgeois society has a more appealing name, say the defenders: liberal society is its name, and liberal culture is its culture. Radical transparency in all human relations is a threat to such a civilization. It is related to the malignant extension of thick relations beyond the scope of close family ties and a few intimate friends, where it really belongs. Selective intimacy, in which individuals share their inner life and deep vulnerabilities, should be shielded even from family relations.

"Why are family gatherings often so exceptionally stifling?" asks Nagel. "Perhaps it is because the social demands of reticence have to keep in check the expression of very strong feelings, and purely formal polite expression is unavailable as a cover because of the modern convention of familial intimacy."[11] His answer provides an astute observation, which can readily be recognized. The lesson I draw from his observation is that for most people, only a tiny fraction of their thick relations are also intimate relations. Families are full of sordid secrets. Even in the family such secrets are kept from the ears of some members. The truth about the mad aunt referred to euphemistically by the family as "the nervous aunt," or the bleak truths about early pregnancies, abortions, suicides, or the army desertion of the black sheep of the family, though known in the family, are hardly acknowledged. Freeing families from the need for sordid secrets is probably part of the plea for transparent relations in which there is nothing to be ashamed of.

In bourgeois society, in which family usually means nuclear family, the menace of squalid secrets is kept under wraps by narrowing the extent of genuine thick relations to a small circle of intimacy.

In any case, a liberal bourgeois culture needs a strong sense of privacy to protect it from the Peeping Toms of Dutch-window society. Communitarianism in this view is an ideology that unjustifiably claims the right to meddle in an individual's private life by talking the language of care, the language of fraternity. It turns thick relations, which should be reserved for a small circle of family and friends, into a sticky collectivist relation between an individual and a self-appointed caring community. By this account, the egalitarian liberal believes that out of the revolutionary triangle one should concentrate only on liberty and equality—that is, on justice—and ignore the fuzzy plea for fraternity. Fraternity, as I already mentioned, should be left to college housing.

One form of life that tried in a serious way to challenge bourgeois culture was the kibbutz. I am talking here in the language of the past, for although the kibbutz movement is still alive, the kibbutz has been greatly restructured and privatized along "bourgeois" lines. The idea was to create a way of life that would manifest the best in family and the best in friendship through communal production and sharing. It was meant to be a sincere society, where information about each other is known but not necessarily acknowledged. But was the kibbutz experiment a success? For some, the historical jury is still out; for others, it is a declared failure—a glorious failure, but a failure nevertheless in not being a genuine alternative to the bourgeois way of life. For one thing, it cannot be an alternative way of life for a large-scale economy and population.

But this is not really the question I am interested in. My question is: Does kibbutz life provide a transparent life immune from betrayal, hypocrisy, and damn lies? Does it produce a sincere society, or does it instead create a sticky, gossipy, wing-clipping society, where petty jealousy masquerades as blatant sincerity, where musical beds due to claustrophobic infidelities are common? Whatever else kibbutz communal life is, it is not an answer to betrayal and hypocrisy. The high ideological and normative demands of kibbutz life nourish both hypocrisy and sincerity: yes, more hypocrisy, but also more denouncements of hypocrisy by acts of rude honesty.

Back to bourgeois civilization, with its insistence on privacy as a condition for liberal culture as a condition for liberal civilization. The private sphere should be protected by opaque windows, literally and metaphorically.

The dialectics here goes in two directions: there is need for privacy to protect liberal civilization, and there is a need for liberal civilization to protect privacy. Privacy justifies liberal civilization, and liberal civilization justifies a strong sense of privacy. The locus of privacy is home, and home should be protected from the public gaze. It is interesting that the words for "home" and for "secret" in German are etymologically connected (*Heim* and *Geheim*). It is when the secret state police, the Geheime Staatspolizei—better known by its acronym, Gestapo—becomes the emblem of the public invading the realm of the private and its treasured secrets that liberal civilization faces a shattering attack. What the Gestapo symbolizes is the totalitarian notion that the state and nothing but the state has a monopoly on secrets. Against this terrifying notion the liberal instinct is to recur to the home-as-castle idea. It is not the inner citadel that matters but home, the inner sanctum of liberal civilization.

Indeed, "a man's house is his castle" is a battle cry for total immunity from intervention in the private sphere, the way sovereignty was meant to provide total immunity from external intervention in affairs of state. But if a man's home is his castle, then in many such castles many petty tyrants rule over their families—and they are almost always men. They reign as heads of families. This criticism of privacy as providing a shield for family tyrants goes under the slogan "the private is political." The feminist movement gave currency to the idea that the private is political, which may justify outside intervention in private homes so as to protect the vulnerable in the family.

The pendulum of interference in privacy on moral grounds goes back and forth. It is very much like the pendulum of intervention in the internal affairs of a sovereign state on humanitarian grounds. The analogy between the microethics of interference in privacy and the macroethics of intervention in sovereignty is pretty suggestive.

In the years following the Second World War a course of events swept the world whereby metropolitan countries handed over authority to their dependent colonies to become sovereign states. "Decolonization" was the term used to describe this course. The fear of neoimperialism—that is, the fear of the old imperial countries regaining hold of their former colonies—was such that any hint of such a possibility was bitterly resented. This attitude applied even to places that were known for their gross violations of human rights. In the name of sovereignty these places acquired immunity from outside intervention. As the bitter memory of colonialism slowly fades and the harsh reality of terror and abusive power in many former colonies slowly descends on earth, calls for intervention in the "internal affairs" of sovereign states, on moral grounds, become more vocal and more real. The moral pendulum is swinging from beatification of sovereignty to sanctification of human rights. Yet the fear of using moral reasons as a pretext for neocolonialism is still a justified fear. And so is the fear of intervention in the private lives of others out of caring. There is no resting point for the privacy pendulum swinging between intervention and nonintervention, for example, in domestic violence.

Social Transparency and Dirty Hands

"Do you suppose that it is possible to govern innocently?"[12]

These words by Hoederer, the fabled Communist Party leader in Sartre's renowned play, give a name to the play, *Les Mains sales,* and, due to Michael Walzer, also to a problem: the problem of dirty hands.[13] The problem of dirty hands is indeed encapsulated in that question.

By "innocent" Sartre probably means free from morally wicked acts, lacking in worldly experience as well as in shrewd cunning as a result of not encountering evil. There is of course a picture of politics that goes with Hoederer's hard line, a picture of revolutionary hardness that is accompanied by the familiar revolutionary bravura: you cannot make an omelet without breaking eggs. Isaiah Berlin thought that this is usually the line of people with a knack for breaking eggs (and, I would add, egg-heads) but with very little idea how to make an omelet. On the revolutionary toughness picture, innocence and morality stand for soppy softness in contrast to the heroic hardness politics requires. Truman's phrase "If you can't stand the heat, get out of the kitchen" is not a revolutionary slogan, but it amounts to the same thing: politics is harsh and hard, morality is soft and sentimental. Morality is sentimentality, and the test of hardness in politics is to overcome moral compunction. When the going gets tough—morally, that is—the tough politicians get going. All this is painfully familiar.

An offshoot of the question "Do you suppose that it is possible to govern innocently?" is the question of whether it is possible to govern transparently. One radical sense of the question is "Can you govern without secrets?" If you can, you must, but can you?

"You" means any potential ruler in democratic society. If the answer to the question is negative and secrets are of the essence of any political order, then the possibility of betraying secrets is endemic to the very running of politics: no secrets, and hence no possible betrayals, means no politics.

Having been born, raised, and lived my life in Israel, it is hard for me to imagine political order without security secrets. But in the year Israel was founded, 1948, the president of Costa Rica abolished that country's army. So doesn't that mean Costa Rica can be governed without state secrets? Maybe there are other secrets in Costa Rica apart from military ones, like the list of soccer players to challenge the Netherlands in the world championship, a secret that may even be elevated to a state secret (this, as we shall see, is no joke). It is clear that the possibility of transparency, as something that can be realistically expected from a political order, depends on each country's sense of security. Transparency, like other good liberal values, goes over well in time of peace, but may go over badly in a time of emergency and war.

Liberalism and social democracy are ideologies of peace. I don't mean ideologies that advocate peace, which they may do as well, but ideologies for time of peace: ideologies the realization of which assumes a state of affairs with no violent conflict. This does not necessarily mean a state of harmony and lack of conflict, but only a lack of violent conflict. Fascism, war communism, and neoconservatism are ideologies of war. By calling an ideology a war ideology, I do not mean that a state run by such an ideology is necessarily a state run by warmongers. There were reckless warmongering fascists such as Benito Mussolini, and there were prudent fascists such as Francisco Franco. The issue is not the character of the leaders but the character of the ideology. For a war ideology, violent conflict, or a threat of violent conflict, is of the essence.

Social democratic parties had to deal with wars, but they dealt with them on a retail basis, usually unsuccessfully. Social democratic parties, unlike nationalist parties of the right, were morally ambushed by the right, who impugned their patriotism. In response, social democrats in power tended to overcompensate for their universal humanism by becoming hyperpatriotic. (Think of the Socialist Party of France during the Algerian War in the 1950s.) The relation between liberalism and imperialism is even more troubling than the record of the social democratic parties. But here too the burden of proof of patriotism was on the liberals' shoulders, whereas conservatives were taken as patriotic by definition. (The liberal John Kerry received a Purple Heart, yet his patriotism is questioned, whereas the conservative

George W. Bush may have received preferential treatment to enter the National Guard so as to avoid the Vietnam draft, yet he is considered ultrapatriotic.)

"The wolf will live with the lamb," says the prophet Isaiah (11:6). "It is fine by me," said Moshe Dayan, "as long as I am the wolf." Security-centered political philosophy doesn't take utopian chances. The wolf should stay a wolf, even if man to man he is a sheep. Even in Costa Rica they should heed security warnings against potential threats. The Soccer War between El Salvador and Honduras (1969) should serve as a reminder to them. The name "Soccer War" is a bit of a misnomer. There were more serious reasons for the war than the one suggested by the name. The name refers to the North American qualifying match between the two countries, a match that was perceived as the immediate cause of the war. Even a quasi-utopian secure situation calls for guarding secrets. Yet security-centered political thoughts, which serve the thoughts of the establishment well, are countered by antiestablishment thoughts, which view secrets as a manipulative mechanism of control. On this line of thought, information is power and those in power try to keep the information only for their own internal consumption by calling it state secrets. The call for radical transparency is directed with deep suspicion toward the establishment in all of its manifestations. This suspicion takes on occasion the form of a conspiracy theory: it is a conspiracy of the people in power against the people. By this account the traitors and the betrayers are the people in power, the "gatekeepers" of state secrets, whereas the saints are the whistle-blowers.

No degree of transparency will convince a believer in a conspiracy theory that what he cares about is all in clear public view. The believer in a conspiracy theory is certain that what is in view is only the tip of the iceberg.

I bring up these two opposite cartoonlike attitudes toward secrecy because they make us aware that we should care more about *accountability* than about unrealistic total *transparency*. You cannot govern without secrets, given the political reality of a world that is far removed from Costa Rica. But this recognition of political reality is not an invitation for government paranoia and witch-hunts to unearth imagined traitors. Nor is it an invitation for antiestablishment paranoia that demonizes governments automatically as evil forces. The issue is how to devise effective institutions of government accountability without having total transparency. This is a timid statement, but, dull as it is, it is the most sensible one in our tangled political situation.

There is another take on the question of whether it is possible to govern innocently, namely, is it possible to govern without myth?

It is the old understanding of the question about innocence in politics. The idea is that to govern is to govern over the multitudes. The multitudes need myth. No regime can be legitimated and hold authority over the masses without a formative shared story. The elite can see through the myth and know that it is nothing but a myth, but the elite shouldn't unmask the myth for fear of losing their freedom to think for themselves freely and safely. The elite should promote myth so as to domesticate the wild beast that is the multitude. The elite mustn't tell the masses that the myth is nothing but a myth, that is, a useful fiction. This should be kept a deep secret. Leo Strauss is an archbeliever in this elitist ruse, but he has the illustrious Cordovan predecessors Ibn Rushd (Averros) and Maimonides to back him up. Behind this version of "double truth," one for the elite and one for the masses, there is a psychological assumption that the multitude is governed by the imagination, whereas the elite are governed by the intellect. Unmasking a myth on this line of thought is an act of betrayal. Unmasking is not a Promethean heroic service to humanity of handing over the divine secret of fire but a pyromaniac disservice to humanity of dangerously playing with fire. The fire is the fickle multitude, which should be kept at bay by a convenient myth.

This double-truth line of thought, one truth for the elite and one for the masses, vitiates our democratic liberal sensibilities, and rightly so. In any case, it should not be conflated with the true worry of defending civilized life from the fantasy of total transparency.

Betrayal and hypocrisy are necessary by-products of civilized life the way urinating is a necessary by-product of drinking.

The relation between betraying secrets and betrayal is not hard to fathom, whereas the relation between uncovering a myth and betrayal is far from straightforward. Yet many people, perhaps too many, find a connection between exposing myth and betrayal. For such people, exposing a myth—that is, unmasking a widely received communal belief as fiction—is an act akin to betrayal. This is particularly true about belief with regard to the birth of the nation taken as an event that constitutes the legitimacy of the community (legitimacy here means "we are like family and not like Mafia family"). But the same holds for other events viewed as constitutive to communal life bonded by thick relations. More often than not, acts of unmasking are taken as betrayal and not as genuine pieces of historical work—revisionist history, yes, but history all the same. In this view, writing history has the role of conferring legitimacy the way chronicles conferred legitimacy on dynastic claims. Hence, demystification is what the bastard does to the legitimate family, washing its dirty linen in public and shaming the family (read the nation). Acting in the

name of transparency in this view is a bastard's deed of undermining legitimacy. (The "bastards" are the insiders who take the
outsiders' posture.) The bastards expose the tendency of legitimacy to shroud itself in the mists of the past, where it can tie the
hegemonic rulers to a story of origin. Unmasking a story of origin is thus perceived as turning a story of immaculate conception into a story of original sin. In short, for many people who
are under the sway of thick relations and who strongly identify
with the community, demystification of the stories their community tells about itself belongs ultimately to the genus of betraying
family secrets, while transparency is nothing but a pretext for
washing the dirty linen in public. This hostile attitude toward
transparency, viewed as inimical to cherishing stories that a
community in thick relations must tell itself, is not my attitude,
but it is so prevalent that no one who deals with betrayal can
safely ignore it—and I don't.

   In my view the issue of transparency in human relations is not
"the truth and nothing but the truth," be it about the past or
about the present. The issue for me is "the whole truth." If transparency requires the whole truth always and everywhere, then
transparency does not get on well with civilized life. If betrayal
is the price we pay for the type of concealment necessary for civilized life, then it is a price worth paying.

NOTES

†

ACKNOWLEDGMENTS

†

INDEX

†

NOTES

1. Why Betrayal?

1. Maximilien Robespierre, *Discours sur l'organisation des Gardes nationales* (1790), Article 16.
2. The saying is by Sebastian-Roch Chamofort as quoted by Carlyle in Norwood Young, *Carlyle: His Rise and Fall* (New York: Morrow, 1927), 153.
3. Erik H. Erikson, *Childhood and Society* (New York: W. W. Norton, 1950), 264–265.
4. United Nations, "The Universal Declaration of Human Rights," Article 18, www.un.org/en/universal-declaration-human-rights.
5. Apostasy is a capital offense in Afghanistan, Brunei, Mauritania, Qatar, Saudi Arabia, Sudan, the United Arab Emirates, and Yemen. See Library of Congress, "Laws Criminalizing Apostasy," www.loc.gov/law/help/apostasy.
6. Russell Hardin, *Trust and Trustworthiness* (New York: Russell Sage Foundation, 2004).
7. Edward C. Banfield, *Moral Basis of a Backward Society* (Glencoe, IL: Free Press, 1958).
8. Shabtai Teveth, *Ben-Gurion's Spy: The Story of the Political Scandal that Shaped Modern Israel* (New York: Columbia University Press, 1996).

2. The Ambiguities of Betrayal

1. Judith N. Shklar, *Ordinary Vices* (Cambridge, MA: Harvard University Press, 1985).

2. W. B. Gallie, "Essentially Contested Concepts," *Proceedings of the Aristotelian Society* 56 (1956): 167–198.

3. "Morris Cohen, 84, Soviet Spy Who Passed Atom Plans in 40's," *New York Times,* July 5, 1995.

4. Nachman Ben-Yehuda, *Betrayals and Treason: Violation of Trust and Loyalty* (Boulder, CO: Westview Press, 2001), 34–38.

5. Barry Clarke, "Eccentrically Contested Concepts," *British Journal of Political Science* 9 (1979): 122–126.

6. Rebecca West, *The Meaning of Treason* (New York: Viking Press, 1947).

7. Myron J. Aronoff, *The Spy Novels of John Le Carré: Balancing Ethics and Politics* (New York: St. Martin's Press, 1999).

8. Edna Ullmann-Margalit, "Big Decisions: Opting, Converting, Drifting," *Royal Institute of Philosophy Supplement* 58 (2006): 157–172.

9. Rebecca West, "The Vassall Affair," *Sunday Telegraph,* April 25, 1963.

10. Christopher Andrew, *Defend the Realm* (New York: Alfred A. Knopf, 2009), 387–389. See also Eric Pace, "Klaus Fuchs, Physicist Who Gave Atom Secrets to Soviet, Dies at 76," *New York Times,* January 29, 1988.

11. E. M. Forster, "What I Believe," *Two Cheers for Democracy* (New York: Mariner Books, 1962).

12. Joseph Conrad, *Under Western Eyes* (Mineola, NY: Dover Publications, 2003), 10.

13. Ibid., 37–38.

14. Victor Navasky, "Elia Kazan and the Case of Silence," *Naming Names* (New York: Viking Press, 1980).

15. "Chelsea Manning," *Wikipedia,* June 11, 2015.

16. Joseph Margulies, "The Promise of May, the Betrayal of June, and the Larger Lesson of Manning and Snowden," *Verdict,* July 17, 2013. See also David Bromwich, "The Question of Edward Snowden," *New York Review of Books,* December 4, 2014.

3. Betraying Thick Relations

1. Willard van Orman Quine, *Word and Object* (Cambridge, MA: MIT Press, 1960), section 53. Quine has argued that the set-theoretical implementation of the concept of the ordered pair is a paradigm for the clarification of philosophical ideas. The general notion of such definitions or implementations is discussed in Thomas Forster, *Reasoning about Theoretical Entities* (Singapore: World Scientific, 2003). Norbert Wiener's paper "A Simplification of the Logic

of Relations" is reprinted, together with a valuable commentary on pages 224ff., in Jean van Heijenoort, *From Frege to Gödel: A Source Book in Mathematical Logic, 1879–1931* (Cambridge, MA: Harvard University Press, 1967). Van Heijenoort states the simplification this way: "By giving a definition of the ordered pair of two elements in terms of class operations, the note reduced the theory of relations to that of classes." Casimir Kuratowski's argument is in "Sur la notion de l'ordre dans la Théorie des Ensembles," *Fundamenta Mathematicae* 2 (1921): 161–171. This differs from Hausdorff's definition in not requiring the two elements 0 and 1 to be distinct from *a* and *b* ("Ordered Pair," *Wikipedia,* June 11, 2015, references 1, 2, 5, 6).

2. William Shakespeare, *Henry V,* IV, iii, 63–64.

3. Carl Gustav Jung, "Ulysses: A Monologue," *The Spirit of Man, Art and Literature* (London: Routledge, 1966), 15:12.

4. Sigmund Freud, "The 'Uncanny,'" *The Standard Edition of the Complete Psychological Works of Sigmund Freud* (London: Hogarth Press, 1919), XVII:218–252.

5. Leon Pinsker, "Auto-Emancipation," 1882, Jewish Virtual Library, www.jewishvirtuallibrary.org/jsource/Zionism/pinsker.html.

6. Ibid.

7. Yuri Slezkine, *The Jewish Century* (Princeton, NJ: Princeton University Press, 2004), 9.

8. Ibid., 41.

9. Virgil, *Aeneid,* Book II, trans. A. S. Kline, 2002, http://freeread.com.au/@rglibrary/virgil/aeneid.html#Aeneid02.

10. John M. Cooper, *Reason and Emotion: Essays on Moral Psychology and Ethical Theory* (Princeton, NJ: Princeton University Press, 1999), chapters 14–16.

11. Patrick Devlin, *The Enforcement of Morals* (Oxford: Oxford University Press, 1965), 12.

12. Ibid., 13.

13. Michael Inwood, "Ethical Life and Custom," *A Hegel Dictionary* (Oxford: Blackwell, 1992), 91–93.

14. Ernest Gellner, *Nations and Nationalism* (Oxford: Blackwell, 1983). See also Anthony D. Smith, *National Identity* (Harmondsworth: Penguin, 1991).

15. Richard Rorty, "Solidarity or Objectivity," *Philosophical Papers,* vol. 1, *Objectivity, Relativism, and Truth* (Cambridge: Cambridge University Press, 1991), 21–34; *Contingency, Irony and Solidarity* (Cambridge: Cambridge University Press, 1989).

16. Ibn Khaldûn, *The Muqaddimah: An Introduction to History,* ed. N. J. Dawood, trans. Franz Rosenthal (Princeton, NJ: Princeton University Press, 1967), esp. 97–99.
17. Gilbert Ryle, *The Concept of Mind* (London: Routledge, 1949), 121.

4. What Is Betrayal?

1. Jorge Amado, *Dona Flor and Her Two Husbands,* trans. Harriet De Onis (New York: Avon Books, 1969).
2. Sophocles, *Oedipus the King,* trans. David Grene, http://abs.kafkas.edu.tr /upload/225/Oedipus_the_King_Full_Text.pdf, line 1105.
3. Theodore Fontane, *Effi Briest,* trans. H. Rorrison and H. Chambers (Harmondsworth: Penguin Classics, 2001).
4. S. Y. Agnon, "The Doctor's Divorce," *A Book that Was Lost and Other Stories,* ed. Alan Mintz and Golomb Hoffman (New York: Schocken, 1996).
5. Bertrand Russell, *The Autobiography of Bertrand Russell,* vol. 1, *1872–1914* (London: Allen & Unwin, 1967), 147.
6. Julian Tuwim, "We Polish Jews," Canadian Foundation of Polish-Jewish Heritage, www.polish-jewish-heritage.org/Eng/RYTM_Tuwim_Eng.htm.
7. Edna Ullmann-Margalit, "Big Decisions: Opting, Converting, Drifting," *Royal Institute of Philosophy Supplement* 58 (2006): 157–172.
8. Michael Stocker, "Values and Purposes: The Limits of Teleology and the Ends of Friendship," *Journal of Philosophy* 78 (1981): 747–765.
9. Ruth Margalit, "The Unmothered," *New Yorker,* May 9, 2014, www .newyorker.com/books/page-turner/the-unmothered.
10. Thomas Scanlon, *Moral Dimensions: Permissibility, Meaning, Blame* (Cambridge, MA: Harvard University Press, 2008).
11. Ralph Linton, *The Study of Man: An Introduction* (New York: Appleton-Century-Crofts, 1936), https://archive.org/details /studyofman031904mbp.
12. Fred Kaplan, "How Did I Get Iraq Wrong? I Trusted Colin Powell and His Circumstantial Evidence—for a Little While," *Slate,* March 17, 2008; "The Tragedy of Colin Powell," *Slate,* February 19, 2004.
13. Richard Rorty, *Contingency, Irony, and Solidarity* (Cambridge: Cambridge University Press, 1989); *Philosophical Papers,* vol. 1, *Objectivity, Relativism, and Truth* (Cambridge: Cambridge University Press, 1991).

14. Edna Ullmann-Margalit, "On Not Wanting to Know," in *Reasoning Practically,* ed. Edna Ullmann-Margalit (New York: Oxford University Press, 2000), 72–84.

15. Yoram Ben-Porath, "The F-Connection: Families, Friends, and Firms and the Organization of Exchange," *Population and Development Review* 6 (1980): 1–30.

16. Adam B. Seligman, *The Problem of Trust* (Princeton, NJ: Princeton University Press, 2000), 16–21, 84–85.

17. James Walsh, *You Can't Cheat an Honest Man: How Ponzi Schemes and Pyramid Frauds Work and Why They Are More Common than Ever* (Aberdeen, WA: Silver Lake Publishing, 1998); Donald Dunn, *Ponzi: The Incredible True Story of the King of Financial Cons* (New York: Broadway Books, 2004).

18. Andrew Kirtzman, *Betrayal: The Life and Lies of Bernie Madoff* (New York: Harper, 2009).

19. David Sinclair, *The Land that Never Was: Sir Gregor MacGregor and the Most Audacious Fraud in History* (Boston: Da Capo Press, 2004).

20. The quotation is from the *Book of Fiefs.* See Marc Bloch, *Feudal Society,* vol. 1, *The Growth of Ties of Dependence,* trans. L. A. Manyon (London: Routledge & Kegan Paul, 1961), 234.

21. Ludwig Wittgenstein, *Philosophical Investigations,* trans. G. E. M. Anscombe (Oxford: Basil Blackwell, 1958), esp. 115–116.

22. I owe this observation to Lee Ross.

5. *Treason*

1. T. S. Eliot, *Murder in the Cathedral* (London: Faber and Faber, 1935), 59.

2. Ibid., 65.

3. Ibid.

4. Ernst H. Kantorowicz, *The King's Two Bodies: A Study in Mediaeval Political Theology* (Princeton, NJ: Princeton University Press, 1957).

5. Jean Anouilh, *Becket* (New York: Riverhead Books, 1995).

6. William Shakespeare, *As You Like It,* II, vii.

7. William Shakespeare, *Julius Caesar,* III, ii.

8. Ibid.

9. Michael Walzer, *Regicide and Revolution: Speeches at the Trail of Louis VI* (Cambridge: Cambridge University Press, 1974).

10. James B. Donovan, *Strangers on a Bridge: The Case of Colonel Abel* (New York: Atheneum, 1964); "Red Files: Secret Victories of the KGB," PBS interview with Svetlana Chervonnya, www.pbs.org/redfiles/kgb/deep /interv/k_int_svetlana_chervonnaya.htm.

11. Albert O. Hirschman, *Exit, Voice, and Loyalty: Responses to Decline in Firms, Organizations, and States* (Cambridge, MA: Harvard University Press, 1970).

12. Cyril Northcote Parkinson, *Gunpowder Treason and Plot* (London: Weidenfeld & Nicolson, 1976); Antonia Fraser, *The Gunpowder Plot: Terror and Faith in 1605* (London: Weidenfeld & Nicolson, 2003).

13. Arthur Miller, *The Crucible* (Harmondsworth: Penguin, 1971).

14. "Treason against the United States, shall consist only in levying War against them, or in adhering to their Enemies, giving them Aid and Comfort. No Person shall be convicted of Treason unless on the Testimony of two Witnesses to the same overt Act, or on Confession in open Court. The Congress shall have Power to declare the Punishment of Treason, but no Attainder of Treason shall work Corruption of Blood, or Forfeiture except during the Life of the Person attainted" (U.S. Constitution, Art. III, Sec. 3).

15. "Espionage Act of 1917," *Wikipedia*, June 11, 2015.

16. Frederick Brown, *For the Soul of France: Culture Wars in the Age of Dreyfus* (New York: Anchor Books, 2011), 195.

17. Ibid., 179.

18. Gisle Tangenes, "The World According to Quisling," *Bits of News*, September 19, 2006.

19. Margret Boveri, *Treason in the Twentieth Century* (New York: G. P. Putnam's Sons, 1963), 64.

20. Robert Ferguson, *Enigma: The Life of Knut Hamsun* (New York: Farrar, Straus & Giroux, 1987).

21. Hans Fredrik Dahl, *Quisling: A Study in Treachery* (Cambridge: Cambridge University Press, 1999).

22. Boveri, *Treason*, 78.

6. Collaboration

1. Philippe Burrin, *France under the Germans: Collaboration and Compromise* (New York: New Press, 1997).

2. Evan Burr Bukey, *Hitler's Austria: Popular Sentiment in the Nazi Era 1938–1945* (Chapel Hill: University of North Carolina Press, 2000).

3. Stanley Hoffman, "Collaboration in France during World War II," *Journal of Modern History* 40 (1968): 375–395.

4. Isaiah Trunk, *Judenrat: The Jewish Councils in Eastern Europe under Nazi Occupation* (New York: Macmillan, 1972).

5. Robert O. Paxton, *Vichy France: Old Guard and New Order 1940–1944* (New York: Columbia University Press, 1972).

6. Michael R. Marrus and Robert O. Paxton, *Vichy France and the Jews* (Palo Alto, CA: Stanford University Press, 1995).

7. Jean-Jacques Rousseau, *The Social Contract* and *The First and Second Discourses* (New Haven, CT: Yale University Press, 2002); *The Social Contract,* book II, book IV, chapter 1.

8. Elitzur A. Bar-Asher Siegal, "Theodor Herzl's Theory of Quasi-Contract: Ideological Background to Theodor Herzl's Theory of the Moral Justification for the Establishment of a State," *Hayo Haya* 4 (2004): 7–23 (in Hebrew).

7. A Collaborator in the Court of History

1. Flavius Josephus, *The Jewish War,* rev. ed., trans. G. A. Williamson (Harmondsworth: Penguin, 1984).

2. Shaye J. D. Cohen, *Josephus in Galilee and Rome: His Vita and Development as a Historian* (Leiden: Brill, 1979).

3. Shaye J. D. Cohen, "Josephus, Jeremiah, and Polybius," *History and Theory* 21 (1982): 366–381.

4. Moshe Halbertal and Avishai Margalit, *Idolatry* (Cambridge, MA: Harvard University Press, 1994).

5. Avishai Margalit, *The Ethics of Memory* (Cambridge, MA: Harvard University Press, 2002), chapter 5.

6. Solomon Schechter and Wilhelm Bacher, "Johanan b. Zakkai," *Jewish Encyclopedia,* 1906, www.jewishencyclopedia.com/articles/8724-johanan-b -zakkai.

8. Apostasy

1. "At the opposite extreme is the strange view held by the early Gnostic sect known as the Cainites described by St. Irenaeus (*Against Heresies* I.31), and more fully by Tertullian (*Praesc. Haeretic.,* xlvii), and St. Epiphanius (*Haeres.,* xxxviii). Certain of these heretics, whose opinion has been revived by some modern writers in a more plausible form, maintained that

Judas was really enlightened, and acted as he did in order that mankind might be redeemed by the death of Christ" ("Judas Iscariot," *Catholic Encyclopedia,* www.newadvent.org/cathen/08539a.htm). The relatively newly found Gnostic Gospel of Judas of the second century has another story to tell, but here too Judas is not a betrayer but rather the only disciple to understand Jesus.

2. Nick Hornby, *Fever Pitch* (London: Victor Gollancz, 1992).

3. Nechama Tec, *In the Lion's Den: The Life of Oswald Rufeisen* (Oxford: Oxford University Press, 1990).

4. Avishai Margalit, *The Ethics of Memory* (Cambridge, MA: Harvard University Press, 2004), 45.

9. Class Betrayal

1. Virgil, *Aeneid,* Book VI, trans. H. R. Fairclough (Cambridge, MA: Harvard University Press, 1916), Loeb Classical Library, www.theoi.com /Text/VirgilAeneid6.html, line 86.

2. H. W. Brands, *Traitor to His Class: The Privileged Life and Radical Presidency of Franklin Delano Roosevelt* (New York: Anchor, 2008).

3. Ralph Chaplin, "Solidarity Forever," 1915, Union Songs, http://unionsong .com/u025.html.

4. Joseph B. Soloveitchik, *Kol Dodi Dofek: Listen, My Beloved Knocks,* trans. David Z. Gordon (New York: KTAV Publishing House, 2006).

5. Julian Tuwim, "We Polish Jews," 1944, Canadian Foundation of Polish-Jewish Heritage, www.polish-jewish-heritage.org/Eng/RYTM_Tuwim _Eng.htm.

6. Emma Orczy, *Scarlet Pimpernel* (London: Hutchinson, 1905).

7. "John Bradford," *Wikipedia,* June 11, 2015.

8. The full text is: "When I saw him standing there at the podium, I said to myself: Rajk was the general secretary of the Hungarian Communist Party, and was shot, or hanged, or garrotted. Kostov was the general secretary of the Bulgarian Communist Party. And when I thought of what happened to them, I thought of the former secretary of the American Communist Party, and I said to myself: There, there but for an accident of geography, stands a corpse!" Earl Browder, C. Wright Mills, and Max Shachtman, "Is Russia a Socialist Country? The Verbatim Text of a Debate," *The New International: A Monthly Organ of Revolutionary*

Marxism 16 (1950): 145–176, www.marxists.org/archive/shachtma/1950/03/russia.htm.

9. Albert Camus, *Algerian Chronicles,* ed. Alice Kaplan, trans. Arthur Goldhammer (Cambridge, MA: Harvard University Press, 2013).

10. Sigmund Freud, *Totem and Taboo,* trans. James Strachey (New York: Norton, 1950), esp. 176.

11. Jean-Paul Sartre, *Critique of Dialectical Reason,* vol. I, trans. Alan Sheridan-Smith (New York: Verso, 2006), book 2, chapter 3.

12. Jean-Paul Sartre and Benny Lévy, *Hope Now: The 1980 Interviews,* trans. Adrian van den Hoven (Chicago: University of Chicago Press, 1996).

13. Georges Lefebvre, *The Coming of the French Revolution,* trans. R. R. Palmer (Princeton, NJ: Princeton University Press, 2005).

14. Hippolyte Taine, *The French Revolution,* vols. 1–3, 1878, trans. John Durand, Online Library of Liberty, http://oll.libertyfund.org/titles/1864.

15. Frantz Fanon, "Concerning Violence," *The Wretched of the Earth,* trans. Constantine Farrington (New York: Grove Press, 1963), 35–106.

16. John Rawls, *A Theory of Justice* (Cambridge, MA: Harvard University Press, 1971).

17. David Rueda, *Social Democracy Inside Out: Partisanship and Labor Market Policy in Advanced Industrialized Democracies* (Oxford: Oxford University Press, 2007).

10. A World without Betrayal

1. Jean Starobinski, *Jean-Jacques Rousseau: Transparency and Obstruction* (Chicago: University of Chicago Press, 1988).

2. Karl Marx, *Capital,* vol. 1 (New York: International Publishers, 1967), 72.

3. Euripides, *Trojan Women and Hippolytus,* trans. E. P. Coleridge (Mineola, NY: Dover, 2002), 47.

4. Euripides, *Medea,* trans. Ian Johnston (Arlington, VA: Richer Resources Publications, 2008), https://records.viu.ca/~johnstoi/euripides/medea.htm, lines 615–618.

5. Pierre Hadot, *The Inner Citadel: The Meditations of Marcus Aurelius* (Cambridge, MA: Harvard University Press, 2001), chapter 6.

6. Hannah Arendt, *On Revolution* (London: Faber & Faber, 1963), 103.

7. Rebecca West, "Sinclair Lewis Introduces Elmer Gantry," *Strange Necessity: Essays and Reviews* (London: Virago Press, 1987).

8. Bernard Williams, *Essays and Reviews 1959–2002* (Princeton, NJ: Princeton University Press, 2014), 227.

9. Nigel Nicolson, *Portrait of a Marriage: Vita Sackville-West and Harold Nicolson* (Chicago: University of Chicago, 1998).

10. Thomas Nagel, *Concealment and Exposure and Other Essays* (Oxford: Oxford University Press, 2004), 4.

11. Ibid., 9.

12. Jean-Paul Sartre, *No Exit and Three Other Plays* (New York: Vintage, 1955), 224.

13. Michael Walzer, "Political Action: The Problem of Dirty Hands," in *War and Moral Responsibility,* ed. Marshall Cohen, Thomas Nagel, and Thomas Scanlon (Princeton, NJ: Princeton University Press, 1974), 145–165.

ACKNOWLEDGMENTS

This book was conceived, in the words of Dylan Thomas, "a grief ago." My wife, Edna, and my sister Tziona, to whom this book is dedicated, were very much alive then.

With the loss of Edna I lost, among other things, my first and foremost reader. She did, however, read the lectures I delivered on betrayal and trust as Bertelsman Europaeum Visiting Professor at the University of Oxford (2001–2002), and her delicate fingerprint can still be found in the book; the indelicacies are all mine. My daughter Ruth Margalit helped me greatly in refining the book's form and content.

The gestation of this book was ridiculously long, and during that time I incurred endless intellectual debts to family, friends, colleagues, and students. My gratitude to all those who shared their time and their minds with me cannot be compressed to a list of names. Two, however, ought to be mentioned: Michael Borns, the language editor of the Federmann Center for the Study of Rationality at Hebrew University of Jerusalem, gracefully and capably helped me arrange my thoughts in a presentable shape; I owe a great deal to the generosity of this unique center for letting Michael assist me. Assaf Sharon, a former student and current friend, read a major chunk of the manuscript and offered his insight and incisiveness.

The happy years I spent as the George F. Kennan Professor at the glorious Institute for Advanced Study in Princeton (2006–2011) made me return to the subject of betrayal—a subject of long interest to me—just as I finished dealing with the topic of compromises and rotten compromises.

The year I spent at the New York University School of Law (at the Straus Institute for the Advanced Study of Law and Justice and the Tikvah Center for Law and Jewish Civilization) provided too much of a distraction, I suppose, to some of the young scholars there. Their infectious enthusiasm for my subject of betrayal persuaded me to turn some rough drafts into a book. The last stop on my foreign tour was at Stanford University, where, as a visiting professor for some years at the Law School and the Philosophy Department, I held lectures and seminars on betrayal. The intellectual intensity of the place, which gives one the impression of Tuscany injected with a Calvinist work ethic, made me rethink some of the positions I had previously taken for granted.

Last but not least in my institutional debt is the Van Leer Jerusalem Institute. For many years, it has been my mission control station and has provided me with an exceedingly pleasant place to work.

INDEX